Literature and Science

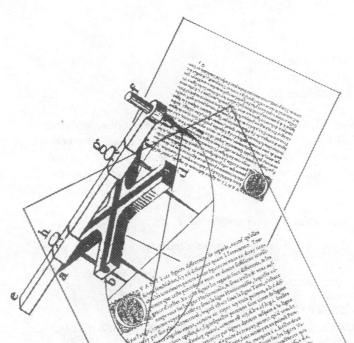

Literature and Science
Theory & Practice

Edited by Stuart Peterfreund

Northeastern University Press   boston

Northeastern University Press

Copyright 1990 Stuart Peterfreund

Library of Congress Cataloging-in-Publication Data

Literature and science / edited by Stuart Peterfreund.
    p. cm.
  Bibliography: p.
  Includes index.
  ISBN 1-55553-058-3 (alk. paper)
  1. Literature and science. 2. Science in literature. 3. Critical theory.
4. Literature, Modern—History and criticism.
I. Peterfreund, Stuart.
PN55.L5 1990   89-33905
801—dc20   CIP

Designed by Mike Fender

This book was composed in Galliard by The Composing Room of Michigan, Inc., in Grand Rapids, Michigan. It was printed and bound by Hamilton Printing Company, Rensselaer, New York. The paper is Miami Vellum, an acid-free sheet.

MANUFACTURED IN THE UNITED STATES OF AMERICA
94 93 92 91 90   5 4 3 2 1

Contents

Practice & Theory

Literature and Science

Introduction

IN THE 1980s, we have witnessed a marked rise of interest in the study of the ideological, social, and cultural relations of science in general and in the study of literature and science in particular. The rising interest in literature and science has been signaled by a number of important book-length studies, among them Michel Serres's *Hermes*, Paisley Livingston's *Literary Knowledge*, Trevor H. Levere's *Poetry Realized in Nature*, Gillian Beer's *Darwin's Plots*, Sally Shuttleworth's *George Eliot and Science*, Ronald E. Martin's *American Literature and the Universe of Force*, and N. Katherine Hayles's *The Cosmic Web*.[1]

A number of book-length essay collections devoted wholly or in part to literature and science have also appeared in this decade. They include Roy Porter and G. S. Rousseau's *The Ferment of Knowledge*; James Paradis and Thomas Postlewait's *Victorian Science and Victorian Values*; Ludmilla Jordanova's *Languages of Nature*; Frederick Burwick's *Approaches to Organic Form*; Andrew E. Benjamin, Geoffrey N. Cantor, and John R. R. Christie's *The Figural and the Literal*; and George Levine's *One Culture*.[2] Journals such as *Annals of Scholarship* and *University of Hartford Studies in Literature* have brought out special is-

3

sues devoted to literature and science.[3] In addition, the study of literature and science is served by a newsletter—*PSLS,* established by the Society for Literature and Science (SLS) at its founding in 1985—as well as by an annual bibliography (formerly published in *Clio,* now in *PSLS*) and a one-hundred-year (1880–1980) cumulated bibliography recently published by the Modern Language Association of America (MLA).[4]

Organizationally, the study of literature and science has also flourished. The Division on Literature and Science of the MLA has long conducted sessions in this interest area at the annual national convention, and they have become increasingly prominent in meetings of MLA's regional affiliates, as well as in meetings of the American Society for Eighteenth-Century Studies and of the International Association for Philosophy and Literature. Founded at the 1985 meeting of the International Congress of History of Science (ICHS), SLS currently boasts an international membership approaching five hundred. At a meeting of the Anglo-American Conference of the History of Science Society and the British Society for the History of Science, in 1988 the panel discussion of literature and science proved both provocative and informative and was warmly received by historians and philosophers of science. There is every indication that one or more sessions at the next quadrennial meeting in 1992 will also be devoted to literature and science.

The flourishing of interest in literature and science constitutes a rousing affirmation of a field of inquiry that, in the late 1970s, had a questionable future, according to one of its foremost scholars and advocates, G. S. Rousseau.[5] The affirmation is due to several factors, among them a calling into question of previous methods of historical scholarship and interpretation, "externalist" accounts as well as "internalist" accounts as they pertain to cultural institutions such as science, and a questioning of previous methods of close literary analysis—the New Criticism to be sure, but also philology—as they pertain to our understanding of literary texts.

These callings into question are, in turn, situated in a larger context of cultural self-interrogation directed at bracketing operative notions such as those of the "natural," the "correct," and the "canonical"—indeed, the very notion of the academic "discipline" itself and the enabling assumptions and methodologies one mobilizes to produce meaning—toward the end of redescribing and reanalyzing the ideological horizons of scholarly praxis in particular and of western culture in general. In terms of this redescription and reanalysis, literature and science are two discourses among other discourses contained, if not constrained, by those ideological horizons. Understood as such, literature and science may be reassimilated in the creation of a new cosmology or, if that claim is too grandiose, may at least be understood as framed discourses, bearing in common the mark of some culturally authorized third term that frames or informs both. If this self-interrogation manifests or implies a politics of discourse, it is the feminist or Marxist discursive politics of scholars such as Sandra Harding or Fredric Jameson,[6] not the hegemonic conservative politics of scholars such as Allan Bloom or E. D. Hirsch.[7]

Flourishing interest and propitious politics notwithstanding, much of what is understood to be the discourse of literature and science has, historically, manifested an egregious lack of ideological, critical, and/or methodological self-consciousness. Given its roots in philology and the history of ideas, the study of literature and science has all too often been, especially prior to the 1980s, a matter of "finding" scientific ideas "in" literature and literary ideas "in" science, in order to demonstrate, in the service of an ideal of cultural unity, that writers have not been hermetic, anachronistic curmudgeons for their part and that scientists have not been illiterate laboratory spooks hovering exclusively over their air pumps and galvanic piles for theirs.[8] The work of such pioneers as Jacob Bronowski, Walter Clyde Curry, Herbert J. Muller, and Marjorie Hope Nicolson is important for establishing the discursive space necessary for "doing" literature and science,[9] but that work never did—indeed, never could—venture meaningful commentary on the foundational assumptions and methodologies used to study literature and science or on the ideological dimension of the resulting discourse. Those who did pay attention to questions of methodology and ideology—usually social historians of the discourse of science such as Boris Hessen and Robert Merton, not those studying the discourse of literature and science—were often as reductive in their application of genetic models of cause and effect as those responsible for the *Quellenforschungen* detailing the scientific "sources" of a major literary figure or work.[10]

Despite the recent flourishing of ideological, critical, and methodological self-scrutiny, most recent essay collections (*The Figural and the Literal* is the notable exception) have not strongly reflected this change of intellectual climate. These volumes have tended to be collections of essays by several hands and little more than that unless, like *Approaches to Organic Form,* they had a common subject. The present volume attempts to retain the synoptic breadth characteristic of the best of these collections while demonstrating the sort of self-scrutiny that has in several instances been wanting. All the contributors make a start out of the assumption that, typically, the discourse of literature and science, like any other discourse of a given culture, is language-bound—logocircumferential, not logocentric—and that language itself is the repository of ideological values and critical and methodological praxis, as well as the boundary between the operational ("doing" science or "doing" literature) and the valuative ("discovering" scientific laws and theories or "arriving at" literary insights or truths). Within this literature and science seek to confront the indeterminacies that lie beyond, although without any false hope of reducing, let alone to-talizing, those indeterminacies.

The boundary between the valuative and the operational is the focus of the present volume. Each of the essays identifies its subject: a problem, topic, or issue in one of the boundary areas of literary-scientific relations. Each essay then proceeds to specify the methodology used to approach its subject. Once specified, the methodology is discussed for the purpose of reaching at least a preliminary understanding of what sort of interpretation its ideological, critical, and/or methodological presuppositions may be expected to generate. The interpretation follows.

The essays themselves are divided into two somewhat arbitrary sections. The essays by Edward Davenport, Charles Anderson, James J. Bono, and Eric C. White, which comprise the first group, all in their various ways address the problem of literary-scientific relations by examining the ideological presuppositions of literature and science as discrete discourses and then proposing models of literary-scientific relations calculated to transcend the disciplinary boundaries posed by those presuppositions. Because they approach the question of literary-scientific relations from a perspective that is specifically historical as well as theoretical, the essays by Mark L. Greenberg, Frederick Burwick, N. Katherine Hayles, and my own essay, which form the second group, complement the essays of the first group by demonstrating the manner in which the theory-and-practice approach can pay scholarly dividends through its reformulation of problems considered "merely" historical (rather than theoretical).

In "The Devils of Positivism," Edward Davenport's purpose, by his own admission, is "to bury positivism, not to praise it." According to Davenport, it is a demotic positivism, wielded by those who would maintain the boundaries between *Naturwissenschaft* and *Geisteswis-senschaft*, that prevents "any attempt to pursue literary theory in a scientific spirit." Such a spirit does not lead one to attempt "to escape metaphysics," for, properly understood, science itself makes no such attempt. Instead, the pursuit of "literary theory in a scientific spirit" entails recognizing the influence positivism has already had on the development of literary criticism, from the time of Spinoza onward, and bracketing that positivist strain and its product, if not putting them under erasure outright. As for boundaries, whether between the natural and human sciences or between other entities: Davenport sees as the underlying agenda of positivism a strong program of social control, a program aimed at putting things in their always discretely separate places. Whether these places are ordained by the ideal of organic unity, as is the case for Comte, or by the ideal of use value, as is the case for Mill, they are ultimately reflexive to the sociopolitical concerns of the individual who bespeaks them. To come to terms with positivism is, for Davenport, to own its influence, transfigured by revisionary ratio to that of Bloom's *apophades* (day of the dead): "we need to reclaim our positivist heritage, while rejecting that positivist hostility to metaphysics . . . which leads only into the cul de sac of Pragmatism. A more sophisticated assessment of positivism will make it easier to begin . . . developing a scientific . . . literary criticism."

In "Literature and Medicine: Why Should the Physician Read . . . or Write?" Charles Anderson undertakes to answer this question by describing "a theory of symbolic interaction which explains, in relatively uncomplicated terms, why patients and physicians seem to speak about such different things when they address the events of sickness." The communication problem to which Anderson alludes "arise[s] directly from conflicts among discursive relationships implied by" the evolving role of the physician throughout the history of medicine. That history is characterized by the physician's withdrawal from dialogue with the patient as medicine moved from a religious and mystical orientation to a scientific one. Implied in the establishment by medicine of "discretionary space, room for exploration, speculation, and even some experimentation" is the onset of a silence between patient and physician and the growth of a "terministic screen" between the two, whose concerns and modes of participation in the life-world of the hospital or clinic have become essentially alienated from one another. The physician should read, then, as the first step in overcoming this alienation. It is, after all, relatively easier for physicians to "learn to come to the medical event both as scientists . . . and as symbolic spectators working with patients to convert scientific facts into human meaning" than it is to train all patients as doctors. The goal, as Anderson sees it, is doctors who are "fully humanized persons" working with "fully humanized patients to heal both the body and the spirit and to bring about the wholeness necessary to health."

In "Science, Discourse, and Literature: The Role/Rule of Metaphor in Science," James J. Bono returns to the much-discussed issue of conceptual change in science to argue that the use of metaphor in science, far from being merely illustrative or ornamental, is fundamentally constitutive of scientific discourse. Moreover, the

> metaphorical aspects of language are essential to understanding the dynamic of conceptual change in science precisely because they ground complex scientific texts and discourses in other social, political, religious, or "cultural" texts and discourses. Rather than mirroring the "legible face" of a reality envisioned by scientists and "deciphered" within a single, dominant paradigm, complex scientific texts and discourses constitute themselves through their intersection with other multiple discourses.

Bono, in other words, proposes situating science in a metaphorically constituted "archaeology of knowledge" of the sort envisioned by Michel Foucault, whose influence Bono freely acknowledges. In framing his argument, Bono questions the strict limits imposed on the constitutive aspect of metaphor in science by Richard Boyd, as well as the attempt to distinguish between the constitutive properties of literary and scientific metaphors undertaken by W. H. Leatherdale. Instead, Bono follows the lead of Mary Hesse and Michael Arbib, who argue that "the development of science and philosophy since the seventeenth century has conspired 'to direct attention away from the concrete facts of ambiguity and change in language,'" especially metaphorical language. Bono concludes by considering "metaphor as a medium of exchange," that is, "as both the site and means for exchanges among not only words or phrases, but also theories, frameworks, and, most significantly, discourses." Exchange implies value, and value in its turn implies an agency to ordain value, which is characteristic of metaphor in science no less than in other discourses. Accordingly, Bono ends with the hope that "science . . . may suffer the rule of its own metaphors and thereby exhibit a genuinely dialogical relationship with literature."

In "Contemporary Cosmology and Narrative Theory," Eric Charles White engages the problematics of narrativity as it applies to the production of cosmological accounts of the origins of the universe. Conceding the validity of the critique of historical narrative of any sort advanced by the likes of Hayden White and Fredric Jameson, Eric White is nevertheless troubled by the implications of that critique for a critical stance and evaluative standards. Accordingly, he attempts "to mediate the dispute concerning the legitimacy of narrative history by turning to a particular case"—natural history in general and cosmology in particular. In so doing, White sees cosmology as a test case for the dispute laid out above, with important implications for how a lay audience should respond to "the tales of cosmic evolution told by the physicists." Faced with "the desire for representational closure" and the imperative of conceiving the unimaginable, the contemporary cosmologist finds himself or herself engaged in an ironic pursuit. The emplotment of the resulting narrative, then, is "a satiric emplotment of cosmic evolution as farce or picaresque. Alone among the traditional armory of narrative forms, farce offers a vision of history that remains cognizant of the sublime unrepresentability of cosmic evolution, a form of narrativity consistent with relativity theory . . . and chaos theory." If there is a narrative strategy that offers the means of moving beyond "a romantic emplotment of history as progressive," it is the picaresque, which allows for a skeptical stance yet eschews the temptation of "plotting the history of reality" as one with either a poetically triumphal or tragic closure. White's picaresque returns its narrator and audience to a world whose history is "a process without a *telos* or goal in which promise and possibility oscillate interminably with the prospect of devolution."

In "Eighteenth-Century Poetry Represents Moments of Scientific Discovery: Appropriation and Generic Transformation," Mark L. Greenberg brings the analysis of literary-scientific relations in the 1700s to a high order of delicacy in demonstrating that the "struggle between 'science,' or natural philosophy, and 'literature' as competing . . . social institutions" was both "fierce" and "encoded," the latter circumstance tending to obscure the former. Rejecting the view that literature and science coexisted easily as different but fully legitimated pursuits in the republic of letters ordained by the classical and humanistic traditions, Greenberg argues that "the language of many eighteenth-century poems devoted to science tropes for poetry and the poet—captures for writing—key instances of scientific discovery while it struggles to represent linguistically that which equations or other purely rational systems can never communicate." As his principal cases in point, Greenberg explores the tropaic moves of John Hughes's "The Ecstacy," James Thomson's "To the Memory of Sir Isaac Newton," Richard Glover's "Poem on Sir Isaac Newton," and Mark Akenside's *Pleasures of the Imagination;* he then turns to "the divergent or contrasting figurations of moments of scientific discovery in the works of such romantic writers as Blake, Coleridge, Wordsworth, and Shelley." In all instances, as Greenberg argues, the tensions between poetry and science seem most fascinating when they appear in poetry considered generally to be supportive of science and scientists.

In my essay, entitled "Blake, Priestley, and the 'Gnostic Moment,'" I attempt to demonstrate how, at one particular instant in the late eighteenth century, a poet and a scientist articulated a response that went beyond the boundaries of their respective discourses to the end of issuing a critique of authority within those discourses and the mechanisms of empowerment leading to such authority. From at least the time of the pre–Nicene Church, gnosticism has been the not-always-loyal opposition, offering a critique of the manner in which established power is promulgated and the epistemological and truth claims that it can legitimately make for how and what it knows. From the start, gnosticism has cast a cold eye on the tropological move in which one who claims "to speak for" some higher authority reifies its own authority through a strategy of metonymic characterization. Following the lead of Elaine Pagels, for example, I should argue that, in the hands of an established Church claiming *ex cathedra* authority to pronounce on the truth of scripture and dogma alike, the creed that endorses as its first principle a belief in "God the Father" becomes the efficient cause of setting in place a patriarchal clergy that relegates women to secondary roles in the practice and promulgation of interpretive and disciplinary authority. Similar moves may be observed in Newtonian scholia on the "true nature" of matter (and the God who, as a transcendent albeit absconded first cause, sets it in motion) and Augustan pronouncements about poetry's imperative to "follow nature." For Blake, who proclaimed his gnostic loyalties, and for Priestley, who was at least superficially far more critical of it, then, gnosticism provides the point of view from which to reveal and criticize the strategy of reification-by-metonymy, as well as the visionary means to present alternative imaginative, cosmological, and scientific accounts of how (and why) "things happen" in the world of human existence.

In "Romantic Drama: From Optics to Illusion," Frederick Burwick explores the development of illusionary stagecraft during the last quarter of the eighteenth century and first half of the nineteenth. Despite resistance from some—Coleridge and Lamb, for example—on the basis of the argument that "stage illusion . . . is not dramatic illusion," the former affecting merely the eye, the latter the imagination, "the acute attention of playwrights and producers to the developments in physical and physiological optics and to experiments in visual perception makes the drama of the period . . . the most intense arena of interaction between aesthetic and scientific concerns." Burwick divides his attention between the techniques of illusion, such as backlighting, forelighting, and projection, and the technology of illusion. As technology improved, progressing from simple oil lamps and mirrors to the magic lantern and limelight, the scale and effectiveness of stage illusion was greatly enhanced. In his conclusion Burwick returns to the objections of Coleridge and Lamb: "What is the nature of dramatic illusion? The answer requires attention to the lambent nature of visual images and the tenuous trust in perception. In exploring the physics of light and the physiology of sight, science has provided new means to challenge both perception and imagination." Seen in a broader context, Burwick's point is that since the late eighteenth century it has not been possible to talk of imaginative activity as the product of scientific or technological thought, or of scientific or technological thought as the product of imaginative activity; rather, the two become a self-sustaining dyad, interdependent modes of thought that have worked in the past and may work in the future each to broaden the horizons of the other.

In "Self-Reflexive Metaphors in Maxwell's Demon and Shannon's Choice: Finding the Passages," N. Katherine Hayles begins with the assumptions that language is ineluctably metaphoric and that the essence of metaphor is in its establishing of relations between words and, ultimately, what those words are taken to signify. As long as metaphor maintains a "twist," that is, a tension compounded of similarity and difference, between the words it relates, a metaphor is considered "live." With the disappearance of such a twist, the metaphor becomes "dead." But this very metaphor equating the mortality of metaphors with that of living creatures is itself an exemplar of how the twist operates, "for metaphors that appear dead may be brought back to active tension again through their interplay with the surrounding context, as the split writing of deconstruction has taught us." Not only "may be brought back to active tension again" but are: Hayles's is "a narrative of metaphors . . . being tightened into tension by changing cultural contexts in interplay with disciplinary traditions." Specifically, Hayles undertakes to trace the manner in which a heuristic metaphor in thermodynamics—that of Maxwell's Demon—having lost its twist with the development (and normalization) of thermodynamics, regains that twist at a "self-reflexive moment" (a "point where the heuristic becomes a metaphor for itself") in information theory. As a metaphor devised to help explain entropy in kinetic systems and to offer some alternative to the specter of universal heat-death (entropy), Maxwell's Demon raised as many questions as it helped answer; as a heuristic, in other words, it demarcated the grounds of disagreement, not the solution to prevent it. So, too, when Leon Brillouin and Claude Shannon revived this heuristic in the discursive context of information theory, it offered grounds for disagreement. Brillouin argues that "information and entropy are opposites and should have opposite signs," denominating information "negentropy," whereas Shannon maintains that information and entropy are identical. Shannon's view has carried the day, but the triumph owes more to his hermeneutical ability to "read" the metaphor convincingly than to his capacity to reduce it to an invariant truth.

The essence of the argument—Maxwell's Brillouin's, Shannon's, and, ultimately, Hayles's and that of the other contributors to this volume—is the interplay between theory and practice, part and whole. Hayles freely owns that she has been talking in circles, hermeneutic circles that are as indispensable to the discourse of science as they are to the discourse of literature (and the discourse of literature and science). Hayles's concluding hope is one that I and, I suspect, most if not all of the other contributors share: to acknowledge the twist, both observed and enacted, to put a torque on that circle that will deform it enough to make its presence visible, and reinforce it enough to demonstrate its inevitability.

Notes

1. Michel Serres, *Hermes: Literature, Science, Philosophy,* ed. Josué V. Harrari and David Bell (Baltimore: Johns Hopkins Univ. Press, 1982); Paisley Livingston, *Literary Knowledge: Humanistic Inquiry and the Philosophy of Science* (Ithaca: Cornell Univ. Press, 1988); Trevor H. Levere, *Poetry Realized in Nature: Samuel Taylor Coleridge and Early Nineteenth-Century Science* (New York: Cambridge Univ. Press, 1981); Gillian Beer, *Darwin's Plots* (London: Methuen, 1983); Sally Shuttleworth, *George Eliot and Science: The Make-believe of a Beginning* (New York: Cambridge Univ. Press, 1984); Ronald E. Martin, *American Literature and the Universe of Force* (Durham: Duke Univ. Press, 1981); N. Katherine Hayles, *The Cosmic Web: Scientific Field Models and Narrative Strategies in the Twentieth Century* (Ithaca: Cornell Univ. Press, 1984).

2. *The Ferment of Knowledge: Studies in the Historiography of Science,* ed. Roy Porter and G. S. Rousseau (New York: Cambridge Univ. Press, 1980); *Victorian Science and Victorian Values,* ed. James Paradis and Thomas Postlewait (1981; rpt. New Brunswick: Rutgers Univ. Press, 1985); *Languages of Nature,* ed. Ludmilla Jordanova (New Brunswick: Rutgers Univ. Press, 1986); *Approaches to Organic Form,* ed. Frederick Burwick (Boston: Reidel, 1987); *The Figural and the Literal: Problems of Language in the History of Science and Philosophy, 1630–1800,* ed. Andrew E. Benjamin, Geoffrey N. Cantor, and John R. R. Christie (Manchester: Manchester Univ. Press, 1987); *One Culture: Essays in Science and Literature,* ed. George Levine (Madison: Univ. of Wisconsin Press, 1987). The Levine volume, it should be noted, is planned as the first in a University of Wisconsin Press series of books on literature and science, a project much like the one on science and the humanities undertaken by David Hull for the University of Chicago Press. A number of other volumes are forthcoming, including a selection of papers from the first annual meeting of the Society for Literature and Science (SLS), to be published by Reidel, and a collection under the editorship of Paul Privateer and G. S. Rousseau, to be published by Cambridge University Press.

3. *Annals of Scholarship* 4,1 (1986); *University of Hartford Studies in Literature*

19,1 (1987). Other journals, including *Studies in the Literary Imagination* and *The Missouri Review,* are planning to do the same.

4. *The Relations of Literature and Science: An Annotated Bibliography of Scholarship, 1880–1980,* ed. Walter Schatzberg, Ronald A. Waite, Jonathan K. Jackson (New York: Modern Language Association of America, 1987).

5. See G. S. Rousseau, "Literature and Science: The State of the Field," *Isis* 69 (1978): 583–91. Rousseau also questioned the future of literature and science in a 1978 MLA convention paper entitled, "Literature and Science: Decoding the State of the Field" (session 553), which itself became the basis of further discussion (session 625).

6. In *The Science Question in Feminism* (Ithaca: Cornell Univ. Press, 1986) and *Fiction and the Political Unconscious* (Ithaca: Cornell Univ. Press, 1981), respectively.

7. In *The Closing of the American Mind: Education and the Crisis of Reason* (New York: Simon and Schuster, 1987) and *Cultural Literacy: What Every American Needs To Know* (Boston: Houghton Mifflin, 1987), respectively.

8. These comments and some that follow draw, in a general sense, on my "Literature and Science: The Present State of the Field," *University of Hartford Studies in Literature* 19,1 (1987): 25–34.

9. See, for example, Jacob Bronowski, *Science and Human Values,* rev. ed. (1965; rpt. New York: Harper & Row, 1972); Walter Clyde Curry, *Chaucer and the Medieval Sciences* (New York: Oxford Univ. Press, 1926); Herbert J. Muller, *Science and Criticism: The Humanistic Tradition in Contemporary Thought* (New Haven: Yale Univ. Press, 1943); and Marjorie Hope Nicolson, *Newton Demands the Muse: Newton's Opticks and the Eighteenth-Century Poets* (Princeton: Princeton Univ. Press, 1946).

10. See, for example, Boris Hessen, *The Social and Economic Roots of Newton's Principia* (1931; rpt. New York: Howard Fertig, 1971); and Robert Merton, *Science, Technology, and Society in Seventeenth-Century England* (1938; rpt. Atlantic Highlands: Humanities Press, 1978).

Theory & Practice

The Devils of Positivism

EDWARD DAVENPORT

Every age has scoffed at its predecessor, accusing it of having generalized too boldly and too naively. Descartes used to commiserate the Ionians. Descartes in his turn makes us smile, and no doubt some day our children will laugh at us. —Henri Poincaré, *Science and Hypothesis* (1905)

However hard we may try, it is scarcely possible to escape from the metaphysical conception of "fact."
—Bertrand Russell, *The Scientific Outlook* (1931)

Introduction: The Burial of Positivism

BY EXPERIMENT I have discovered that literati read (quite correctly) a note of irony in my title—"The Devils of Positivism"—and so expect that I have written a defense of positivism. I will begin, therefore, by stating that I come to bury positivism, not to praise it. Decent burial is what any great but dead intellectual movement deserves; the remains of positivism, however, have lately been hung up for display, as a scarecrow to frighten young literary theorists.

What this melancholy spectacle is supposed to frighten us away from is twofold: first, any attempt to pursue literary theory in a scientific spirit. The idea implied seems to be that the only kind of scientific approach possible is the worst kind of positivism. A good example of such scarecrow tactics is provided by Richard Rorty's essay, "Science as Solidarity." As the title suggests, one thing Rorty does in the essay is to redefine science "as" something new. A scientist in Rorty's new pragmatist dispensation would, and I quote, "rely on a sense of solidarity with the rest of her profession, rather than a picture of herself as

17

battling through veils of illusion, guided by the light of reason."[1] But even with this presumably improved definition of science, in which he has substituted the pursuit of solidarity for the pursuit of truth, and substituted a feminine for a masculine scientist, Rorty still feels compelled to sharply distinguish natural science from literary criticism. One consequence of pragmatist views, he says, is that "perhaps 'the human sciences' *should* look quite different from the natural sciences. This suggestion is based . . . on the observation that natural scientists are interested primarily in predicting and controlling the behavior of things, and that prediction and control may not be what we want from our . . . literary critics."[2]

Rorty's view of science as dedicated to prediction and control is positivistic in the worst sense. Rorty rejects as naive the contention of scientists like Galileo and Einstein that they were not primarily seeking such instrumental ends as prediction and control, but were rather striving to understand the mystery of the universe and to explain reality. Rorty rejects the realism of Galileo and Einstein, just as the narrowest positivists had done.[3] Realism is a metaphysical concept, and narrow positivism was opposed to all metaphysics. To play devil's advocate for a moment, let me say that, in a sense, positivist opposition to metaphysical ideas can be seen as not narrow but liberal and antidogmatic. The dogmatically held ideas upon which various earlier systems had been based were all metaphysical—that is, open to no test by fact. Where opposition to metaphysics became narrow, however, was in the mistaken assumption that metaphysical ideas could not be held undogmatically and could not be examined critically, even if they were open to no empirical test. Narrow positivism held the equally mistaken assumption that it was possible to think at all without some metaphysical ideas—note the epigraph above from Bertrand Russell, indicating that the concept of "fact," basic to positivism, is itself metaphysical.

Rorty rejects attempts to make literary criticism more scientific as being foolish metaphysical dreams. He promises that through pragmatism we can escape metaphysics. I do not think literary criticism wants to escape metaphysics so much as to find out how its metaphysical conflicts can usefully be debated and honestly be resolved.

This brings me to the second item that the sport of positivist-bashing is meant to distract young literary theorists from noticing—namely, that we are all the true heirs of literary positivism, both those pursuing scientific criticism and today's antiscientific avant-garde. One could argue that, ironically, all the theorists who today pride themselves on opposing both reason and theory, such as Stanley Fish, Jacques Derrida, Michel Foucault, and Richard Rorty, are the strictest positivists, precisely in their hostility to metaphysics and in their assumption that we can in some sense escape metaphysics, rather than being required, as I think, to do our metaphysics more critically—more scientifically.

Another implication of speaking of positivists as "devils" is to suggest that positivism has taken on mythical dimensions and exercises spellbinding power over various fields of inquiry. This is indeed felt to be the case in many fields, especially in the social sciences, where not a day passes without a new article protesting the suffocating effect of outworn yet powerful positivist methodology. For examples of such protest see the essays in John Nelson et al.'s *Language and Argument in Scholarship and Public Affairs*.[4] The humanities have never fallen as fully under the spell of positivist methodology as have the social sciences, yet Rorty's protest of Lovejoy's program for philosophy and Wellek's protest of positivism in literary scholarship indicate fears that even the humanities could fall prey to positivism's dangerous and mythic spell.[5]

The major threat positivism might pose to the humanities may be seen in the following quotation from Feigl: "the logical positivists were adamant in excluding as *nonsense* any question that, in the light of logical analysis, revealed itself to be absolutely unanswerable."[6] The humanities bristle with such questions and so, in the light of positivism, risk looking like nonsense, though clearly much depends here on the criteria of the answerability of questions. For those who will accept anecdotes, images, metaphors, and literature generally as answers, many problems are solved. For others, either the humanities or positivism itself become nonsense.

Richard Rorty's contention that the realism of Galileo and Einstein was metaphysical is not wrong. Karl Popper's *Logik der Forschung* of 1934 made clear that scientific realism is a metaphysical, which is to say untestable, notion. But more than that, Popper showed that science was metaphysical through and through.[7] All scientific laws, all attempts to generalize from singular observations, involve us in conjecture, in guesswork, so that Popper calls scientific laws themselves conjectures or guesses, which in turn depend upon metaphysical assumptions about order, causality, and so on. Popper was not without precursors in seeing science as metaphysical. Bertrand Russell had been forced to acknowledge that the notion of "fact" was metaphysical, yet he did not think it any the less necessary for that.

Popper also eventually became convinced that we could not escape metaphysics, even in science, and so, unlike Rorty, Derrida, and others, he rejected the positivist search for an escape from metaphysics. Instead, he said, we have to learn how to do our metaphysics more scientifically, more critically. We have to seek ways to make metaphysical notions testable. Popper argued that the development of physics had been precisely such a discovery of how to test metaphysical notions, an argument developed more fully in Joseph Agassi's Popperian essay, "The Nature of Scientific Problems and Their Roots in Metaphysics."[8]

In a section of that essay called "The Anti-Metaphysical Tradition Is Outdated," Agassi writes, "In my undergraduate days I used to resent the hostility toward metaphysics displayed by my physics teachers; my present view is in a sense an inversion of theirs. They derided all metaphysics as the physics of the past; I extol some metaphysics as the physics of the future."[9]

It should be emphasized that Agassi says "some metaphysics," for as he explains, the positivists were right to notice that much metaphysics immunizes itself against all possible criticism or test, and so cannot become scientific. But they were wrong to suppose that therefore all metaphysics was bad. Popper had argued that human sciences, such as psychology, had before them the task, not of rejecting metaphysics as the positivist psychologists had tried to do, but of making metaphysical psychology testable.[10]

The implications for literary criticism and the human sciences are enormous. We all know that the human sciences are shot through with metaphysical assumptions, not only value assumptions but even descriptive assumptions about the nature of mind, the nature of literary texts, and so on. For centuries, ever since the scientific revolution began, there has been a tendency to separate the human sciences from science proper, or to unite the human sciences with science only at the cost of their metaphysical content. This was the single biggest failure of positivism. Note that the first chapter of A. J. Ayer's classic neo-positivist text, *Language, Truth, and Logic,* is entitled "The Elimination of Metaphysics."[11] Positivism meant basing inquiry only on positively established or verified facts. Positivism therefore initially ruled out any scientific study of areas like literature, in which the "facts" were so different from those in physics, chemistry, and so on. Positivism ultimately had to reject both realism and causality as unverifiable; Hume's need to reject realism and causality on positivist grounds is discussed by Popper.[12]

When literary positivists attempted to make criticism more scientific, they tended to do so by eliminating as much as possible the metaphysical content of literature. This often resulted in a sterile formalistic or statistical approach to literature; perhaps I should add that I do not think either formalism or statistics have to be sterile if used in a way that respects the metaphysical content of literature. René Wellek gives examples of what it would mean or has meant not to respect the metaphysical content of literature. When he discusses the literary positivism of Georg Brandes's *Main Currents of Nineteenth Century Literature,* he complains, "But of course Brandes' psychology has a reductive result: he cannot understand Kierkegaard's religion or philosophy. . . . Kierkegaard is often criticized for not sharing Brandes' outlook: he 'cannot and will not understand that the history of modern literature is identical with the liberation from the moral and religious conceptions of the tradition.' "[13]

Popper's conjectural philosophy of science offers a new program for scientific criticism—one that does not sacrifice the metaphysical content of literature and criticism, but does not abandon the pursuit of testability either. For those interested, I have written about this at greater length elsewhere,[14] but now I must return to the burial of positivism.

Positivism and Literary Criticism

First of all, then, who were the positivists, and especially the literary positivists? *Positivism* has represented many different things in its time. René Wellek uses the term broadly to cover much of nineteenth-century literary scholarship, under the influence of science, and he mentions as typical Taine's slogan of "race, milieu, moment"[15]—suggesting that literature is determined by external forces—although he argues elsewhere that Taine was not really a positivist ("in the sense of believing in the doctrines of Comte, Mill or Spencer"[16]). Nicola Abagnano says, "Through its acceptance of the concept of the infinity of nature and of history, and therefore, of necessary and universal progress, positivism had affinities with the other important nineteenth-century philosophical movement, absolute idealism, and belongs with it in the general range of romanticism."[17]

This somewhat counterintuitive subsumption of positivism within romanticism has much to recommend it in considering positivism's excesses, but we must keep in mind that positivism can also be opposed to absolute idealism, as René Wellek notes apropos of Taine: "Still admitting Taine's rejection of many of the central doctrines of the most eminent positivists, one could argue that he was a positivist in a wide and loose sense. The worship of the natural sciences and their methods points in this direction: seen in the wide perspective of 19th-century intellectual history, Taine seems to belong to the reaction against early idealism."[18]

In addition, positivism both predates and postdates romanticism. Ian Hacking identifies four epochs of positivism: Hume's positivism (1739), Comte's positivism (1830–42), logical positivism (1920–40), and the contemporary positivism of Bas van Frassen's *The Scientific Image* (1980).[19] Positivism's most characteristic thesis is that the methods of science should be applied to all areas of inquiry, including the study of literature. As John Stuart Mill puts it in his famous volume on logic and scientific method, "The backward state of the moral sciences can only be remedied by applying to them the methods of physical science, duly extended and generalized."[20] I agree with Mill here, although as I have said, I do not agree with Mill's antimetaphysical understanding of science.

This central idea of the unity of the scientific method of inquiry actually predates Hacking's first epoch (that is, Hume's epoch, 1739), for it was already put forward in Spinoza's pioneering work on the scientific approach to biblical interpretation, his *Tractatus Theologico-Politicus* (1670). Spinoza writes, "I may sum up the matter by saying that the method of interpreting Scripture does not widely differ from the method of interpreting nature—in fact, it is almost the same."[21] He goes on to show that the great scandal of interpretation is the willingness of scholars to read the Bible literally or figuratively depending on which reading supports their overall assumptions. Those who wanted to prove that the Bible was right and science was wrong would read it literally. Those who wanted to prove that the Bible never conflicted with science would read it figuratively. Such an ad hoc system of reading placed interpretation beyond criticism and so made it worthless for Spinoza. The scientific way, he argued, was to follow a strict methodological rule, such as always to prefer a literal interpretation unless that was overruled by evidence internal to the text. He says, "If we would know whether Moses believed God to be a fire or not, we must on no account decide the question on grounds of the reasonableness or the reverse of such an opinion, but must judge solely by the other opinions of Moses which are on record."[22] Only by following such a strict methodological rule could interpreters provide others with the opportunity to refute them and so be scientific. Possibly, Spinoza's motivation in preferring this rule was not concern with openness to refutation, but rather his belief that evidence found in the Bible was divinely revealed and therefore true, and thus the only basis for scientific deductions (according to his rationalistic view of science).

Spinoza's thesis of the unity of scientific and literary critical method had profound influence, not only on Mill, but on Lessing and Coleridge before Mill, and on Hippolyte Taine and I. A. Richards afterward.[23] The limitation of Spinoza's idea of scientific criticism was that it was purely rationalist and not at all empiricist—that is, Spinoza thought one could obtain certain knowledge in the human sciences through deductive reasoning from self-evident axioms, and he was not interested in experimental testing of the conjectures of literary criticism or ethics. A later positivist, Hans Reichenbach, was to notice precisely this limitation of Spinoza's approach:

> There is no geometrical necessity, only a logical necessity concerning the consequences that follow from a given set of axioms; the mathematician cannot prove the axioms to be true. Had Spinoza foreseen this result of the modern philosophy of mathematics, he would not have attempted to construct his ethics after the pattern of geometry. He would have been horrified at the idea that a non-Spinozistic ethics could be constructed which would possess the same kind of cogency that his own system possessed, and that if his axioms were of the nature of geometrical axioms, they could not be given a demonstrative proof. It would not have helped him to turn them into results of experience, like the axioms of geometry, for empirical truth is not what he wanted. He wanted to establish ethical axioms that are unquestionable. He wanted axioms that are necessary.[24]

Positivism is thus intimately tied, through Spinoza, to the birth and development of modern literary criticism. From the start, positivism presented a problem and a challenge to literary criticism. The problem was how to apply (appropriately and fruitfully) the methods of science to studying texts—a problem to which Spinoza's *Tractatus* provided the first brilliantly detailed solution. The challenge was to equal or at least approximate the successes of natural science in discovery, explanation, and testability. This is a challenge that Mill thought the moral or human sciences had not yet met nearly two centuries after Spinoza, whose work on scientific interpretation had been forced underground because of its implications for religious orthodoxies. In response to Mill (and to Spinoza, whose fame had spread, as is often the case with authors forced underground), nineteenth-century and twentieth-century literary critics adapted the rigor and knowledge of various social sciences, beginning with psychology and sociology, to literary criticism. This process has been studied by such historians of science and criticism as Stanley Edgar Hyman and Herbert J. Muller.[25]

Such adaptations of social science to criticism (beginning with Saint-Beuve's use of psychology and Taine's of sociology) are characteristic of the best and worst in modern criticism. They represent a partial success in meeting the positivist challenge, for as Hyman argued more than forty years ago, no critic would want to forgo the wealth of new discoveries about literature already made possible by the application of psychological, sociological, economic, and anthropological approaches.[26] And since that time the application of linguistics to literary study, via formalism, through structuralism, to semiotics and poststructuralism, has only continued the scientific effort in criticism originated by positivism (paradoxically so, in the case of poststructuralism).

Given that even poststructuralist theory is made possible by the investigation of the connections of criticism to linguistic science, an investigation stimulated by the positivist thesis of the unity of the method of inquiry, we can see that the quarrel of critical theory with positivism is really a family quarrel. Yet this is not to deny that positivism bought its unity of method at too high a cost—namely, the exclusion of metaphysics. Within literary criticism the adaptations of social science to criticism have sometimes led into scientistic dead ends that have bred skepticism about the basic assumption of the unity of scientific method.

Even René Wellek, who is basically sympathetic to the rational critical tradition within which positivism arose, was moved by such excesses to dismiss the scientific approach to criticism rather sweepingly in his 1946 essay "The Revolt against Positivism in Recent Literary Scholarship." Wellek starts by praising literary positivism: "the many attempts to transfer the methods of natural science to the study of literature . . . was the intellectually most coherent and respectable movement in nineteenth century scholarship." Yet he finds that many of these literary positivists were overreachers:

> There was the effort to imitate the methods of natural science by a study of causal antecedents and origins which, in practice, justified the tracing of any kind of relationship as long as it was possible on chronological grounds. Applied more rigidly, scientific causality was used to explain literary phenomena by determining causes in economic, social, and political conditions. Other scholars even tried to introduce the quantitative methods of science: statistics, charts, and graphs. And finally there was a most ambitious group which made a large-scale attempt to use biological concepts in the tracing of the evolution of literature. Ferdinand Brunetiere and John Addington Symonds conceived of the evolution of genres on the analogue of biological species.[27]

Reacting to the hubris with which such causal explanations were pressed, Wellek denies that there can be a science of criticism. Yet Wellek's understanding of science in this essay is undeniably positivistic—that is, he assumes that a scientific approach must exclude metaphysics. He says, "A science of literature which divorces literary study from criticism (i.e., value judgment) is impossible."[28] I would agree. But both science and criticism have passed beyond the need of such positivism.

Wellek described the antipositivist revolt in criticism, the revolt in defense of the metaphysical content of literature, as being already a half-century old when he wrote. He dated it from the writings of Wilhelm Dilthey in 1883 and of Benedetto Croce in 1917. That the revolt should still be going strong a century later is evidence that science is still equated in the literary and philosophical mind with positivism. More recent attacks on positivism have far exceeded Wellek's skeptical strictures and have attacked the very notion that criticism is a rational enterprise. Geoffrey Hartman was to argue in his *The Fate of Reading* that reason is an idealistic disorder.[29]

The Radical Origins of Positivism

Hartman, like many others today, attacks reason, science, and positivism as if they were equivalent, and attacks them for being anti-human, indifferent to human values or to anything that cannot be empirically measured. This blatantly disregards the explicit statements by both Comte and Mill that they were developing their systems to rescue scientific thought from a narrow empiricism. Both were utopian social reformers, and the social reformer Saint Simon was the inventor of the term *positivism*.[30] Comte's positivist system, which was the first to bear the actual name of positivism, began with the problem of the failure of the French Revolution to alleviate human misery and oppression. Comte took the revolution to be the crucial experiment refuting the eighteenth-century radicalism of Voltaire and Bentham. Social revolution, he argued, could not take place simply by raising the consciousness of the masses to perceive injustice. In addition, we needed a proper understanding of the laws of social change, and he, like Marx afterward, hoped to set forth what those laws were, so that the social revolution could proceed. Popper, in his *Poverty of Historicism,* was later to criticize the notion of the application of laws of motion to social institutions as being based on an erroneous analogy.[31]

Far from being indifferent to human values, Comte ultimately designed a positivist religion to go along with his positivist state. Comte's religion included a roster of positivist saints, whose contributions to human progress were to be celebrated in annual festivals according to the new positivist calendar. Those who hindered human progress were to be excommunicated from the positivist church, hence becoming the original devils of positivism. When Comte's contemporaries, like Mill himself, objected to Comte's positivism, the objection was not that positivism was indifferent to values, but rather that it took values for granted in a very uncritical manner and then proceeded to legislate those values in a very undemocratic manner. The notion that positivism is indifferent to values has a basis in fact, since as I have said,

now claimed by antipositivists in their attacks on positivism must include the following:

1. The self is fictional.
2. Causal explanation is a delusion.
3. Observation is always mingled with ideology.
4. Facts cannot even be perceived without prior theory.
5. Blind empiricism (fact gathering) leads nowhere.
6. Metaphysics and theology are to be rejected.
7. Science must be seen in social context.
8. Scientistic (blindly inappropriate) applications of science to other areas of inquiry must be avoided.

All of these theses can be found in Comte or Mill and were further developed or modified by Taine, Mach, and Russell. The significance of such theses ought to be not whether they are positivist or antipositivist, scientific or antiscientific, but whether they are true and lead to fruitful research in various areas of inquiry, including literary criticism. To explore this question, we need to reclaim our positivist heritage, while rejecting that positivist hostility to metaphysics which somehow still flourishes among our literary critical avant-garde and which leads only into the cul de sac of pragmatism. A more sophisticated assessment of positivism will make it easier to begin the task of developing a scientific, which is to say testable, literary criticism.

Notes

1. Richard Rorty, "Science as Solidarity," in *Language and Argument in Scholarship and Public Affairs,* eds. John Nelson et al. (Madison: Univ. of Wisconsin Press, 1987), 51.

2. Ibid., 46.

3. Richard Rorty, *Consequences of Pragmatism* (Minneapolis: Univ. of Minnesota Press, 1982), 191–94.

4. Madison: Univ. of Wisconsin Press, 1987.

5. Rorty on Lovejoy is found in *Consequences of Pragmatism,* 169–71; for René Wellek on literary positivism see "The Revolt Against Positivism in Recent European Literary Scholarship," rpt. in *Concepts of Criticism,* ed. Stephen G. Nichols, Jr. (New Haven: Yale Univ. Press, 1963), 256–81.

6. Herbert Feigl, "The Origin and Spirit of Logical Positivism," in *The Legacy of Logical Positivism,* eds. Peter Achinstein and Stephen F. Barker (Baltimore: Johns Hopkins Univ. Press, 1969), 5.

7. A succinct discussion of what Popper means by metaphysics as well as what he means by critical discussion of irrefutable metaphysical claims can be found in his *Conjectures and Refutations,* rpt. in *Popper Selections,* ed. David Miller (Princeton: Princeton Univ. Press, 1985), 209–19.

8. Agassi's essay can be found in his *Science in Flux,* eds. R. S. Cohen and Marx Wartofsky (Dordrecht: D. Reidel, 1975), 208–39.

9. Ibid., 211.

10. For Popper on psychoanalysis see "The Problem of Demarcation" rpt. in *Popper Selections,* ed. David Miller (Princeton: Princeton Univ. Press, 1985), 128.

11. A. J. Ayer, *Language, Truth and Logic* (New York: Dover, 1945).

12. Popper's discussion of Hume's positivist rejection of realism and causality is in his "The Problem of Induction" in *Conjectures and Refutations,* rpt. in *Popper Selections,* ed. David Miller (Princeton: Princeton Univ. Press, 1985), 106ff.

13. René Wellek, *A History of Modern Criticism* (New Haven: Yale Univ. Press, 1965), 4:363.

14. Edward Davenport, "Why Theorize about Literature?" in *What Is Literature?* ed. Paul Hernadi (Bloomington: Indiana Univ. Press, 1978) 35–46; "Wilhelm Dilthey Updated: Values and Objectivity in Literary Criticism," *Mosaic* 14,4 (Fall, 1981): 89–105; "Scientific Method as Literary Criticism," *Et Cetera* 42,4 (Winter, 1985): 331–50; "Pursuing Truth in Criticism," *Publication of the Society for Literature and Science* 2,2 (March 1987): 1–5; "The New Politics of Knowledge: Rorty's Pragmatism and the Rhetoric of the Human Sciences," *Philosophy of the Social Sciences* 17,3 (September 1987): 377–94; "The Scientific Spirit," in *Literary Theory's Future(s),* ed. Joseph Natoli (Champaign: Univ. of Illinois Press, 1989) 151–80.

15. Wellek, "Revolt against Positivism," 256.

16. Wellek, *A History of Modern Criticism* (New Haven: Yale Univ. Press, 1965), 4:35.

17. Nicola Abagnano, s.v. "Positivism" in *The Encyclopedia of Philosophy* (New York: MacMillan, 1967), 5:414–19.

18. Wellek, *History of Modern Criticism,* 4:35.

19. Ian Hacking, *Representing and Intervening* (Cambridge: Cambridge Univ. Press, 1983), 41–57.

20. John Stuart Mill, "A System of Logic," 1844, in *J. S. Mill's Philosophy of Scientific Method,* ed. Ernest Nagel (New York: Hafner, 1950), 307.

21. Benedict Spinoza, *Theologico-Political Treatise* (1670: rpt. New York: Dover, 1951), 99.

22. Ibid., 102.

23. For Spinoza's influence see Thomas McFarland, *Coleridge and the Pantheist Tradition* (Oxford: Oxford Univ. Press, 1969).

24. Hans Reichenbach, *The Rise of Scientific Philosophy* (Berkeley: Univ. of California Press, 1951), 278–79.

25. Stanley Edgar Hyman, *The Armed Vision* (New York: Random House, 1947–55); Herbert J. Muller, *Science and Criticism: The Humanistic Tradition in Contemporary Thought* (New Haven: Yale Univ. Press, 1943).

26. Hyman, *The Armed Vision.*

27. Wellek, "Revolt against Positivism," 257–58.

28. René Wellek, "The Concept of Evolution in Literary History" in *Concepts of Criticism,* ed. Stephen G. Nichols, Jr., 37–53.

29. Geoffrey H. Hartman, *The Fate of Reading and Other Essays* (Chicago: Univ. of Chicago Press, 1975).

30. See *The Encyclopedia of Philosophy* (New York: Macmillan, 1967) 5:414.

31. Karl Popper, "The Poverty of Historicism" 1944/45 in *Popper Selections,* ed. David Miller (Princeton: Princeton Univ. Press, 1985), 300.

32. Bertrand Russell, *The Scientific Outlook* (New York: W. W. Norton, 1931), 260.

33. Ian Hacking, *Representing and Intervening,* 43.

34. E. D. Hirsch, *Validity in Interpretation* (New Haven: Yale Univ. Press, 1967); Gerald Graff, *Literature against Itself* (Chicago: Univ. of Chicago Press, 1979).

35. W. J. T. Mitchell, ed., *Against Theory: Literary Studies and the New Pragmatism* (Chicago: Univ. of Chicago Press, 1985).

36. Thomas S. Kuhn, *The Structure of Scientific Revolutions* (Chicago: Univ. of Chicago Press, 1962; rev. ed., 1970).

37. Richard Rorty, *Consequences of Pragmatism* (Minneapolis: Univ. of Minnesota Press, 1982).

Bibliography

ABAGNANO, NICOLA. "Positivism." In *The Encyclopedia of Philosophy*. New York: Macmillan, 1967. 5:414–19.

AGASSI, JOSEPH. "The Nature of Scientific Problems and Their Roots in Metaphysics." In *Science in Flux,* ed. R. S. Cohen and Marx Wartofsky. Dordrecht: D. Reidel, 1975. 208–39.

AYER, A. J. *Language, Truth and Logic*. New York: Dover, 1945.

DAVENPORT, EDWARD. "The New Politics of Knowledge: Rorty's Pragmatism and the Rhetoric of the Human Sciences." *Philosophy of the Social Sciences* 17,3 (September 1987): 377–94.

_____. "Pursuing Truth in Criticism." *Publication of the Society for Literature and Science* 2,2 (March 1987):1–50.

_____. "Scientific Method as Literary Criticism." *Et Cetera* 42,4 (Winter 1985): 331–50.

_____. "The Scientific Spirit." In *Literary Theory's Future(s)* ed. Joseph Natoli. Champaign: University of Illinois Press, 1989. 151–80.

_____. "Why Theorize about Literature?" In *What Is Literature?* ed. Paul Hernadi. Bloomington: Indiana University Press, 1978.

_____. "Wilhelm Dilthey Updated: Values and Objectivity in Literary Criticism." *Mosaic* 14,4 (Fall 1981): 89–105.

FEIGL, HERBERT. "The Origin and Spirit of Logical Positivism." In *The Legacy of Logical Positivism,* ed. Peter Achinstein and Stephen F. Barker. Baltimore: Johns Hopkins University Press, 1969.

FISH, STANLEY. *Is There a Text in This Class? The Authority of Interpretive Communities*. Cambridge, Mass.: Harvard University Press, 1980.

GRAFF, GERALD. *Literature against Itself.* Chicago: University of Chicago Press, 1979.

HACKING, IAN. *Representing and Intervening*. Cambridge: Cambridge University Press, 1983.

HARTMAN, GEOFFREY H. *The Fate of Reading and Other Essays*. Chicago: University of Chicago Press, 1975.

HIRSCH, E. D. *Validity in Interpretation.* New Haven: Yale University Press, 1967.

HYMAN, STANLEY EDGAR. *The Armed Vision.* New York: Random House, 1947–55.

KUHN, THOMAS S. *The Structure of Scientific Revolutions.* Chicago: University of Chicago Press, 1962; rev. ed., 1970.

MCFARLAND, THOMAS. *Coleridge and the Pantheist Tradition.* Oxford: Oxford University Press, 1969.

MILL, JOHN STUART. "A System of Logic." 1844. In *J. S. Mill's Philosophy of Scientific Method,* ed. Ernest Nagel. New York: Hafner, 1950.

MILLER, DAVID, ed. *Popper, Selections.* Princeton: Princeton University Press, 1985.

MITCHELL, W. J. T., ed. *Against Theory: Literary Studies and the New Pragmatism.* Chicago: University of Chicago Press, 1985.

MULLER, HERBERT J. *Science and Criticism.* New Haven: Yale University Press, 1943.

NAGEL, ERNEST, ed. *J. S. Mill's Philosophy of Scientific Method.* New York: Hafner, 1950.

NELSON, JOHN, et al. eds. *Language and Argument in Scholarship and Public Affairs.* Madison: University of Wisconsin Press, 1987.

POINCARÉ, HENRI. *Science and Hypothesis.* 1905. Trans. New York: Dover Publications, 1952.

POPPER, KARL. *The Logic of Scientific Discovery.* New York: Harper & Row, 1959. Originally published as *Logik der Forschung* (Springer, 1934).

————. *Objective Knowledge.* 1934. Reprint. Oxford: Oxford University Press, 1972.

REICHENBACH, HANS. *The Rise of Scientific Philosophy.* Berkeley: University of California Press, 1951.

RORTY, RICHARD. *Consequences of Pragmatism.* Minneapolis: University of Minnesota Press, 1982.

————. "Science as Solidarity." In *Language and Argument in Scholarship and Public Affairs,* John Nelson et al. eds. Madison: University of Wisconsin Press, 1987.

RUSSELL, BERTRAND. *The Scientific Outlook.* New York: W. W. Norton, 1931.

SPINOZA, BENEDICT. *Theologico-Political Treatise.* 1670. Reprint. New York: Dover, 1951.

WELLEK, RENÉ. *A History of Modern Criticism.* New Haven: Yale University Press, 1965.

————. "The Revolt against Positivism in Recent European Literary Scholarship." 1946. Reprinted in *Concepts of Criticism,* ed. Stephen Nichols, Jr. New Haven: Yale University Press, 1963.

Literature and Medicine
Why Should the Physician Read . . . or Write?

CHARLES ANDERSON

A way of seeing is also a way of not seeing.
—Kenneth Burke, *Permanence and Change*

DURING THE DECADE of the 1980s, literature and medicine has become a legitimate, if modest, field of study. Its practitioners teach in and out of medical schools, present papers at national and regional conferences, publish articles in journals ranging from *Literature and Medicine* to *Annals of Internal Medicine* to *College English,* write books, and compile bibliographies and collections of teaching materials. Although work in the field is wonderfully varied and has grown remarkably sophisticated, it continues to be dominated by crucial questions that bedevil physicians, writers, advocates, and critics: What, after all, is the point? How do medicine and literature relate? Why *should* the physician read?

Answers to these basic questions range from the highly abstract to the very practical, from what Kathryn Montgomery Hunter calls "the enlightenment model" to "the engineering model."[1] On the abstract end, literature is believed to help "sensitize medical students to the inner needs and attitudes of their patients,"[2] to help physicians "look with feeling for the subject of [human experience],"[3] to "enlarge imagination and educate sensibility,"[4] and to enable its physician readers "to comprehend and celebrate the mystery of the human condition."[5] On a more pragmatic level, literature serves to help "the doctor to read, explicate and interpret, as well as control language,"[6] to reinforce the physician's ability to read and interpret the "signs" of the patient's body in a way analogous to the way the literary critic interprets the "signs" of the literary text,[7] and to alter, perhaps to improve, the taking of more useful or more meaningful medical histories.[8]

These and other reasons offered for the incorporation of literature into medical education and clinical practice stem from a long and complex history of medical progress which has enabled physicians to make enormous advances in the treatment of serious diseases. Such advances have, simultaneously, spawned widespread criticism from patients who feel alienated, who feel their doctors have become distant, uncommunicative, and unable to address crucial aspects of sickness which most concern the patients. Philosopher S. Kay Toombs, describing her own encounters with physicians attempting to treat her multiple sclerosis, relates a typical experience.

> In discussing my illness with physicians, it has often seemed to me that we have been somehow talking at cross purposes, discussing different things, never quite reaching one another. This inability to communicate does not, for the most part, result from inattentiveness or insensitivity but from a fundamental disagreement about the nature of illness. Rather than representing a shared reality between us, illness represents in effect two quite distinct realities, the meaning of one being significantly and qualitatively different from the meaning of the other.[9]

Even the briefest survey of the literature shows that the study of such encounters has become the staple of not only literature and medicine, but of most of the medical humanities. It also shows that, though most studies involve more or less specific calls for change in the practice and/or teaching of medicine, relatively few involve specific plans for implementation or even suggestions for starting points. In fact, most writers seem content to set forth a more or less complicated plan for patient-physician interaction[10] and then to assume that merely setting forth an alternative will bring it into being. This is not, unfortunately, the case. "Without the necessary definitions, tools and skills," says Eric Cassell, "all that has been created is a moral injunction: 'Go thou and do likewise.' "[11]

Scholars who do attempt to set forth a more detailed plan most often base it upon the discourse of literary criticism, a highly academic discourse that valorizes the analysis of literature and encourages the reader, in order to understand the text, to interpose some form of aesthetic distance between himself or herself and the work, seeing it in terms of a more or less coherent literary theory. In many recent plans, the patient becomes a metaphorical text and the physician becomes a metaphorical critic reading the text under the influence of one or another of the literary schools—hermeneutics, phenomenology, or deconstruction, for example.[12]

Although there seems little doubt that such applications shed light upon the events of sickness and health and patient-physician interaction, it also seems to me that they reinforce, in subtle but crucial ways, exactly those behaviors that have created such a powerful insistence upon changes in the medical profession, behaviors Toombs calls "habits of mind." If the point of literature and medicine, as a discipline, is to encourage physicians to trade the objective, scientific constraints of cause and effect and simple linearity for those of, say, hermeneutics, "the medieval fourfold sense of scripture . . . [which] has the advantage of neatly organizing the various elements of interpretive activity in a logically progressive fashion,"[13] then the study of literature and medicine will not lead to a more humanistic medicine. Instead, it will contribute to further alienation of both physician and patient by providing physicians with new tools to systematize, to objectify, and finally to appropriate not only the disease but also the human experience and particular meaning the disease holds for the patient.

But this need not be the case. If Toombs is correct in asserting that the patient and the physician experience the medical event as existing in qualitatively distinct realities, an attempt to change the nature of the encounter must involve a change in the "habit of mind" producing the particular reality within which the physician or the patient dwells. If we shift our focus to literary discourse, seeing it not as words about literature but as all of the interchanges, transactions, and symbolic experiences taking place as the reader engages the literary text, we will soon discover that the importance and power of literature stem from the fact that it lives at the intersection of language and experience out of which Toombs's "quite distinct realities" arise. Furthermore, we will see that the literary experience provides an essential doorway into the symbolic, interpretive, and humanistic processes that provide the energy, the impetus, and the empathic potential necessary to create a common reality inhabited by physician and patient. And finally, we will begin to see ways in which literature can help to bring about needed changes in the practice of medicine.

In the pages that follow, I will describe a theory of symbolic interaction which explains, in relatively uncomplicated terms, why patients and physicians seem to speak about such different things when they address the events of sickness. I will then relate that theory to the histo-

ry of medicine and show that many of the current difficulties in medicine arise directly from conflicts among discursive relationships implied
by that history. And finally, I will suggest specific ways in which literature, literary discourse, and literary experiences may help to reshape
the "habits of mind" of physicians seeking to address the illnesses of
their patients.

In *An Essay on Man,* Ernst Cassirer describes what may be the most
basic attribute of human beings: our reliance upon a *"symbolic system"* to
respond to the world.

> No longer in a merely physical universe, man lives in a symbolic universe.
> Language, myth, art, and religion are parts of this universe. They are the
> varied threads which weave the symbolic net, the tangled web of human
> experiences. All human progress in thought and experience refines upon and
> strengthens this net. No longer can man confront reality immediately; he
> cannot see it, as it were, face to face. . . . Instead of dealing with the things
> themselves man is in a sense constantly conversing with himself. . . . He
> lives rather in the midst of imaginary emotions, in hopes and fears, in illu-
> sions and disillusions, in his fantasies and dreams. "What disturbs and
> alarms man," said Epictetus, "are not the things, but his opinions and fancies
> about the things."[14]

Because we depend upon symbols to mediate our responses to the
things of the world, "man lives not merely in a broader reality; he lives,
so to speak, in a new *dimension* of reality."[15] Reality itself, in our sense
of the word, moves from the external world to the internal, becoming
an issue of interpretation and meaning rather than simple reflexes responding to unmediated stimulation, an issue of language at work upon
the "things of the world."

Although there are commonalities, each of us understands world experience in a unique way, different enough from others so that each
particular conversation about the things of the world is likely to differ
from others in important respects. Out of these differences arise what
psychologist George A. Kelly calls "personal constructs," elaborate
symbolic and verbal models that represent or encode the way in which
each particular human being construes or represents or has made sense
of past experience. Personal constructs are important because they make
past experience available to present time and thereby enable each of us
to predict the outcome of current events in order to act toward the
future. Personal constructs thus provide continuity and a paradigm or
schema for making sense of the events of one's life. They comprise our
immediately available theories of how the world is, what its rules are,
and where we fit in.[16]

Building upon the work of Kelly and others, rhetorician and educational theorist James Britton suggests that each personal construct, or representation, becomes a storehouse of experience and that one of its most important qualities is that it "lasts in time in a way events don't. So you can work on it. You go back over experiences and work on them."[17] But you cannot return to the event itself, except in memory and only through language about it. If the event is one that fits the expectations generated by the representation, then talking or writing or perhaps reading about it or about similar events will allow it to be smoothly incorporated into the representation as a confirmation of and further evidence for the fit between inner reality and outer world. But if the event is one that challenges important aspects of the representation, then either the representation must be altered in such a way that the event can become a part of how one knows the world to be or the event, as we understand it, must be changed in order to preserve the representation.

In either case, the process is unmistakably literary and symbolic in nature, engaging its participants in what Britton calls the spectator role: "Going back over things in order to come to terms with them—to deal with as yet undigested events."[18] In this role, the primary need and end is to create a story or a narrative or to engage in a dialogue in which characters and events interact in ways that lend themselves to interpretation and lead to understanding. If the story can be "written" or the drama "experienced" in a way that makes sense, the event can be "digested," and those involved can go on about the business of living. If it cannot, then it must be rewritten again and again until it is dealt with. The spectator role is removed from actuality because events happen, are done, and cannot be changed. Nonetheless, spectatorship is essential to incorporating events into the representation that comprises the symbolic dimension of reality in which we, as human beings, must live. It is where we work out our values and is, therefore, a necessary prelude to dealing with events in the future.

But we do not live alone. We are, in fact, insatiably social creatures, needing the support of and interaction with other human beings. Because language is dialogical by definition, we need to belong to communities of persons with whom to share our talk. If there is no such community, we will find others and create one. Because of this need, our sense or senses of reality are not simply a matter of individual preference. To belong to a given community (most of us belong to many) is to participate in its conversation about the things of the world and to agree, explicitly or implicitly, with its sense of what those things signify, which ones affect us, and how we will respond to them. Benjamin Lee Whorf addresses this aspect of reality-building and describes the processes by which language and community act upon the perceptions and practices of us all.

> We dissect nature along lines laid down by our native languages. The categories and types that we isolate from the world of phenomena we do not find there because they stare every observer in the face; on the contrary, the world is presented in a kaleidoscopic flux of impressions which has to be organized by our minds—and this means largely by the linguistic systems in our minds. We cut nature up, organize it into concepts, and ascribe significances as we do, largely because we are parties to an agreement to organize it in this way—an agreement that holds throughout our speech community and is codified in the patterns of our language.[19]

Because particular languages select from the "kaleidoscopic flux of impressions" precisely those elements that validate their views or representations of the world, Whorf holds that "every language is a vast pattern-system, different from others, in which are . . . ordained the forms and categories by which the personality not only communicates, but also analyzes nature, notices or neglects types of relationship and phenomena, channels his reasoning, and builds the house of his consciousness."[20]

While Whorf is concerned with communities the size of natural language groups, Kenneth Burke describes similar processes at work within narrower communities comprising particular professions and fields of study. Over time and through conversations about the things of the world which concern the members of a given profession, each field selects from the sum of possibilities its own particular concerns and develops its own particular set of terms through which members may legitimately "talk" about those concerns.

> Not only does the nature of our terms affect the nature of our observations, in the sense that the terms direct the attention to one field rather than to another . . . [but] *many of the "observations" are but implications of the particular terminology in . . . which the observations are made.* In brief, much that we take as observations about "reality" may be but the spinning out of possibilities implicit in our particular choice of terms.[21]

The combination of all the particular terms within a given field constitute that field's "terministic screen," which comprises both a way of seeing and an elimination of other ways incompatible with its particular terminology. According to Burke, "we *must* use terministic screens" if we are to participate in the events of a particular field or profession.[22] Although terministic screens are not rigidly determinative—we can change professions and, clearly, professions do shift perspectives—they serve to shape the reality we perceive and in which we live as long as we are a part of the community speaking its particular language and using its particular set of terms.[23]

The representations, or constructs, out of which we find personal meaning and a sense of personal reality differ significantly from those in which we locate our public selves. Although both emerge from a complex environment of negotiations among self, community, profession, experience, and the things of the world, our personal constructs arise from our need to make sense of past events in order to focus our values and to plan action in the future. In this realm, we depend upon the stories of others to help us overcome the limits of our immediate environments. Such stories enable us to extend our range of experience and to incorporate events into our world that we have not experienced, but we are free to take or leave them. Within the terministic screens of our professional communities, however, we depend upon the experiences of others to teach us the rules by which we must behave in order to be members of the club. Stories involving our colleagues are most likely to contain exemplars of successful or unsuccessful behavior designed to affirm the values of the field within which we work. If we expect to change those values and the reality they describe, we must first learn them and be bound by them. In Britton's terms, as members of professional communities, we engage in the role of the participant, the person whose thought and action is directed not toward integration of past or virtual experience, but toward doing things in the outside world. What we do in the outside world has important implications for what we do in the interior world of our personal constructs, but it is a different linguistic and symbolic process.[24] In medicine, recognizing and elaborating upon the differences between personal constructs and terministic screens opens a way of understanding Toombs's sense that she and her physician were speaking from two qualitatively different realities. They were.

Although individual physicians vary in their specific understandings of the terministic screen with which their professional community deals, everything they do is heavily influenced by the presence of that screen, which is an enormously powerful one reaching back more than twenty-five centuries. By tracing the historical development of the terministic screen, or symbolic reality, with which physicians are most concerned, one may see the ways in which patients, physicians, and medicine have been construed by that reality. Understanding this construal leads directly to an understanding of why Toombs and other patients feel as they do and what effect literary discourse might have on the situation and why.

In its earliest forms, medicine was an adjunct to myth and religion.

Its "cures" consisted of strictly defined and practiced rituals, medications, and surgical procedures designed to appease various deities and to drive evil spirits, demons, devices, and so on from the bodies of sick persons. In ancient societies, the healing function of medicine was intimately related to a larger symbolism manifesting cultural and religious beliefs about the nature of the world, the cosmos, and the powers that controlled them.[25] A crucial element of ancient medicine was a belief in the power of the spoken word, of dialogue between the sick person and others, as a cure for or palliative to disease. The highly verbal nature of healing served to cast patients into roles of central significance, making them speaking partners, full participants in the cultural, religious, and philosophical milieu of their respective societies. Even those who could not be cured or who were cast out of their communities because of their diseases played important, well-defined, though often cruel roles in the cosmic dramas by which those communities lived and through which their members found meaning in their lives.

Medicine lost many of its ties with religion and mysticism when it became "a part of pre-Socratic Ionian natural philosophy, from which it imbibed an interest in the explanation of the natural world through reason, as well as a fascination with the ideas of cause and effect and change."[26] Such an interest created discretionary space, room for exploration, speculation, and even some experimentation. It weakened the ties between medicine and religion and strengthened those with natural philosophy (science). During the fifth century B.C., the Hippocratic school of medicine in Greece significantly extended this process. As Edmund Pellegrino and David Thomasma explain,

> the Hippocratic physician insisted on freedom from magico-religious and even philosophical constraints. Observation, reason, and moral considerations became the bases for his actions . . . reason based on observation . . . [promised] new knowledge; and thus the expansion of human capabilities. As a result, a wide variety of theories of medicine and therapeutics emerged in the Hellenic and Roman world. They replaced the carefully standardized modes of treatment to which the medicine man-priest had been previously confined.
>
> Technical authority was established so that the physician might judge what was best for his patient, not just what ritual he might apply.[27]

Disease became an objective phenomenon that doctors worked to isolate, observe, describe, and treat. According to Cassell, the Hippocratic physicians believed that "causes of diseases could be found within the constitution of men and in disturbances in their inner and outer equilibrium resulting from diet or heredity or from a maladaptation to their inner or outer environments."[28] Disease was no longer understood to be a visitation of the gods, and the Greek rationalist physicians did all they could to ensure that it was not treated as such by confining their inquiries into its workings to what Cassell calls "the narrower class" of questions.

> Before Hippocrates, and probably for most of the other cultures of our present world, *only* the problem of fate, the wider question "Why *me?*" was pertinent, and the answers were provided by religion or mysticism.
>
> When Hippocrates introduced the rational basis of medicine, he did not deny the cogency of the wider question. Rather, he introduced a systematic method of understanding and answering the narrower questions. What is the matter with the ankle? What should one do for the ankle? What will happen to the ankle?[29]

This emphasis upon observation and reason was directly responsible for great advances in the treatment of disease. In addition, the Hippocratic writings defined the proper and just relationship between the patient and the physician, thereby prescribing a code of ethics and creating an ideal of the kindly, concerned, competent physician which endures to this day.

> Greek medicine . . . defined for itself a moral framework which made the patient-physician relationship a private affair. The physician became a benign, paternalistic figure who still retained his old hieratic as well as his new rational capabilities. He determined what was good for his patient and disclosed only so much of his reasons or his art as he thought appropriate. He assumed moral as well as technical authority, declaring his relationship with the patient a sacred precinct—guarded by confidentiality and not to be intruded upon by anyone beyond the patient or his family.[30]

The Hippocratic physicians effectively isolated themselves and their patients from the larger cultural, philosophical, and religious milieu of their time, leading to the designation of medicine as the "silent art." This silence was important because the Hippocratic writers were highly conscious of the use of language in earlier rituals of healing and wished to dissociate themselves from what they considered poor practice. Their treatments were based upon objective measurement that "included the information of the senses, [but] it decidedly did not include much of what the patient said, since that was merely opinion."[31] Thus, the Greek physicians became more and more concerned with the somatic or the physical, and in the process, according to Pedro Lain Entralgo, the psychological, philosophical, or symbolic aspects of the medical event, crucial parts of earlier forms of treatment, were reduced to such a degree that the physicians finally came to view all sickness as disruption or abnormality in the physical nature of the sick person. Even dreams were considered to be functions of the four humors.[32]

In terms of the theory developed earlier in this discussion, the Hippocratic physicians, as a community, began developing a terministic screen in which the most critical elements of the medical event were outward signs or symptoms of the diseases from which their patients suffered. This lead to tremendous growth in treating the ailments of patients, but it also worked to exclude other representations from the medical event. Issues of fate and meaning, the larger questions comprising the patients' personal constructs, the individual symbolic representations by which they understood their lives and planned their courses of action were, at least in theory, excluded. More importantly, physicians began the process of excluding the patient from dialogical involvement in the medical event. The physician might listen, but he would not hear.

Medieval Christian physicians, philosophers, and theologians did much to reintegrate the scientific and the symbolic aspects of the medical event by affirming at once the absolute individuality and worth of each person, the spiritual implications of suffering associated with disease and the tending of the sick, and the somatic or physical origins of bodily ailments. For the medieval physician, disease was both physiological and symbolic, having significance and meaning in the lives of sufferers and those who tended them which went far beyond the narrowly defined relationship of physical causes and their effects as prescribed and treated by classical medicine.[33] Medieval medicine provided a compelling restatement of Plato's insistence that the body not be separated from the soul in medical treatment and that "good words" be an integral and central part of all treatment.[34] It was through words and words only that the medieval Christian achieved the balance and harmony of being that might produce health of the whole person. As Lain Entralgo, quoting Clement of Alexandria, puts it,

> "Medicine cures the ills of the body; but wisdom, the *Logos* of the Father, the creator of mankind, takes care of the creature as a whole, and heals the body and the soul. . . . That is why we call the *Logos* 'savior,' because it has discovered spiritual remedies for the welfare and salvation of men; it preserves health, discovers harm, points out the causes of illness, cuts out the roots of unreasonable appetites, ordains the regimen, prescribes all the antidotes to cure the patient. . . ."[35]

The medieval doctor had to be both a naturalist, treating the causes and symptoms of diseases, and a shaman of sorts, applying "good words," the "*Logos* of the Father," to the soul.

The effect upon western medicine as a whole, even upon physicians with no Christian faith, has been to create a view of the human being "as a 'person,' as a living, rational, free individual, capable of inner reflection and endowed with true inwardness."[36] However, the fact that medieval medicine also, by and large, embraced the classical diagnosis and treatment of the body as an object different from the soul or the personality of the sufferer served ultimately to preserve rather than resolve the dichotomy between the symbolic or psychological and the physical or scientific sides of medicine. This dichotomy created tremendous tension in a profession dominated by three conflicting imperatives: (1) the need to find causes and cures for the ills of the physical body; (2) the urge to explore the mysteries of the human body through dissection and experimentation, both of which had already begun to question classical anatomical dogma supported by the Church and the universities; and (3) the human and Christian imperatives to relieve suffering or at least to do no harm to the living, breathing persons under treatment. Physicians often did great harm, sometimes killing patients in the process of trying to effect cures, patients whose worth in the cosmology of the medieval community was infinite.

Into this highly tensive situation entered perhaps the most important single influence upon the development of medical discourse, René Descartes, who "was most interested" in "paving the way to a purely mechanical physics, biology, and medicine" based upon geometrical and mathematical principles.[37] In Descartes's philosophy, according to Etienne Gilson, "man alone has both a body and a mind; as to physical bodies, they are nothing but bodies . . . variously shaped particles of extension, arranged according to various orders, and occupying certain places in space. Even living bodies, animals for example, are mere machines, and our human body itself, when considered apart from the mind to which it is united, is nothing but a machine."[38] Through a process of "feature" transfer described by Owen Thomas in *Metaphor and Related Subjects,* Descartes's body machine metaphor became one of medicine's central working definitions. The attributes or features of "a machine" (inanimate, made of separate parts, breakable, fixable) became the defining characteristics of the body. And "our human body" became a machine to be understood, managed, and treated as one.[39]

The patient remained the center of the medical event, his return to health being its raison d'être, but in a working sense, the patient as a person came to have little place at all in the events of medicine, being merely attached to the machine delivered up for repair. The physician, as the mechanic (the image of the watchmaker would probably be more accurate), was free to manipulate, tinker with, or adjust the mechanism in whatever way seemed advisable to restore it to proper working order, ultimately, if all went well, restoring the patient to health.[40]

Descartes's metaphor, in combination with the overall power of his philosophy, thus created a conceptual context that rearticulated and finally legitimized the "objective" the patient-physician relationships at the center of the scientific medicine of the Greek naturalists. At the same time, it released the pressure exerted upon the physician by the need to relate to the living beings who might suffer terribly because of the physician's actions. In the end, an irreparable machine is not a dead person.

Of course, for most of the following three centuries, all of this was highly theoretical. As Stanley Reiser argues, the physicians of the seventeenth and eighteenth centuries depended primarily upon "unsatisfactory" reports from their patients for the diagnosis of disease. This was so primarily because physicians lacked sufficiently sophisticated technologies for looking beyond patients' reports to the anatomical events upon which those reports were based. Although Descartes legitimized the splitting of the patient from the body and the treatment of the body in the way a watchmaker might treat a broken watch, it took the invention of such technical devices as the stethoscope and various visual technologies to bring practice into line with theory.[41]

As medical technology and further experimentation began to produce tangible, positive results, among which was the theory of disease and the emergence of modern clinical method in early-nineteenth-century France,[42] the role of the physician shifted from one of mechanic to one of experimental scientist, an increasingly appealing conceptual metaphor in which the body retained its machinelike qualities but became a machine to be understood through and manipulated by the power of experimental science.[43] This view of the body further reduced the role of symbolic discourse within the medical event by creating a demand for scientific certainty—what could not be proved through experimentation was simply not worth examining. The only appropriate reality for the physician became that represented in the language of science, a representation in which physicians come to disease from outside and reduce the particulars of this or that patient's suffering to preestablished categories of causes, effects, and treatments, a representation that finally eliminates the participation of the patient. As Reiser puts it,

> auscultation helped to create the objective physician, who could move away from involvement with the patient's experiences and sensations to a more detached relation, less with the patient but more with the sounds from within the body. Undistracted by the motives and beliefs of the patient, the auscultator could make a diagnosis from sounds that he alone heard emanating from body organs, sounds that he believed to be objective, bias-free representations of the disease process.[44]

Like the Hippocratic school, Cartesianism and the scientific world view, with its emphasis upon certainty, reason, mathematics, and experimentation, was responsible for huge gains in understanding and treating the body and its diseases.[45] These gains pushed medicine to become more and more scientific and to concern itself increasingly with the anatomy and physiology, the physics and chemistry of the body, but not in any essential or mainstream way with the spiritual, symbolic, or psychological aspects of the sick person's illness, except as those aspects could be used to consolidate and to extend the scientific. This has led, according to Pellegrino and Thomasma, to

> the concept of a quantifiable, experimental, and mechanistic reductionistic enterprise. . . . The modern positivistic and reductionistic bias of medicine, and the believers in medicine as high technology, are their linear descendants. The unprecedented successes of the scientific method in medicine are strong arguments in favor of their presuppositions. The ethic which emerges from this conception of medicine places its greatest emphasis on competence, scientific certitude, and the advancement of knowledge and clinical experiment. It tends to depreciate caring and in its most severe form would assign the nonscientific aspects of care to others—not to physicians.[46]

By the middle of the twentieth century, the machine and experimental science metaphors were so deeply embedded in the language of medical practice and training that they had become virtually the only ways of understanding, of talking about, and of practicing medicine.[47] To train as a physician, it was (and still is) necessary to develop into something of an experimental scientist.

Even now, medical students' first significant job is to dissect, to study the human machine as an incredibly complex set of interlocking systems, each of which must be meticulously and repeatedly disassembled so that when the students become doctors and the time comes to practice medicine, they will know exactly how the mechanism fits together. When surgeon-writer Richard Selzer describes his dissecting experiences, he focuses upon the "dead, enduring their daily measure of shredding, pulling, gouging. Before long . . . they were meatwrecks, something made of leather, something unfinished, a strange collage of wallets, pouches and lanyards, only part of which had been crafted, and the rest being in a state of emergence, an unruly hanging of strips and thongs and flaps."[48] Selzer's particular expression of his reaction to the dissecting experience is not likely to match that of most medical students, but it does articulate important elements that lie at the very beginning of every physician's training. The first is the simple fact that the first bodies the students encounter are dead ones rather than living ones. They are bodies shorn of the possibilities of pain and pleasure and language, lifeless bodies that serve as objects for study and as the focal points of the students' first officially sanctioned conception of the locus of their lives' work. The second element has to do with the nature and the end of the work, the "shredding, pulling, gouging" that reduce already reduced human beings to an even more basic form, until they finally do not resemble anything human at all, but become "meat-wrecks," "wallets, pouches and lanyards."

These two elements combine to create an initial view of medicine as primarily concerned with manipulating bodies that play no part in the events of which they are in fact the very center, a view at once complex in the amount of "pure" information it makes available and forces the student to master and simplistic in that it ignores life, the one element essential to all medical activity. Students learn how the parts of the body fit together but cannot see how they work together with a human spirit to produce a living person. By the time contemporary medical students have learned enough of what Selzer appropriately calls "this knowledge that is ours and no one else's" to be identified by their teach-ers, their colleagues, their patients, and themselves as doctors, "they have," according to Cassell, "acquired a world view and the mode of thought that produced that view. They have learned a special language that at once reveals their knowledge of the new world but at the same time locks them into the mode of thought and the special picture of that world . . . whose success and efficacy seem proved on all sides."[49] The importance of language to this world view, to this terministic screen, cannot be overemphasized, because it is through the language of scien-tific medicine that physicians gain access to the knowledge they seek and to the lives they wish to live, and it is only in terms of this language and the reality it creates that they can have the knowledge that makes them full and fully certified members of the medical profession. To be a physician is to be a scientific physician.

Physicians trained to be experimental scientists are likely to treat their patients, consciously or not, as objects to be manipulated, research to be conducted, or sets of facts to be mastered and controlled. The pa-tient-physician relationship that naturally arises from such an under-standing is likely to be one-sided, with physicians assuming the pre-rogative to exercise the powers of their science to act upon disease in the best interests of patients, which they will naturally equate with the best interests of the science they practice. If the disease is a relatively straightforward one that matches an established set of diagnostic facts, it can be named, and the treatment is a matter of administering the appropriate medication to take care of the problem.[50] Here, the best interests of patients genuinely coincide with those of the science of medicine, a cure is effected, and the fact that patients play only "objective" roles can be traded for a certain cure. This is the ideal working relationship between scientific physicians and sick patients.

But when the disease is more complex, physicians are faced with "problems" very much like the problems that provoke experimental scientists into designing and conducting new experiments. The more difficult the disease, the more strictly scientific the approach tends to become, and as the highly technical apparatus of modern diagnosis and treatment is brought to bear, patients become more and more objects and less and less persons. Like the cadavers with which medical training begins, patients are poked, prodded, and gouged by a growing corps of specialists and technicians, intent on "finding out for sure" and on "doing everything possible." In extreme cases, patients may be reduced by a single variable, becoming "the stomach in room 215," "the liver in 104," or "the tumor in 224." In such a reduced reality, physicians have all the options. They act. Their patients are acted upon.

Meanwhile, patients experience a highly personalized form of the scientific reduction to which physicians and technicians subject their bodies. "In health," writes Cassell,

> we know we are alive by our connectedness to the world. . . . by numerous physical phenomena—touch, sight, balance, smell, taste, hearing—and also by our interest in things and in others, by our feelings for people, by what we do and how necessary we are, by our place in the social scheme. . . . In illness, however slight, some of these contacts are lost. . . . As illness deepens, connections are increasingly cut off by the symptoms of sickness and by the forced withdrawal from society.[51]

When patients enter a hospital or a care facility, most remaining connections are broken immediately. The highly technical nature of scientific medicine serves to further the process by distancing them from their physicians, who become obscured behind a screen of tests, technical apparatus, and terminology patients seldom have the knowledge or the experience to comprehend. They may even become disconnected from their diseases, which become the "property" of the physicians, technicians, and care personnel who treat them.

While patients are constrained by the imposition of disease upon their lives, they are not completely controlled by it, nor are the effects of their illnesses, which are a result of, but not the same as, their diseases. As Anthony Moore describes them,

> the experiences of illness are protean. In some cases disease can dignify, in others it creates heroic capacities. It can lead to self-realization; it can level unequal men; it can be thought of as an agent of retribution. . . .

Even patients who see disease as a despoiler often experience sentiments of greater complexity. They see illness as an ever-present reminder of the unexpected, and of man's fundamental vulnerability. . . . A single motor accident, one hospital laboratory test, and emergency operation, each can raze to ruin all that was raised by the total of a man's life.[52]

Illness thus transcends both the disease and the physical concerns of the scientific physicians' language and perspective. It is brought on by the disease, but illness is not a disease process. It is a symbolic one, a highly charged, critically important form of spectatorship out of which patients, helpless to alter the facts of disease, work through language to alter their symbolic representations of the world to account for, to incorporate, and to make real those facts. Although their lives may not depend upon their success, living their lives does.

"In illness," says Cassell, describing the struggle to incorporate the facts of disease,

we attempt to understand, but the disease process is beyond our control and the significance of events is often beyond our knowledge. Because . . . lack of understanding threatens our completeness and exposes us to unknown dangers, we make new and repeated interpretations with added emotional content to compensate for a deficient reality. Rather than bringing comfort, each new interpretation only shows more clearly the tattered edges of our understanding.[53]

The intensity of the effort arises from the fact that patients have experienced serious challenges to fundamental aspects of their personal constructs. According to Toombs,

the loss of wholeness experienced in illness not only incorporates a perception of bodily impairment and loss of integrity but also includes the loss of certainty in its most profound form. In the experience of illness the individual is forced to surrender his most cherished assumption, that of his personal indestructability. . . . "It could happen to ME" is felt . . . as a concrete actuality, and not as an amorphous possibility.[54]

Patients thus focus their energy not upon the causes and effects of medical science, but upon the larger questions we examined earlier.

Because physicians operate within a terministic screen whose control, simplicity, statistical significance, and passively voiced, objective syntax argue that the world is stable, knowable, and manipulable and that it makes sense—and because who they are is so intimately woven into those arguments—they have no resources for sharing the struggles of patients. The rules say they must always live in the participant role, in the role of doing things, of being the agent. The evaluative, value-laden dimensions of spectatorship which absorb their patients' attention exist in a wholly different order of reality. Engagement in such struggles would necessarily involve physicians in events leading to questions about the rules of medical practice, would confront them with the limitations and uncertainties of the human condition, and would finally invite them to consider medicine not as fact and experimental verification of fact, but as probability and possibility laced with a certain but unpredictable amount of uncertainty. It would suggest that doctors' authority over disease and over patients may also be uncertain, an uncertainty that has the power to "raze to ruin" all that medical training has enabled them to understand about themselves, their patients, and medicine itself. And given that the medical event demands action, it is no wonder they insist upon a margin of safety, a measure of "detached concern," a measure whose purpose is to protect physicians, but whose effect is to isolate them, locking them into a reality apart from that of the patient, a reality focused on the disease, unable to address illness and powerless to heal, in the most important sense of the word, which is to make whole again.

I think it is here that literature and medicine as a field can make an important contribution, because it is here that literary discourse can help physicians overcome their reluctance to enter the struggles of their patients by providing models of symbolic experience in which compassion, the ability to "feel genuinely the existential situation of the person who is bearing the burden and who has undergone the insult of sickness to his whole being," can be developed.[55] It is also here that practitioners of literature and medicine often substitute literary criticism for literary discourse, falling victim to the powerful analogy between the literary critic, who maintains a necessary aesthetic distance, and the physician, who maintains a necessary emotional one. If this is where literature and medicine stops, then it will only serve to legitimize, in nonscientific but equally scientistic terms, the distance between patient and physician, a distance that created the difficulties literature is supposed to alleviate. It will have missed the point.

But if we understand the act of reading a literary work to be the sum total of all experiences—physical, emotional, and symbolic—taking place as we work our way from the first to the last word of the text, and if we see the point of reading as opening ourselves to the workings of that text rather than analyzing it according to one or another critical school, then we can see that what we do as readers is precisely what happens when we engage in the spectator role listening to the story of another's life in order to expand the possibilities of our own personal constructs. By absorbing and responding to the story, we work upon ourselves, upon how we represent the world to ourselves, upon our values and our assumptions about the things of the world, and upon the decisions we will ultimately make in response to those things. In the process, we become so deeply immersed in the reality represented by the work, in its events, emotions, and ideas, that we become collaborators in the act of creating that world, resonating in a metaphorical way to the conjunction of our lives and the words of the writer. The distance between self and other is diminished, reduced, and finally disappears altogether as we round out and complete the work in greater detail and complexity that any mere words on a page can hope to do.[56] In a very real sense, reading becomes a literary event becomes a composing activity, and we become writers as well as readers.[57]

On the one hand, the events depicted in a novel such as Mary Shelley's *Frankenstein* are not real at all because we do not have to, indeed we cannot, directly participate in them. Everything in the novel works to make us aware of its disjunction with the everyday—the language is archaic, the situation is impossible (though not improbable), the very world in which it takes place has long since ceased to be. On the other hand, precisely because our reading of the novel is "free of the constraints of the day-to-day world,"[58] we are invited to experience new and unexpected possibilities, and we are free to make of those possibilities whatever sense we will or can, depending upon how we choose to stand in relation to the events of the text, how we choose to compose those events into our own lives. We may, for example, experience the novel as the story of a weak man's inability to accept responsibility for his actions and thereby alter our own understanding of the definition of responsibility. Or we may suffer the bitter, tragic decline of a great potential gone to waste. Or we may wait, expecting the flashing lights of the laboratory and leaving disappointed when they never appear. But we do not, under normal circumstances, read *Frankenstein* as a behavior handbook or as an illustration of the influence of Goethe's *The Sorrows of Young Werther* on the literature of the early nineteenth century or as an illustration of the methodology of the fourfold interpretation of Scripture. We may do all these things, but we do them at a point subsequent to the experience of reading the text. As normal, uncoerced readers, what we learn from *Frankenstein,* we learn apart from the immediate need to act. If we act in accord with what we learn, we do so later, in another context, out of the change the novel has wrought in our reality.

The literary experience, then, is a form of spectatorship which allows us to suspend our ordinary, everyday activities and to reach past who we must be to touch who we might be. As readers, we experience a form of catharsis that does not purge our feelings as we might purge our bodies of unwanted or dangerous substances, but purges in a very rare sense of the term defined by the *Oxford English Dictionary* as "to reach out, extend, put forth," or "to issue forth," making it possible for us to imaginatively leave our everyday selves and become willing participants in the events of other realities. We experience what Louise M. Rosenblatt calls a *"living-through,* not simply *knowledge about,"* the radically different houses of consciousness within which other characters in the human drama reside.[59] It is this process that the study of literature and medicine can promote, and it is this process alone that will humanize medicine for both the physician and the patient.

By providing physicians with symbolic experiences that draw them out of their own worlds and into those of the texts they read, literary discourse teaches doctors, in a very powerful though indirect way, to overcome their reluctance to engage in the messy, painful reality-building that absorbs their patients. Because literary discourse invites a form of Britton's spectatorship, it encourages physicians to make sense of the world in ways other than those legitimized by the participatory terministic screen of medical discourse. Being removed from the imperative to act, literary experiences lead to identification with fictional characters but do not endanger physicians in the way identification with a terminally ill patient might endanger their ability to respond to a critical situation or their willingness to continue practicing medicine. Out of this identification comes the potential to and the knowledge of how to connect with patients on the most basic of human levels and to create with them the shared reality within which healing may take place.

I recognize that my aims and goals sound very much like those I complained about at the beginning of this chapter—moral imperatives with little direct applicability. How, one must ask, can physicians be taught to engage in the processes I have described? I do not believe they can be *taught,* but they can be placed in situations in which literary discourse happens and out of which they may make the necessary connections to change the rules by which they normally live. Although I think there are many ways to accomplish this—not the least important of which is simply to allow them time and space in their training for intensive composing activities, both reading and writing—I want to focus here on one published example that strikes me as a particularly important and powerful approach to placing literary discourse in the medical profession. It involves composing fiction.

In an article entitled "To Render the Lives of Patients," Rita Charon describes an experiment she conducted involving the use of fiction as a counter to the dehumanization her medical students and their patients suffer in the context of a teaching hospital. Charon describes listening to one of her students presenting a case and realizing that both he and the patient had become dehumanized by the difficulties they had experienced over the course of the night during which the patient had been admitted. Fear of not living up to the "stringent requirements" under which the student had to operate as an initiate into the medical profession led to feelings of incompetence directed at himself and to feelings of anger directed toward the patient. Because he had no means of dealing with those feelings, the student's ability to perform his required medical tasks was impeded, and care for the patient was jeopardized. The patient, because she had not cooperated fully with the student, became an enemy against whom the student felt compelled to fight in order to render care, an enemy to be coerced through the use of force if necessary. She had no voice in the student's presentation and was consequently reduced to the categories of the case history and to the cause of the student's potential failure before his teachers and peers. In an attempt to rehumanize both the student and the patient, Charon asked that he "present that case in the first person. Tell it as if you're the patient, and explain to me what happened before you fainted, and what you think is going to happen next." Unknown details were to be made up.[60]

Charon calls her assignment an attempt to engage the imagination of the student, but in reality she gave the student permission to engage in a process of literary spectatorship. By creating a literary experience in which the student left the stringent, day-to-day requirements of the teaching hospital, his entry point into the terministic screen of medical discourse, and entered a fictive version of the life of the patient, Charon's assignment enabled the student to enter a significantly different reality in which he could "live through" the patient's illness apart from his own need to act so that he might come to understand why she was reluctant and uncooperative the night before. In addition, because storytelling and story "hearing" are crucial to maintenance of each personal construct, the student was able to focus the event in order to "digest" it for himself. In this case, "he knew . . . something was wrong with his treatment of the patient. He knew that his feelings of dismay toward her compromised his ability to make reasonable judgments in her care. He couldn't reach her. She seemed actually to fear him. His idealized self-image as an empathetic and powerful doctor was at stake."[61]

The fictive rendering of the patient's life which the student produced was inaccurate in several respects and had virtually no diagnostic or therapeutic value. But the act of doing it enabled the student to assess his own personal construct, to see that the patient's reluctance was not an attack on his identity but stemmed from an inability to comprehend the meaning of her disease. It engaged him in exactly the same symbolic process she was experiencing and created a bridge between their very different construals of the same set of events, between their qualitatively different realities. The fiction enabled the student to find new energy for this very particular and suddenly very human patient. It revealed what Burke calls a fundamental "collective revelation" upon which human interaction is based: "we . . . cannot relate to one another sheerly as things in motion. Even the behaviorist, who studies man in terms of his laboratory experiments, must treat his colleagues as *persons,* rather than purely and simply as automata responding to stimuli. . . . we think of one another (and especially of those with whom we are intimate) as *persons.* . . . the human race cannot possibly get along with itself on the basis of any other intuition."[62]

Charon's experiment in literary discourse heralds the next generation of scholarship in literature and medicine, a generation in which practitioners work not only to empower physicians to read and to respond to literary texts, but also to engage in literary discourse in a rich and fundamental way by creating it directly out of their own experience as the poet or the novelist creates literature and as the patient creates meaning out of the facts of disease and the experience of illness. Writing the short story did not teach Charon's physician specific, explicit rules for dealing with patients, for conducting himself in the surgical theater, for presenting cases at Grand Rounds, or for publishing a critical study in *Literature and Medicine,* but it did enable him to engage fully in the symbolic processes implicit in literary discourse. From this engagement, he and others may learn to come to the medical event both as scientists tracking down the causes of disease and as symbolic spectators working with patients to convert scientific facts into human meaning. They may learn to understand medicine as patients understand it, as both disease and illness, science and symbol. Virtual experience may become actual experience. When this happens, physicians will become doctors, fully humanized persons working with fully humanized patients to heal both the body and the spirit and to bring about the wholeness necessary to health. Literature and medicine will not have missed the point.

Notes

1. Kathryn Montgomery Hunter, "Literature and Medicine: Standards for Applied Literature," in *Applying the Humanities,* ed. Daniel Callahan, Arthur L. Caplan, and Bruce Jennings (New York: Plenum Press, 1985), 289–304.

2. Joanne Trautmann, "Can We Resurrect Apollo?" *Literature and Medicine* 1 (1982): 6.

3. Edmund D. Pellegrino, "To Look Feelingly—The Affinities of Medicine and Literature," *Literature and Medicine* 1 (1982): 19.

4. Ronald Carson, "Literature and Medicine," *Literature and Medicine* 1 (1982): 45.

5. Angela Belli, "The Impact of Literature upon Health: Some Varieties of Cathartic Response," *Literature and Medicine* 5 (1986): 107.

6. G. S. Rousseau, "Literature and Medicine: Towards a Simultaneity of Theory and Practice," *Literature and Medicine* 5 (1986): 161.

7. Hunter, "Literature and Medicine: Standards," 300–302.

8. Larry R. Churchill and Sandra W. Churchill, "Storytelling in Medical Arenas: The Art of Self-Determination," *Literature and Medicine* 1 (1982): 73–79.

9. S. Kay Toombs, "The Meaning of Illness: A Phenomenological Approach to the Patient-Physician Relationship," *Journal of Medicine and Philosophy* 12 (August 1987): 219–20.

10. See Toombs, "Meaning of Illness"; Stephen L. Daniel, "The Patient as Text: A Model of Clinical Hermeneutics," *Theoretical Medicine* 7 (1986): 195–210; and Richard J. Baron, "Bridging Clinical Distance: An Empathic Rediscovery of the Known," *Journal of Medicine and Philosophy* 6 (February 1981): 5–23.

11. Eric J. Cassell, "The Place of the Humanities in Medicine," in *Applying the Humanities,* 178.

12. Edward L. Gogel and James S. Terry, "Medicine as Interpretation: The Uses of Literary Metaphors and Methods," *Journal of Medicine and Philosophy* 12 (August 1987): 205–17.

13. Daniel, "The Patient as Text," 200.

14. Ernst Cassirer, *An Essay on Man: An Introduction to a Philosophy of Human Culture* (1944; rpt. New Haven: Yale Univ. Press, 1974), 25.

15. Ibid., 24.

16. George A. Kelly, *A Theory of Personality: The Psychology of Personal Constructs* (1955; rpt. New York: W. W. Norton, 1963), chap. 3.

17. James Britton, "Writing to Learn and Learning to Write," chap. 10 in *Prospect and Retrospect: Selected Essays of James Britton,* ed. Gordon M. Pradl (Montclair, N.J.: Boynton/Cook, 1982), 101. Also see Britton's *Language and Learning* (Coral Gables, Fla.: Univ. of Miami Press, 1970), chap. 3.

18. Britton, "Writing to Learn," 104.

19. Benjamin Lee Whorf, "Science and Linguistics," in *Language, Thought, and Reality: Selected Writings of Benjamin Lee Whorf,* ed. John B. Carroll (1956; rpt. Cambridge, Mass.: MIT Press, 1982), 213.

20. Whorf, "Language, Mind, and Reality," in *Language, Thought, and Reality,* 252.

21. Kenneth Burke, "Terministic Screens," in his *Language as Symbolic Action: Essays on Life, Literature, and Method* (Berkeley: Univ. of California Press, 1966), 46; emphasis mine.

22. Ibid., 50.

23. For a detailed elaboration of the tendency of such specialized language

communities to shape reality in particular ways, see Peter L. Berger and Thomas Luckmann, *The Social Construction of Reality: A Treatise in the Sociology of Knowledge* (Garden City, N.Y.: Doubleday, 1966), and Richard Rorty, *Philosophy and the Mirror of Nature* (1979; rpt. Princeton: Princeton Univ. Press, 1980).

24. Britton, "Writing to Learn," 94–100.

25. Eric J. Cassell, M.D., *The Healer's Art: A New Approach to the Doctor-Patient Relationship* (New York: J. B. Lippincott, 1976), 15.

26. Edmund D. Pellegrino and David C. Thomasma, *A Philosophical Basis of Medical Practice: Toward a Philosophy and Ethic of the Healing Professions* (New York: Oxford Univ. Press, 1981), 15.

27. Pellegrino and Thomasma, *Philosophical Basis of Medical Practice,* 157.

28. Cassell, *Healer's Art,* 55.

29. Ibid., 57.

30. Pellegrino and Thomasma, *Philosophical Basis of Medical Practice,* 158.

31. Cassell, *Healer's Art,* 56.

32. Pedro Lain Entralgo, *Mind and Body, Psychosomatic Pathology: A Short History of the Evolution of Medical Thought,* trans. Aurelio M. Espinosa, Jr. (New York: P. J. Kenedy and Sons, 1955), 64.

33. Edmund D. Pellegrino, *Humanism and the Physician* (Knoxville: Univ. of Tennessee Press, 1979), 44–46.

34. Lain Entralgo, *Mind and Body,* 45–46.

35. Ibid., 110–11.

36. Ibid., 112.

37. Etienne Gilson, *The Unity of Philosophical Experience* (New York: Charles Scribner's Sons, 1937), 161.

38. Gilson, *Unity,* 200–201.

39. Owen Thomas, *Metaphor and Related Subjects* (New York: Random House, 1969), 40.

40. See Cassell, *Healer's Art,* chaps. 1 and 2, for a more detailed examination of factors in medical history and philosophy which both reflected and contributed to the progressive isolation of the patient's self from the medical event.

41. Stanley Joel Reiser, *Medicine and the Reign of Technology* (Cambridge: Cambridge Univ. Press, 1978), chaps. 1–3.

42. I. R. McWhinney, "Are We on the Brink of a Major Transformation of Clinical Method?" *CMAJ* 135 (15 October 1986): 873–74.

43. Pellegrino and Thomasma, *Philosophical Basis of Medical Practice,* 197.

44. Reiser, *Medicine and the Reign of Technology,* 38.

45. Cassell, *Healer's Art,* 55–62.

46. Pellegrino and Thomasma, *Philosophical Basis of Medical Practice,* 197.

47. See Jonathan Miller, *The Body in Question* (New York: Random House, 1978), for a popularized example of just how deeply embedded the machine metaphor is. Note especially the preface.

48. Richard Selzer, speech notes. These notes were acquired from Selzer in April 1984 at his home in New Haven, Conn.

49. Cassell, *Healer's Art,* 101.

50. Harold Bursztajin, M.D., et al., *Medical Choices, Medical Chances: How Patients, Families, and Physicians Can Cope with Uncertainty* (New York: Dell, 1981), 112.
51. Cassell, *Healer's Art,* 27.
52. Anthony R. Moore, *The Missing Medical Text: Humane Patient Care* (Victoria, Australia: Melbourne Univ. Press, 1978), 36.
53. Cassell, *Healer's Art,* 35.
54. Toombs, "Meaning of Illness," 230–31.
55. Pellegrino, *Humanism and the Physician,* 225–26.
56. William H. Gass, "In Terms of the Toenail: Fiction and the Figures of Life," in his *Fiction and the Figures of Life* (1958; rpt. New York: Alfred A. Knopf, 1970), 55–76.
57. See Robert J. Tierney and P. David Pearson, "Toward a Composing Model of Reading," in *Composing and Comprehending,* ed. Julie Jensen (Urbana, Ill.: NCTE, 1984), 45.
58. Cassell, "The Place of the Humanities," 173.
59. Louise M. Rosenblatt, *Literature as Exploration,* 4th ed. (New York: MLA, 1983), 38.
60. Rita Charon, "To Render the Lives of Patients," *Literature and Medicine* 5 (1986): 58–59.
61. Charon, "To Render," 60.
62. Burke, "Terministic Screens," 53.

Bibliography

BARON, RICHARD J. "Bridging Clinical Distance: An Empathic Rediscovery of the Known." *Journal of Medicine and Philosophy* 6 (February 1981): 5–23.
BELLI, ANGELA. "The Impact of Literature upon Health: Some Varieties of Cathartic Response." *Literature and Medicine* 5 (1986): 90–108.
BERGER, PETER L., and THOMAS LUCKMANN. *The Social Construction of Reality: A Treatise in the Sociology of Knowledge.* Garden City, N.Y.: Doubleday, 1966.
BRITTON, JAMES. *Language and Learning.* Coral Gables, Fla.: University of Miami Press, 1970.
———. "Writing to Learn and Learning to Write." In *Prospect and Retrospect: Selected Essays of James Britton,* ed. Gordon M. Pradl. Montclair, N.J.: Boynton/Cook, 1982.
BURKE, KENNETH. *Language as Symbolic Action: Essays on Life, Literature, and Method.* Berkeley: University of California Press, 1966.
BURSZTAJIN, HAROLD, M.D., et al. *Medical Choices, Medical Chances: How Patients, Families, and Physicians Can Cope with Uncertainty.* New York: Dell, 1981.
CARSON, RONALD. "Literature and Medicine." *Literature and Medicine* 1 (1982): 44–46.
CASSELL, ERIC J. *The Healer's Art: A New Approach to the Doctor-Patient Relationship.* New York: J. B. Lippincott, 1976.

————. "The Place of the Humanities in Medicine." In *Applying the Humanities,* ed. Daniel Callahan, Arthur L. Caplan, and Bruce Jennings. New York: Plenum Press, 1985.

CASSIRER, ERNST. *An Essay on Man: An Introduction to a Philosophy of Human Culture.* 1944. Rpt. New Haven: Yale University Press, 1974.

CHARON, RITA. "To Render the Lives of Patients." *Literature and Medicine* 5 (1986): 58–74.

CHURCHILL, LARRY R., and SANDRA W. CHURCHILL. "Storytelling in Medical Arenas: The Art of Self-Determination." *Literature and Medicine* 1 (1982): 73–79.

DANIEL, STEPHEN L. "The Patient as Text: A Model of Clinical Hermeneutics." *Theoretical Medicine* 7 (1986): 195–210.

GASS, WILLIAM H. "In Terms of the Toenail: Fiction and the Figures of Life." In his *Fiction and Figures of Life.* 1958. Rpt. New York: Alfred A. Knopf, 1970.

GILSON, ETIENNE. *The Unity of Philosophical Experience.* New York: Charles Scribner's Sons, 1937.

GOGEL, EDWARD L., and JAMES S. TERRY. "Medicine as Interpretation: The Uses of Literary Metaphors and Methods." *Journal of Medicine and Philosophy* 12 (August 1987): 205–17.

HUNTER, KATHRYN MONTGOMERY. "Literature and Medicine: Standards for Applied Literature." In *Applying the Humanities,* ed. Daniel Callahan, Arthur L. Caplan, and Bruce Jennings. New York: Plenum Press, 1985.

KELLY, GEORGE A. *A Theory of Personality: The Psychology of Personal Constructs.* 1955. Rpt. New York: W. W. Norton, 1963.

LAIN ENTRALGO, PEDRO. *Mind and Body, Psychosomatic Pathology: A Short History of the Evolution of Medical Thought.* Trans. Aurelio M. Espinosa, Jr. New York: P. J. Kenedy and Sons, 1955.

McWHINNEY, I. R. "Are We on the Brink of a Major Transformation of Clinical Method?" *CMAJ* 135 (15 October 1986): 873–74.

MILLER, JONATHAN. *The Body in Question.* New York: Random House, 1978.

MOORE, ANTHONY R. *The Missing Medical Text: Humane Patient Care.* Victoria, Australia: Melbourne University Press, 1978.

PELLEGRINO, EDMUND D. *Humanism and the Physician.* Knoxville, Tenn.: University of Tennessee Press, 1979.

————. "To Look Feelingly—The Affinities of Medicine and Literature." *Literature and Medicine* 1 (1982): 18–22.

PELLEGRINO, EDMUND D., and DAVID C. THOMASMA. *A Philosophical Basis of Medical Practice: Toward a Philosophy and Ethic of the Healing Professions.* New York: Oxford University Press, 1981.

REISER, STANLEY JOEL. *Medicine and the Reign of Technology.* Cambridge: Cambridge University Press, 1978.

RORTY, RICHARD. *Philosophy and the Mirror of Nature.* 1979. Rpt. Princeton: Princeton University Press, 1980.

ROSENBLATT, LOUISE M. *Literature as Exploration.* 4th ed. New York: Modern Language Association, 1983.

ROUSSEAU, G. S. "Literature and Medicine: Towards a Simultaneity of Theory and Practice." *Literature and Medicine* 5 (1986): 152–81.

SELZER, RICHARD. Speech Notes. These notes were acquired from Selzer in April 1984 at his home in New Haven, Conn.

THOMAS, OWEN. *Metaphor and Related Subjects.* New York: Random House, 1969.

TIERNEY, ROBERT J., and P. DAVID PEARSON. "Toward a Composing Model of Reading." In *Composing and Comprehending,* ed. Julie Jensen. Urbana, Ill.: NCTE, 1984.

TOOMBS, S. KAY. "The Meaning of Illness: A Phenomenological Approach to the Patient-Physician Relationship." *Journal of Medicine and Philosophy* 12 (August 1987): 219–40.

TRAUTMANN, JOANNE. "Can We Resurrect Apollo?" *Literature and Medicine* 1 (1982): 1–17.

WHORF, BENJAMIN LEE. *Language, Thought, and Reality: Selected Writings of Benjamin Lee Whorf.* Edited by John B. Carroll. 1956. Rpt. Cambridge, Mass.: MIT Press, 1982.

Science, Discourse, and Literature
The Role/Rule of Metaphor in Science
JAMES J. BONO

IN "THE DISCOURSE ON LANGUAGE," Michel Foucault insists that western thought, in the course of its history since Greek antiquity, has enforced the "elision of the reality of discourse" in its pursuit of what Foucault labels "true knowledge."[1] One task for the field of literature and science, arguably, is to unmask the reality of the discourse(s) of science. For the elision of discourse of which Foucault speaks is perhaps nowhere more deeply ingrained than in science. Popular and professional images of science, reinforced by philosophical tradition stretching back to Plato and Bacon, differentiate between a science striving to "mirror Nature" and literature enmeshed, if not mired, in language.[2] As a "mode of expression," literature cannot disengage itself from language, whereas to science, language in this view is merely a transparent vehicle through which it transmits to others its encounter with a lawful universe. The world presents itself to science not obliquely through language, but directly "with a legible face, leaving us merely to decipher it."[3]

As a result, we regard science as marked by difference: as separate from literature, from language, from the discourses inhabiting the

59

imagined and constructed worlds of social practices and cultural forms. Another related task thus facing the field of literature and science is to remember, and deconstruct, the differences that have separated science from literature.[4] In particular, we need to challenge systematically and carefully the ingrained assumption that language is, or that it can unproblematically be made to function as, a transparent medium for scientific inquiry and theory. This task will lead us back to the discursive nature of science, to that very reality of the *discourse* of science—the materiality and textuality of the languages of science—which Foucault's remarks about western thought in general help us remember. By remembering, then, the differences that have separated science from literature and language, we may be able to re-member—to join together— those ignored or insufficiently acknowledged elements (and disjecta membra) that constitute the discourse of science. Such a theoretical enterprise has, I believe, significant consequences for the practice of both literature and science and the history of science.

Crucial to this theoretical enterprise is an adequate understanding of the textuality of scientific discourse and of the metaphoricity of the languages of science. In my view, metaphorical—or, more broadly speaking, tropological—language figures centrally in both exposing and understanding the textuality of scientific discourse. I therefore propose in this essay to examine the place of metaphor in science.

Metaphor is closely linked to arguments about whether language is constitutive of science itself, of what scientists do, and of the theories they construct. Since the early 1960s, a small but growing contingent of theorists has argued for the constitutive nature of language and metaphor.[5] But even among these theorists, apparent consensus masks often fundamental disagreements concerning what it *means* to say that language, or metaphor, is constitutive of science. In my view, these frequently submerged disagreements are symptomatic of the power that the "metaphorics" of the text of western science still wields to subvert the potentially radical implications of understanding language as constitutive of science.[6] The ancient trope of science as a special kind of "seeing," as exhibiting an "insight" that privileges it with respect to other discourses,[7] serves to elide the reality of its own discourse by recuperating the notion of language as constitutive of science. Thus, for some theorists, the constitutive dimension of scientific language (including metaphors), while exerting a shaping influence upon theory, remains within the explicit domain, and control, of specific scientific communities. As a specialized and socially restricted discourse, the language of science does not, as a result, risk unwieldy, and unruly, dissemination of meanings. According to this view, the special insight of scientists contains and controls the language and metaphors constituting scientific discourse. This recuperation of language lies implicit, for example, in Brian Vickers's remarks contrasting early-modern science and magic:

> In the scientific tradition, I hold, a clear distinction is made between words and things and between literal and metaphorical language. The occult tradition does not recognize this distinction: Words are treated as if they are equivalent to things and can be substituted for them. Manipulate the one and you manipulate the other. Analogies, instead of being, as they are in the scientific tradition, explanatory devices subordinate to argument and proof, or heuristic tools to make models that can be tested, corrected, and abandoned if necessary, are, instead, modes of conceiving relationships in the universe that reify, rigidify, and ultimately come to dominate thought. One no longer uses analogies: One is used by them. They become the only way in which one can think or experience the world.[8]

Vickers's study of language and metaphor during the Scientific Revolution in effect establishes a sharp dichotomy between science and nonscience. Science controls language, whereas language controls occult modes of thought.

To the rule of metaphor such critics oppose a strictly delimited, even domesticated, role of metaphor. By contrast, I believe that it is fruitful to examine more radical implications of the constitutive role of language in science which give full weight to the dense reality of discourse and to the dissemination and proliferation of meanings within and beyond the boundaries of science itself. Indeed, I shall argue that such metaphorical aspects of language are essential to understanding the dynamic of conceptual change in science precisely because they ground complex scientific texts and discourses in other social, political, religious, or "cultural" texts and discourses. Rather than mirroring the "legible face" of a reality envisioned by scientists and "deciphered" within a single, dominant paradigm, complex scientific texts and discourses constitute themselves through their intersection with other, multiple discourses. Such intersection sets up interferences among various discourses leading to the dissemination of various meanings with the power to disrupt, to resist, and to transform the metaphors and deeply embedded tropological features of the languages of a given discourse.

How are metaphors constitutive of science? Discourse about metaphor and science enjoys a long, indeed ancient, history. To situate the view I wish to propose of metaphor as a medium of exchange which may function both generatively and transformatively, let me first crudely articulate a "standard" view of metaphor in science and survey some attempts at framing revisionist positions.

The standard view and its variants start from the conventional distinction we have seen Vickers use: that between literal and metaphorical, or figurative, language. Such a view originates with the notion that there are proper, or literal, meanings we can attribute to a given term and that metaphorical usages involve using a word in a distorted or deviant—that is to say, nonliteral—manner. One finds such a distinction embedded in the earliest authoritative definitions we have of metaphor in the western tradition, for example, that of Aristotle.[9] Of course, this deviant metaphorical use of language could prove valuable and was, indeed, often regarded as a device of considerable power in, for example, poetry and rhetoric. The "standard" view of metaphor in science, in fact, represents a decisive break of philosophy and science from rhetoric. This separation and consequent identification of science with the literal or nonmetaphorical gained much momentum from the theories of language championed by the likes of Hobbes, Locke, and such "official" apologists for the new science as Thomas Sprat, official historian of the Royal Society.[10]

In the view of these theorists, metaphor introduces inappropriate, nonliteral meanings into science, contaminating the precise and stable meanings science attempts to discover behind the terms it uses. Such metaphoric contamination compromises scientific inquiry and the integrity of propositional logic and deductive reasoning in scientific theory and explanation. In short, the way of metaphor becomes, in seventeenth-century philosophy and science, the way of error. Metaphor is to be avoided. Where its use enters into science, one must reduce the meaning of such metaphors to some stable, literal sense.[11]

Revisionist views of metaphor and science have, in the Anglo-American world at least, largely stemmed from the new understandings of metaphor espoused by I. A. Richards and, following Richards, Max Black.[12] Black's "interaction theory of metaphor," which explicitly opposes views such as the "substitution theory" in which metaphors can be replaced by literal statements, provides some theorists with a starting point for articulating the role of metaphor in science. Accordingly, scientific metaphors, in some circles at least, have won a modicum of respect as constitutive elements of scientific theory, rather than mere ornaments—dangerous ones at that—as in the standard view.

If the standard view takes as its bedrock the distinctions between metaphorical and literal terms, rhetoric and science, and the figural and the literal, revisionist theories call such dichotomies into question, though not, as we shall see, to the same degree. In the following discussion, I shall examine but four examples of revisionist views as a backdrop for my own discussion of the role, or rule, of metaphor in science.

Richard Boyd has argued, in an important article,[13] that metaphors have a significant role to play even within the highly specialized and precise languages of mature sciences. That role, for Boyd, is an essential one: essential, that is, to the process of theory construction. More specifically, Boyd identifies a special class of scientific metaphors and claims that there are cases

> in which metaphorical expressions constitute, at least for a time, an irreplaceable part of the linguistic machinery of a scientific theory: cases in which there are metaphors which scientists use in expressing theoretical claims for which no adequate literal paraphrase is known. Such metaphors are *constitutive* of the theories they express, rather than merely exegetical.[14]

As examples, Boyd points to the proliferation of metaphors drawn from computer science and information theory in the "relatively young science" of cognitive psychology. Moreover, he suggests that "the metaphorical statement that the brain is a sort of computer" which one finds used in the theories of psychology "share[s] with more typical interaction metaphors, at least for a time, the property that their cognitive content cannot be made explicit."[15]

Despite the claim that metaphors are constitutive of scientific theories, Boyd severely limits the power of metaphorical language in science by adopting two related strategies that, together, counterbalance his claim by reasserting science's control over its metaphors. His first strategy is to introduce a sharp dichotomy between "literary" and "scientific" metaphors. Literary metaphors, in Boyd's view, are the creation, and property, of individual creative authors and their texts; they are explicated, not typically by their authors, but by practitioners of literary criticism; and finally, they do not generate "strategies for future research" or lead to complete (literal) explication, but are characterized by "conceptual open-endedness."[16] By contrast, Boyd claims that scientific metaphors "undergo a sort of public articulation and development that is uncharacteristic of literary metaphors" and thus become "the property of the entire scientific community" rather than of specific authors.[17] As a result, the explication of scientific metaphors "is an essential part of the task of scientific inquiry."[18] This professional and social fact, in turn, generates a further consequence, namely, that scientific metaphors function to produce "strategies for research." Here Boyd's first strategy of dichotomizing "literary" and "scientific" metaphors intersects with his second strategy of claiming that theory-constitutive metaphors ultimately become fully explicated as the result of "scientific inquiry" or "strategies for research":

> Finally, whatever the merits of the claim that the cognitive content of literary metaphors can never be captured by literal paraphrase, there seems to be no reason to doubt that such explication is possible in the case of theory-constitutive metaphors, nor is there any reason to doubt that complete explications are often the eventual result of the attempts at explication which are central to scientific inquiry.[19]

The assumptions and consequences of Boyd's strategies merit some examination. If I read Boyd correctly, he suggests a fundamental divergence of aims in science and literature. Literature, he assumes, values invention, the free, imaginative production of a highly individualized—indeed, subjective—*insight*. Hence, the purpose of literary metaphors is to exhibit a continually shifting, even disruptive, point of view. Stable images and meanings, the domestication of metaphors implicit in their repetitive use and adoption by a network of individual authors, signal the decline of literature and literary genius. Under such circumstances, literary metaphors become "trite or hackneyed," losing "their insightfulness through overuse."[20] Effective literary metaphors would, then, appear to be unruly precisely insofar as they are subjective: representing, in language, the eruption of a private "insight" into the public arena.

By contrast, "successful" scientific metaphors are neither unruly nor subjective. Rather, they are the product of a scientific community's collective insight. That is to say, the "articulation and development" of theory-constitutive metaphors result from the scientific community's growing *perception* of the world. The scientific community, in Boyd's account, finds itself driven toward the use of theory-constitutive metaphors because of its evolving conviction that there are "features of the world whose existence seems probable, but many of whose fundamental properties have yet to be discovered."[21] Metaphors, in such a situation, allow the scientific community to articulate hypotheses and theories for the exploration and explanation of such probable features of the world. Metaphors provide, in a sense, linguistic tools for obtaining a purchase upon the empirical world. In Boyd's view, "theory-constitutive metaphors, in other words, represent one strategy for the accommodation of language to as yet *undiscovered causal features* of the world."[22]

From this account, it is clear that Boyd attributes not only a special significance, but also a privileged status, to what might be termed the *inductive consensus* of the scientific community. By *inductive consensus*, I mean to suggest that Boyd appears to ground the special status of theory-constitutive scientific metaphors, in contrast to literary metaphors, in the scientific community's shared experience and perception of some, as yet partially explored, features of the world. Where literary metaphors are the product of a highly subjective imagination expressing a personal insight about experience, scientific metaphors are chosen for their aptness in capturing an as yet unspecifiable *range* of interconnections among potential features of the empirical world which observations lead us to believe exist.

This view of scientific metaphors limits sharply the degree to which language may be said to shape scientific discourse. Metaphors are consciously chosen or "introduced"[23] by scientific communities driven by inductively grounded perceptions of the world and by established theoretical frameworks. Rather than the world's accommodating itself to language, Boyd regards scientific metaphors as part of the process whereby language accommodates itself to the world so that, in the end, "our linguistic categories 'cut the world at its joints.' "[24]

Apart from the epistemology and philosophy of language and science implicit in Boyd's belief that language can "cut the world at its joints," I want to point to several questionable features of Boyd's argument. First, his distinction between literary and scientific metaphors rests, in part, upon a caricature of literature and literary creativity bristling with assumptions that have been undermined by postmodern theorists. The notions of authorship, of the autonomous creativity of the "individual talent" or Cartesian "mind," have been subjected to close scrutiny and severe criticism by philosophers and literary theorists such as Michel Foucault, Jacques Derrida, Paul de Man, Fredric Jameson, Edward Said, and Stephen Greenblatt.[26] In addition, critical literary historians have begun to show that the characterization of literary texts and language (including metaphors) as the exclusive product of an autonomously acting author—as acts of pure imagination and subjectivity—is itself a culturally bound historical phenomenon.[27] As such, that characterization has served the interests of post-Enlightenment and post-romantic society and éven, it has been argued, the interests of the rising profession of literary criticism and the academic literary establishment in modern times.[28] Moreover, as premodern literature, or traditions outside the modern canon such as Native American literature, attest, the idea of individual, autonomous authorship is not a necessary feature of what we call literature. At the very least, recent theoretical perspectives suggest that the emphasis upon the creative author who exercises subjective control over texts and language be balanced by an understanding of how authors and their texts are themselves socially and culturally constructed. More radically, such perspectives suggest the demise of the author caught within the web of textuality or within the "prisonhouse of language."

Second, if such views make Boyd's distinction between literary and scientific metaphors somewhat difficult to retain, one can also question the control he implicitly grants science, or the scientific community, over its use of metaphors. The unruliness of literary metaphors stems, in Boyd's account, from their subjective, personal provenance. By contrast, postmodern literary theory would situate the unruliness of metaphors in language itself. Texts defy the efforts of their authors to control them in large measure because the tropological and rhetorical dimensions of language—which cannot be bracketed or stripped away—ensure a multiplicity of meanings and the possibility of continual reinterpretation. Hence, if Boyd's attempt to distinguish literary from scientific metaphors requires that literary metaphors "belong" to individual authors in a way that scientific metaphors do not, postmodern theories of language and textuality call that distinction into question. At some fundamental level, linguistic tropes—literary *and* scientific—belong to language, not to individuals, not even to the "authors" of literary language. As a result, the "public articulation and development" of theory-constitutive scientific metaphors do not ensure that science retains control over such metaphors, since the unruliness of metaphors does not depend on their subjective provenance as opposed to public articulation so much as it depends upon the characteristics of language, discourse, or textuality.

To justify the implicit claim that science controls its theory-constitutive metaphors, then, one must directly confront such characteristics of language, discourse, and textuality and show how science curtails the multiplicity of meanings and interpretations of its metaphors. Science does, I believe, continually attempt to do this. The question, however, is whether it is successful in its efforts. Here, I think, Boyd's response is, once again, insufficient. Rather than addressing issues raised by a postmodern account of language and discourse, Boyd skirts them: (1) by suggesting that the employment of theory-constitutive metaphors follows from, and is dependent upon, the agreement of a scientific community, based upon its experience of the world, that certain probable features of the world can potentially be explicated through the similarities and analogies suggested by the metaphor. This view privileges the special insight, perception, or mode of seeing of a scientific community and fails to consider that such modes may themselves be the result of metaphorical or linguistic *interpretations* of the world. It therefore assumes a vantage point, outside of language, from which science may choose and control its metaphors; (2) by choosing only a limited class of scientific metaphors, those he calls theory-constitutive metaphors, which have the characteristic of constituting the explicit object of research strategies. As a result of this choice, Boyd can maximize our sense of science's control of its metaphors, since he can claim that the *meaning* of such metaphors becomes subject to increasing specification. Such metaphors, through research efforts, generate complete explications, or "literal paraphrase[s]";[29] and (3) by emphasizing the borrowing of metaphors from other domains of science, rather than from nonscientific discourses. As we shall see, issues of the unruliness of metaphors are especially acute where such "alien" discourses are involved.

W. H. Leatherdale, in contrast to Boyd, asserts a more radically metaphorical view of science.[30] Metaphor enters nearly every major aspect of science and is not restricted to certain special cases of theory construction. Speaking metaphorically himself, Leatherdale argues that science needs a nonliteral dimension, that a literal interpretation of the terms and concepts of scientific theories impoverishes and disempowers them.

> Such an interpretation of theories would threaten to make science die of clinical antisepsis. For science needs the inoculation of ambiguity and the semantic haze that surrounds the neutral analogy of a model or the unexplored resources of a metaphor if it is to marshal its resources for survival and growth. Too doctrinaire an axiomatization, or literal reconstruction, even supposing this were possible in any neutral untheoretically-infected way, might free science from the infection of error due to uncritical reliance on a model or metaphor, but it would kill it stone dead in the process.[31]

Science, in short, is a "metaphorico-deductive" system, from which it derives its vitality and powers of growth.[32]

Leatherdale's provocative analysis suggests many important respects in which the practice and discourse of science draw their power from metaphors. Intertwined with his suggestive remarks, however, are scattered statements and arguments that introduce decided tensions into his account of scientific metaphors. Particularly noteworthy, I think, are the tensions introduced when Leatherdale attempts to compare literary and scientific metaphors. They are not, he asserts, the same.[33] Literary metaphors differ from scientific in their "greater diffuseness," in their "emotive and affective tone," in the particularity of their "context of metaphoric description," in their typical lack of concern "with any objective reality," and, finally, in their desire "to shake off the routine and familiar"[34]—the last-mentioned echoed by Boyd's characterization of literary metaphors as always seeking inventiveness and novelty.

Each of the differences Leatherdale adduces requires a detailed response that I cannot provide in the present essay. However, detailed responses to these differences certainly must constitute part of a more comprehensive theory of scientific metaphors. That there are differences between literary and scientific metaphors I do not doubt. Whether these differences constitute substantive and theoretically significant distinctions, or whether they are, rather, attributable to differing rhetorical or ideological functions of scientific and literary discourses seems to me the essential question for debate.[35] Rather than responding in a comprehensive way, I should like to reply to a few specific points. Leatherdale's claim that "emotive and affective tone" is "irrelevant to the scientific use" of metaphor, while perhaps commonsensical, strikes me as an unnecessary and misleading concession. For, in addition to the cognitive content of scientific metaphors accepted to varying degree by revisionist accounts, such metaphors importantly traffic, at times, in just such emotive and affective associations. These associations may be submerged, or even deliberately veiled by rhetorical ploys aimed at enforcing the objectivity and authority of a given scientific discourse, but nevertheless they reveal, under scrutiny, the values-implications embedded in a particular discourse. For example, the use of spirit-matter and microcosm-macrocosm analogies in the Middle Ages and Renaissance, the use of mechanistic metaphors since the seventeenth century, and, more recently, the use of racial and gender analogies in biology and medicine all combine overt cognitive assertions of similarity or difference with more subtle emotive and affective appeals to an underlying structure of social, political, cultural, and/or religious values.[36] These dimensions of scientific metaphors are essential to understanding the discursive, intertextual nature of science.

Leatherdale's remarks concerning literary metaphors and "objective reality" appear to be especially in tension with his larger claims concerning the metaphorical nature of science. Though his remarks are neither sustained nor analytical, they seem to suggest the existence of a non- or extrametaphorical dimension to science. "Thus the 'meaning' of a literary metaphor is circumscribed by all the particular details of subject matter, event, aim, circumstance and style which belong to the poem or other work in which they occur. They are therefore designed to integrate with the author's total descriptive and aesthetic intention and not with *independent neutral cognitive criteria*."[37] One may infer that the concluding phrase, though obscure, applies to scientific metaphors. Leatherdale implies here, I think, that scientific metaphors are designed not to fulfill some self-expressive function, but, rather, to fulfill the function of "capturing" some aspect of "objective reality" as identified by, or in accordance with (here the sense is obscure), some "independent neutral cognitive criteria." The difficulty here is to understand how such "independent . . . criteria" present themselves to us so that they can serve, somehow, to validate scientific metaphors. One possibility is, as Leatherdale opines a few pages later, that "there really does seem to be a language which is neutral to theory and which may be regarded as the literal language, and I have suggested that it is the language of direct perception or of 'ostensivity.' "[38] But this opinion only serves to reintroduce the notion that science is a privileged activity with special access to a kind of seeing, or insight, that reveals the literal contours of objective reality. Such a view reinforces the divide between the literal and the metaphorical, thus rendering obscure the claim that science is metaphorical.

However, Leatherdale juxtaposes assertions regarding this "literal language" with a different view, namely, that "in a sense language creates the world of phenomena, and all cognition no matter how purely 'phenomenal' is 'Worthäftigkeit,' word-laden. For example, even the tendency to 'see' the world in terms of thing, property and process springs from the noun, adjective and verb structure of our language."[39] To further complicate matters, Leatherdale seems to retract in large measure his earlier insistence upon the distinction between literary and scientific metaphors when he notes that "there are even in literature recurrent metaphors which achieve some permanence and . . . which approach the systematic complexity and fertility of scientific metaphors."[40] After citing specific examples, Leatherdale concludes:

> Such a use of metaphor in literature demonstrates that the difference between literary and scientific metaphors is, in cognitive terms (and disregarding any aesthetic or affective tone), essentially one of degree rather than of kind. If it is true that metaphors can be permanent . . . then there seems to be no place where one can draw the line between the more transient and local metaphors of literature and the established and systematic metaphors of science.[41]

More consistent and thoroughgoing, I think, is the analysis of metaphor in science that Mary Hesse has developed in a series of books and articles on the philosophy of science.[42] In particular, Hesse articulates a rich and subtle view of scientific metaphors in a chapter entitled "Language, Metaphor, and a New Epistemology," part of a book jointly authored with Michael Arbib.[43] Although I cannot examine Arbib and Hesse's theory in detail in this essay, certain features of their discussion are worth mentioning here. Arbib and Hesse's rejection of the "literalist view of language" is complete and fundamental to their account of scientific metaphors.[44] In their view, the development of science and philosophy since the seventeenth century has conspired "to direct attention away from the concrete facts of ambiguity and change in language."[45] As a result, the story of language, meaning, and representation—particularly in science—has, capitally in the Anglo-American world, relied on a literalist account of language emphasizing the importance of "precise and stable meanings." Metaphorical language, then, becomes problematic, for "if metaphor is to be taken seriously, it implies changing meanings; in a literalist theory, however, there is no room for understanding metaphor as implying continual shifts of meaning."[46]

This polarity between stable versus shifting meanings is, I would argue, central to an understanding of scientific change and the role/rule of metaphor in science. For Arbib and Hesse, the Anglo-American tradition's insistence on a literalist view of language and its corollary, precise and stable meanings, in the face of "pervasive" evidence of meaning changes in the way we actually use language leads them to propose as their fundamental thesis that "all language is metaphorical."[47] By this thesis they mean to assert that "metaphorical shifts of meaning depending on similarities and differences between objects are pervasive in language, not deviant, and some of the mechanisms of metaphor are essential to the meaning of any descriptive language whatever."[48]

Several consequences of their thesis are significant for the view of metaphor in science I wish to propose. First, for Arbib and Hesse, "metaphorical shifts in meaning" result in "the interaction and redescription of domains" brought together through metaphorical association.[49] Second, attention to such interactive dimensions of language, to the way in which meaning shifts and domains undergo redescription through metaphoric associations, can lead to "critique, evaluation, and perhaps replacement." In this and perhaps other senses, then, "metaphor is potentially revolutionary."[50] Third, Arbib and Hesse note that their general account of language as metaphorical translates with special force to the domain of science:

> if we look at the implications of recent discussions of the theory ladenness of observation, of realism and the use of scientific models, we find that the use of language in scientific theory conforms closely to the metaphoric model. Scientific revolutions are, in fact, metaphoric revolutions, and theoretical explanation should be seen as metaphoric redescription of the domain of phenomena.[51]

In fact, Arbib and Hesse rephrase Kuhn's language of scientific revolutions to conform to their own idiom. "In the development of science a tension always exists between normal and revolutionary science: normal science seeks to reduce instability of meaning and inconsistency and to evolve logically connected theories; revolutionary science makes metaphoric leaps that are creative of new meanings and applications and that may constitute genuine theoretical progress."[52] Such rephrasing of Kuhn, however, is more than a "mere" rhetorical transposition. Rather, the change in idiom itself constitutes a metaphorical shift that redefines the notion of scientific revolutions in a manner, I would suggest, that is far more fitting to a view that seeks to re-member the *discourse* of science.

As a final example of revisionist views, an article by historian Nancy Leys Stepan makes a very important contribution toward a theory of scientific metaphors.[53] Building upon the interaction theory of Max Black, Stepan sees metaphors in science as evoking associations among "specially constructed systems of implications."[54] Furthermore, she suggests that "what makes" a metaphor or "analogy suitable for scientific purposes is its ability to be suggestive of new systems of implications, new hypotheses, and therefore new observations."[55] Stepan grounds her analysis in the example of analogies between race and gender in the biological sciences of the nineteenth and twentieth centuries.

Stepan's example is especially telling since it indicates both how complex and how powerful the role of metaphors in science can be. The analogy between race and gender involved more than just the transfer of meanings of inferiority associated with the black to women, for it allowed, in turn, the characteristics of the female to be projected back upon the black as further signs of inferiority. Such complex analogies, then, drawing upon cultural stereotypes and popular metaphors, acted powerfully upon scientific inquiry by constructing the very categories, and hence "facts," that scientists used to frame and test hypotheses. Thus, for Stepan, metaphor or analogy is constitutive both of scientific theory and of the categories of experience that underlie scientific discovery—which both highlight and suppress features of the perceived world.[56]

Stepan also notes two other interconnected features of scientific metaphors which supplement in quite important ways other, including revisionist, views. First, Stepan notes that metaphors do not just have intellectual or cognitive roles in science, but also carry "social and moral consequences."[57] Scientific metaphors can and do shape our actions in the world. This consequence of metaphors is of more than practical interest. It has significant theoretical implications as well, for it suggests ways in which scientific change, through changing metaphors, may be linked to broader social and cultural factors. Indeed, in my opinion, a second important feature of scientific metaphors noted by Stepan is the potential "role of social, political, or economic factors in

the generation of new metaphors, and therefore new meanings, in science."[58] Stepan suggests, without sustained explication, that scientific
metaphors, far from remaining isolated and insulated from other domains of social action and discourse, actually may provide links for the
interaction between those domains and scientific practice and discourse. As noted at the beginning of this essay, I want to argue that the
very power of metaphors to disseminate meanings within and beyond
the boundaries of science can enable us to understand the dynamics of
scientific change, but only if we attend to how scientific metaphors
interact with other discourses. As a medium of exchange among discourses, metaphors generate and transform scientific discourse and expose its textuality.

The question of how metaphor is constitutive of science does not permit a simple, or single, answer. In the remainder of this essay I want to
explore an important, if largely neglected, dimension of scientific metaphors—namely, metaphor as a medium of exchange—that, in my opinion, is central to this question. I believe that understanding this dimension of metaphor may help us understand the generative and
transformative power metaphor has in scientific discourse and, as a
consequence, may affect our understanding both of scientific change
and of the relationship between science and literature, broadly conceived. Such a perspective, moreover, carries with it a number of possibilities for the *practice* of literature and science and of the history of
science which I hope the several examples used in the course of my
argument will suggest.
    The very concept of metaphor has since antiquity implied as an es-
sential part of its meaning the idea of transfer. Taken in its most common sense, the idea is that metaphor involves a transfer of meaning
from one term, to which that meaning attaches properly or literally, to
another, where the meaning becomes improper, deviant, or metaphorical. While acknowledging the ability of metaphors to transfer
meanings, this traditional account serves the interests of a western philosophical—in origin, an Aristotelian—tradition in positing universal
terms with fundamentally stable, proper, and literal meanings.[59] The
capacity of metaphor to disrupt stable meanings, to disseminate meanings across and beyond the boundaries marking a specialized discourse,
and, in short, to act generatively and transformatively was little acknowledged and less explored. In the wake of profound critiques of the
literalist view of language echoed from within both the Anglo-American tradition[60] and the world of poststructuralist theory,[61] a broader
appreciation of metaphorical transfer of meaning is both possible and
necessary.

To capture the wider significance of such transfer, I have chosen to look at metaphor as a medium of exchange. For metaphor functions—interactively, if you will, as Max Black and those who have extended his analysis prefer—as both the site and means for exchanges among not only words or phrases, but also theories, frameworks, and, most significantly, discourses.[62] Such exchanges trade on the capacity of metaphorical language to shift meaning. Rather than ineluctably resulting in anarchic instability—a chaotic flux of meanings—such exchanges, I want to suggest, function within, or rather create, an "ecological" network driven by the tension-fraught need or desire both to "fix" meanings and to disrupt, generate, and transform them. In science, I contend that metaphor functions as a medium of exchange in at least two, interconnected, domains: (1) the intrascientific and (2) the extrascientific.[63]

The intrascientific functioning of metaphors represents, relatively, the simplest example of metaphoric exchange in science and also constitutes the category of metaphors that have most commonly elicited critical attention and analysis. By *intrascientific*, I mean those metaphors in scientific discourse which one typically can trace back to an "original" use *within* science itself. That is to say, the metaphoric exchange occurs either within one scientific discipline or between two or more disciplines of science and technology. One example of intrascientific metaphoric exchange is the analogy Boyd notes in cognitive psychology between the human brain and a computer. Here metaphorical exchange occurs between the discipline of cognitive psychology and those of computer science and information theory. In addition, the metaphor trades on meanings associated with the relatively recent technology of computers. Although some of these meanings may have broader cultural resonances—one thinks, for example, of the social meaning that the language and technological capacities of the computer increasingly carries in western culture—for the most part intrascientific metaphorical exchanges give the appearance of being contained or delimited in their range of association, even if, as Boyd notes, one cannot readily specify their precise cognitive content.

Moreover, this appearance of delimitation translates into the common perception that such metaphorical usages in science are, or can be, controlled. Specification, through research, of how the brain is like a computer, or how the human organism, in the language of early-modern biology, is like a machine, seems to limit the range of meanings associated with the metaphor. However, this view of intrascientific metaphorical exchange rests, I shall argue below, on an uncomplex and historically naive understanding of how the discourses of particular scientific disciplines are actually constituted. Only by limiting the role of metaphor in science largely to cases of intrascientific exchange have theorists been able to produce relatively persuasive arguments for science's control over its metaphors.

In order to illustrate these points and to introduce more complex modes of metaphoric exchange in science, let us take as an example William Harvey's use of a mechanistic metaphor, in which the heart is likened to a machine, in his *De motu cordis* of 1628.[64] At one point Harvey argues that the movement of the auricles and ventricles of the heart

> is comparable with what happens in machines in which, with one wheel moving another, all seem to be moving at once. It also recalls that mechanical device fitted to firearms in which, on pressure to a trigger, a flint falls and strikes and advances the steel, a spark is evoked and falls upon the powder, the powder is fired and the flame leaps inside and spreads, and the ball flies out and enters the target; all these movements, because of their rapidity, seeming to happen at once as in the wink of an eye.[65]

Harvey's use of the machine analogy is highly specific. The heart is like a machine only in the restricted sense that the movements of its various component parts are, like certain machines, synchronized and of such rapidity that they appear to occur simultaneously. As employed here, Harvey's machine analogy might seem to be an instance of an intrascientific metaphor. Yet it is worth noting that this metaphor, while effecting a limited transfer of meaning between the notions of machine and heart, in fact fails to function in any significant way as a medium of exchange between theories, frameworks, or discourses. Harvey's use of language does not, in his seventeenth-century Aristotelian context, evoke the theoretical trappings or discursive horizons of mechanism. His restricted, even controlled, introduction of the machine metaphor represents neither the site nor the vehicle of shifts of meaning. The metaphor, indeed, is neither fraught with tension between two contesting discourses nor productive of change of an exchange of meaning through linguistic slippage that results in the disruption or transformation, however subtle, of a scientific discourse.

This is not to say that Harvey, the scientist, completely controls his metaphors: rather, we must look to other uses of metaphor in Harvey's discourse to find instances of true metaphoric exchange. More particularly, Harvey's use of metaphors associated with the blood, spirits, soul, the macrocosm and microcosm, circulation, and the like provides examples of metaphoric exchange as vehicles for profound shifts of meaning resulting in the disruption and transformation of Renaissance scientific discourses.[66] By contrast, machine analogies in Harvey's works are relatively simple and unproductive precisely because they tend to stand outside the tension between animistic versus vitalistic and transcendent versus immanent discourses, a tension which informs Harvey's biological speculation.

Curiously, many of Harvey's admirers, especially nineteenth- and twentieth-century scholars, have placed far greater weight upon his mechanistic metaphors than upon the others. The notion that the heart might be like a machine—more specifically, like a pump—has prompted reinterpretations of Harvey's work. In the course of such interpretation, Harvey's machine metaphors were reinscribed in such a fashion as to become media of exchange between different theoretical frameworks and discourses. Starting, perhaps, with Descartes,[67] the machine metaphor became the vehicle for shifting the meaning of such biological terms—and "entities"—as blood, spirits, the heart, and organs generally. Thus, in comparing the heart to a machine, Harvey's restricted analogy gave way to a wholesale metaphoric exchange in which the meaning of the term *heart*—biologically, ontologically, and metaphysically—shifted dramatically to become embedded in a systematic discourse of mechanism. The shift entailed not only a redescription of the function of the heart in the theoretical, scientific terms of mechanism, but also transformations of the religious, social, cultural, and psychological meanings and values associated with the heart.

The example of the machine metaphor suggests several important points about metaphoric exchange. First, not all analogies drawn from within science or technology necessarily serve as a medium of exchange. To do so, the analogy must implicate the subject in question in the system of meaning from which the analogy is drawn. Harvey's use of the machine analogy, while illustrating his observations of the heart's movements, stops short of implicating the term *heart* in any "mechanistic" system of meaning. As a result, no significant shift of meaning occurs. This observation is reinforced not only by the restricted and detailed nature of the analogy itself, but also by its discursive context. Though ultimately opposed to mechanism, Harvey's own scientific discourse emerges not in contestation to it, but rather from the dialogical interaction of other discourses.

Hence, second, to function as a medium of exchange, an intrascientific metaphor must occasion shifts of meaning by facilitating the interaction of different discourses. Such interaction can occur as a direct result of a scientist's dialogical struggles with contesting discourses or contesting features of a single, dominant discourse. Or, as in the above example, it can occur subsequently as a result of the reappropriation and reinterpretation of a metaphor by those who bring to it a new system of meaning, or discourse.

Third, though one can speak of intrascientific metaphors as facilitating the exchange of meaning between scientific discourses, in practice it is difficult to restrict exchanges occasioned by scientific metaphors to shifts in scientific meaning alone. Rather, intrascientific exchange is closely linked with extrascientific exchange.

The last two points demand illustration, however brief. Taken together, they hint at an understanding of how scientific discourses are constituted and how they change. This understanding is one that I shall first explicitly articulate and only then illustrate. Implicit in the above discussion is the notion that scientific discourses are inherently unstable. That is to say, a scientific discourse, though striving to enforce stable meanings and an orderly pattern of relationships among natural entities, nonetheless finds itself combating, if not repressing, conflicting tendencies. This inherent tension, which contributes to the instability of meaning in scientific discourses, represents an indelible mark, if you will, of the rude origins of scientific discourses. That mark is a mark of difference—of the impure, hybrid nature of such discourse, of its construction out of the forced mingling of diverse and often divergent systems of meaning.

The tensions inherent in scientific discourses, and their rude origins, are, I would argue, the result of the concrete, historical processes through which they are constituted as culturally and socially situated discourses. Too often, critics have depicted the origins of scientific discourses as autonomous acts of genius, or as the ineluctable unfolding of a rational framework of explanation over time, or, alternatively, as the revolutionary grasping of a new vision of nature. All of these historiographical models of scientific development and change cut scientific discourse off from some pertinent aspect of its highly specific, local, and self-reflexive—or dialogical—historical origins. Scientific metaphors, with their shifts of meaning occasioned by metaphoric exchange, represent telling traces of such repressed, or forgotten, origins.

To recapture such origins, to re-member the discourse of science, we should attend to such traces, to such metaphors. Doing so, I think, will lead us to the synchronic dimensions of scientific change, to the constitution of scientific discourses as synchronic systems of meaning within a constellation of other cultural and social systems. Such a view would insist that scientific discourses do not arise solely from internal articulation of inherited scientific traditions, nor from their wholesale rejection through conversion to a new system.

Instead, this view would insist upon the complex reception and reshaping of diachronically inherited scientific languages in the production of "new" scientific discourses. In this view, a diachronic, or disciplinary, history of science—still the dominant form of historical scholarship—would require extensive rewriting in order to capture the intersection and interference of such inherited scientific languages with other, synchronically situated, extrascientific discourses. How might such a history be (re-)written?

I would suggest that we need to look below the level of conscious scientific theory to the metaphors and tropes informing its discourse. Metaphors and tropes may be transmitted over time, but their meaning must always be reconstituted synchronically. That is to say, such meanings are socially and culturally situated, carrying resonances that speak forcefully to individual members of specific communities. But this very process of reconstituting the meaning of metaphors subjects them to the interference of other discourses—and, I might add, other metaphors—which, indeed, allows them to speak resonantly to communities of individuals. Such meaning is synchronically constructed: the metaphors and tropological features of extrascientific discourses—whether religious, political, social, economic, or "literary"—through individual acts of interference and interaction work to "fix" the meanings of inherited terms, and metaphors, within a newly constituted scientific language. By fixing meanings in highly specific, local, though still plastic, ways, the diachronic dimensions of scientific discourse come to constitute a synchronically coherent, if now metaphorically reordered and situated, language. Such a language constitutes a particular discourse and makes possible its production of theories.

This view of the construction of scientific languages can account, I believe, for what may seem mutually exclusive phenomena. On the one hand, some scientific discourses appear insular and objective; on the other, all such discourses, it has been claimed, are socially and culturally constructed. To the extent that apparently timeless and autonomous scientific traditions diachronically constitute a given scientific discourse, such discourses can give the appearance of being isolated from the external "contamination" of society and culture. However, once one accepts the proposition that the role of the metaphorical restructuring and reception of such traditions is critical to the emergence of a synchronically situated scientific language, various possibilities for the social and cultural construction of science become evident.

This view also offers a potential release from the most glaring shortcoming of Foucault's early emphasis upon discursive practices: its tendency to regard particular texts and authors as merely exemplary of a larger discourse. Foucault's essentially ahistorical practice disregards the tensions inherent within historically constituted scientific languages precisely because he fails to see them as *hybrid*, as constructed out of earlier frameworks and culturally significant metaphors. Since scientific languages are necessarily hybrid, even the most coherent of them will contain inherent tensions, if not contradictions, which are usually kept submerged but are never completely hidden. If particular authors and texts reflect such scientific languages or discourses, they also more importantly *refract* them. That is, they selectively and individually highlight or suppress the tensions and contradictions within a shared scientific discourse.

Indeed, the very embeddedness of scientific discourses in other, synchronic languages ensures that they harbor not just the possibility for harmony among communities of scientists, but also the very seeds of their own destruction. The yoking of different frameworks and discourses, often in tension with one another, through the dominance of certain shared metaphors, opens scientific languages to the interpretive practice of individual scientists. Here again cultural and social factors come into play. Though accepting a common scientific language or discourse, the individual scientist uses it in a way shaped by social and cultural commitments external to that language. Indeed, these commitments are themselves revealed by yet other languages, not always shared by a scientist's colleagues in his or her professional community, a mediation that results in a selective and idiosyncratic highlighting of the tensions and metaphors contained within the shared scientific language. Given a particular configuration of socially and culturally conditioned hermeneutic principles, a scientific discourse can thus prove inherently unstable. As a result, scientific change, rather than representing an inexplicable gestaltlike change as with Kuhn and Foucault, can be rooted in the destabilizing tendencies inherent in a scientific language. When exacerbated by the interference of social, cultural, or ideological factors, such tendencies can prove disruptive and productive of change.

Two final examples point toward a conclusion. My study of the term *spiritus* in medieval medical discourse illustrates how intra- and extra-scientific metaphors interact to transform received scientific languages and thus constitute a scientific discourse.[68] Although historians describe medieval medicine as "Galenic," medieval medical discourse actually represents a transformation of Galen's system reinscribed within a highly specific cultural setting. Galen's medical spirits—the Greek *pneuma*—assumed for medieval theorists far more significance than they had for Galen. The latter considered spirits a rarefied form of matter especially suited to certain key functions in the body. For example, the vital spirits, because of their lightness and rapidity, were well adapted to conveying life-giving warmth from the heart—the source of vital spirits—to the rest of the body.

By the twelfth and thirteenth centuries *spiritus* had become not merely a suitable instrument for life-giving warmth, but a quasi-independent, active substance and the singular medium of life itself. What happened to elevate the status of Galen's medical spirits and, as a result, subtly to transform medical discourse as a system of meaning? I have argued elsewhere for the central role of metaphors in transforming and then reconstituting medical discourse. At one level, the intrascientific, one could argue that analogies between two "scientific" disciplines, medicine and psychology, provided the key. That is to say, Galenic spirits, by analogy either to the Greek conception of soul in Aristotelian or Platonic psychology or to the processes of perception and cognition in ancient psychology, acquired new meanings as either the source or medium of life itself. In this case, shifts of meaning in medical discourse are linked to interactions between that discourse and the discourse of psychology occasioned by intrascientific metaphoric exchange. In quite precise, and increasingly specifiable, ways, analogies between medical spirits and psychological discourse become constitutive of medical theory.

What we find, however, is that such neat and controlled use of metaphor in medieval science gives way, instead, to an array of culturally significant shifts of meaning. The very metaphors that linked the two received languages of medicine and psychology subjected those discourses to the interference of other, extrascientific discourses, which, in turn, reconstituted and transformed those metaphors, producing a synchronically resonant and culturally situated system of medieval medicine. The metaphors that implicated *spiritus* in the system of meaning associated with psychology—the Aristotelian discourse of soul—became the sites and vehicles of yet more complex and unruly dissemination of meanings. The traditional medical term *spiritus* became enmeshed in a web of metaphors which extended and transformed its meaning. Its intrascientific metaphorical associations with *soul* and *medium* provided vehicles for injecting *spiritus* into yet other, extrascientific, systems of implication. The biblical image of Jacob's ladder, which became a trope for the soul's ascent to the divine, provided, for example, a theologically resonant metaphor for spirits as a ladder joining the mortal body with the divine soul. Other images and metaphors—the biblical trope of flesh and spirit, the Neoplatonic and Christian/Gnostic use of spirit/matter dichotomies and analogies—transformed medical spirits from mere material instruments of bodily functions into something far more noble and powerful. Such metaphors revealed the textuality of medieval medical discourse, its links to poetry, theology, biblical exegesis, and the like.

As a result, this new medieval discourse of medicine generated a host

of problems and implications which served to redirect theoretical speculation while introducing socially and culturally pivotal tensions that all
but defied resolution within its own system of discourse. Hence, the
metaphorical reception and transformation of the diachronic tradition
of Galenic medicine provided fertile ground for theoretical speculation
during the Middle Ages and Renaissance. But it also ensured the instability of medical discourse and its potential destruction in the seventeenth century as tensions between immanent versus transcendent and
animistic versus material tendencies proved explosive within the new
cultural ecology of post-Reformation Europe.

Since extrascientific metaphoric exchange implicates scientific discourse in other systems of meaning, metaphors can have the effect of
linking scientific discourse, to varying degrees, with social and cultural
change and the meanings, values, and ideological interests associated
with them. Although the transformations within medicine from the
Middle Ages to the early modern period can illustrate these points,
Stepan's discussion of gender and race analogies provides a telling example that readers may want to consult.

Indeed, what I have termed *extrascientific metaphorical exchange* is
central to Stepan's story. According to her account, the eighteenth-
century passion for classificatory schemes, when focused upon the
intersecting domains of biology and anthropology, drew upon common—that is, extrascientific—cultural metaphors to produce a discourse that encompassed and explained racial difference. Longstanding
metaphoric association of the black "with baseness, sin, the devil, and
ugliness"[69] established a common cultural system of implication which
defined the black as "other" and provided an underlying foundation of
unexamined assumptions for the later construction of a discourse of
racial difference. Such metaphoric associations, with their implications
of inferiority, savageness, and low rank in the chain of being, provided
a kind of cultural currency that the emerging discourse of biological
classification and anthropology drew upon when establishing "scientific" foundations for racial distinctions. Thus common racial beliefs,
when transferred metaphorically to science, led to identification of the
black with, for example, apes and, consequently, to a program of empirical research that sought "objective" verification of such beliefs
through comparative intra- and interspecies measurements of physical
characteristics.[70]

Stepan shows how, during the nineteenth century, the biological
"signs" of black inferiority were transferred to women. Women, after
all, were in cultural terms analogous to blacks: both were "innately
impulsive, emotional, imitative rather than original, and incapable of

the abstract reasoning found in white men."[71] Not surprisingly, anthropologists and biological scientists found that both the black and women shared the physical signs of low status—for example, low brain weights and protruding jaws.[72] In effect, scientists of the late eighteenth and nineteenth centuries, I would suggest, reappropriated both the ancient metaphor of nature as a hierarchical scale from lower to higher beings and the nearly-as-hallowed analogy between natural and social hierarchies. These inherited metaphors gained specificity and acquired culturally resonant meaning through interference—or interaction—with the synchronically situated discourses of race and gender. In essence, scientists, as members of certain specific extrascientific communities, reconstituted the dominant metaphors of inherited scientific tradition to reflect not only the cognitive content of their own socially situated extrascientific discourse, but, significantly, the values and ideologies that informed it as well.

The power of such metaphors in science is considerable. Narrowly construed, metaphors can direct scientists to explore links that would otherwise remain obscure. In some instances, such as those of metaphors associating brains and computers or disease and military invasions, the links suggested by metaphors can prove enormously productive of theoretical advances and empirical observations. In others, such as those of race and gender analogies, the links are misleading, mistaken, embarrassing, or worse. More broadly understood, metaphors represent sources of inherent instability within scientific discourse, with the capacity to forge links with other discourses, exchanging meanings that can shift the import of key theoretical terms. Once particular metaphors become part of the very fabric of scientific discourses, in other words, the capacity of individuals, or even scientific communities, to control them is, at best, limited. Rather than exhibiting unerring conscious design and authorial control, such scientific metaphors adapt themselves to a larger ecology of contesting social and cultural values, interests, and ideologies. Although subject to change—to reinterpretation, to refutation, to critique, exposure, and the effects of changing norms and ethos—the import of such ingrained and accepted scientific metaphors is not easily delimited. Once metaphors are dislodged and discarded, replaced by others, metaphoric exchange can assume the mantle of "revolution." But though their effects may appear like that of a sudden shift of gestalt, such metaphoric "revolutions" are grounded in interpretation, not, I would argue, in an unmediated perceptual shift.[73] Given the complexity of metaphoric exchange underlying scientific change, a more fitting model for scientific change might be that of negotiation rather than revolution.[74]

The process of negotiation, indeed, reflects more adequately the textuality of scientific discourse, its implication through the metaphoricity of its language in the "text" of other discourses. To the extent, then, that this theoretical analysis implicates scientific discourse in the languages of other, extrascientific discourses, science can no longer regard itself as separate from literature, nor as in complete control of its metaphors and analogies. Science, in short, may suffer the rule of its own metaphors and thereby exhibit a genuinely dialogical relationship with literature.

Notes

1. Michel Foucault, "The Discourse on Language," in *The Archaeology of Knowledge and the Discourse on Language* (New York: Pantheon, 1972), 227.

2. Richard Rorty, *Philosophy and the Mirror of Nature* (Princeton: Princeton Univ. Press, 1979).

3. Foucault, "Discourse," 229.

4. James J. Bono, "Literature, Literary Theory, and the History of Science," *Publication of the Society for Literature and Science* 2, 1 (November 1986): 5–9.

5. My discussion below treats but four such theorists: Richard Boyd, W. H. Leatherdale, Mary Hesse, and Nancy Leys Stepan. Other relevant works include Roger S. Jones, *Physics as Metaphor* (Minneapolis: Univ. of Minnesota Press, 1982); Thomas S. Kuhn, "Metaphor in Science," in *Metaphor and Thought,* ed. Andrew Ortony (Cambridge: Cambridge Univ. Press, 1979), 409–19; Richard Olson, ed., *Science as Metaphor* (Belmont, Calif.: Wadsworth, 1971); Paul Ricoeur, *The Rule of Metaphor,* trans. Robert Czerny, with Kathleen McLaughlin and John Costello, S.J. (Toronto: Univ. of Toronto Press, 1977); Stephen Toulmin, "The Construal of Reality: Criticism in Modern and Postmodern Science," *Critical Inquiry* 9 (1982): 93–111; Colin Murray Turbayne, *The Myth of Metaphor* (1962; rpt. Columbia: Univ. of South Carolina Press, 1970); Philip Wheelwright, *Metaphor and Reality* (Bloomington: Indiana Univ. Press, 1962).

Several bibliographies and other essay collections should also be noted: Warren A. Shibles, *Metaphor: An Annotated Bibliography and History* (Whitewater, Wis.: The Language Press, 1971); J. P. Van Noppen et al., *Metaphor: A Bibliography of Post-1970 Publications,* Amsterdam Studies in the Theory and History of Linguistic Science, Series V, Library & Information Sources in Linguistics (Amsterdam/Philadelphia: John Benjamins, 1985); Mark Johnson, ed., *Philosophical Perspectives on Metaphor* (Minneapolis: Univ. of Minnesota Press, 1981); Sheldon Sacks, ed., *On Metaphor* (Chicago: Univ. of Chicago Press, 1978); David S. Miall, ed., *Metaphor: Problems and Perspectives* (Atlantic Highlands, N. J.: Humanities Press, 1982).

6. See Bono, "Literary Theory." I shall discuss some of these disagreements below.

7. Jacques Derrida, "White Mythology: Metaphor in the Text of Philosophy," in *Margins of Philosophy,* trans. Alan Bass (Chicago: Univ. of Chicago

Press, 1982), 207–71; Derrida, "The *Retrait* of Metaphor," trans. F. Gasdner et al., *Enclitic* 2, 2 (1978): 5–33. On Derrida and metaphor, see also Rodolphe Gasché, *The Tain of the Mirror: Derrida and the Philosophy of Reflection* (Cambridge, Mass.: Harvard Univ. Press, 1986); Dominick LaCapra, "Who Rules Metaphor? Paul Ricoeur's Theory of Discourse," in his *Rethinking Intellectual History: Texts, Contexts, Language* (Ithaca: Cornell Univ. Press, 1983), 118–44.

8. Brian Vickers, "Analogy versus Identity: The Rejection of Occult Symbolism, 1580–1680," in *Occult and Scientific Mentalities in the Renaissance*, ed. Vickers (Cambridge: Cambridge Univ. Press, 1984), 95–163, esp. 95.

9. The basic texts are Aristotle, *Poetics* (1457b) and *Rhetoric* (1405a). For a brief review of metaphor in the history of thought, see Mark Johnson, "Introduction: Metaphor in the Philosophical Tradition," in *Philosophical Perspectives on Metaphor*, 3–47.

10. Hans Aarsleff, *From Locke to Saussure: Essays on the Study of Language and Intellectual History* (Minneapolis: Univ. of Minnesota Press, 1982). I shall treat the relationship between language theory and science in a book I am preparing for the University of Wisconsin Press, *The "Word of God" and the "Languages of Man": Interpreting Nature and the Classical Tradition in Early-Modern Science and Medicine*. A recent collection of essays touches upon many important points: Andrew E. Benjamin, Geoffrey N. Cantor, and John R. R. Christie, eds., *The Figural and the Literal: Problems in the History of Science and Philosophy, 1630–1800* (Manchester: Manchester Univ. Press, 1987). The essay by Geoff Bennington, "The Perfect Cheat: Locke and Empiricism's Rhetoric," pp. 103–23, takes its start from Locke's noted remarks from Book III of his *Essay Concerning Human Understanding*: "If we would speak of Things as they are, we must allow, that all the art of Rhetorick, besides Order and Clearness, all the artificial and figurative application of Words Eloquence hath invented, are for nothing else but to insinuate wrong *Ideas*, move the Passions, and thereby mislead the Judgment; and so indeed are perfect cheat." Quoted from Bennington, 103.

11. See Mark Johnson's exposition of what he calls the *literal-truth paradigm* in his "Introduction," pp. 12–13.

12. I. A. Richards, *The Philosophy of Rhetoric* (Oxford: Oxford Univ. Press, 1936); Max Black, "Metaphor," *Proceedings of the Aristotelian Society*, n. s. 55 (1954–55): 273–94; Black, *Models and Metaphors* (Ithaca: Cornell Univ. Press, 1962); Black, "More About Metaphor," in Ortony, *Metaphor*, 19–43.

13. Richard Boyd, "Metaphor and Theory Change: What Is 'Metaphor' a Metaphor For?" in Ortony, *Metaphor*, 356–408.

14. Ibid., 360.

15. Ibid., 361.

16. Ibid., 361–63.

17. Ibid., 361.

18. Ibid., 362.

19. Ibid.

20. Ibid., 361.

21. Ibid., 364.

22. Ibid.; emphasis added.

23. Ibid., 363.

24. Ibid., 358.

25. Thomas Kuhn's response on this point is worth noting in his reply to Boyd. See his "Metaphor in Science."

26. See, for example, Michel Foucault, "What Is an Author?" in *Language, Counter-Memory, Practice: Selected Essays and Interviews,* ed. Donald Bouchard, trans. Donald Bouchard and Sherry Simon (Ithaca: Cornell Univ. Press, 1977), 113–38.

27. For example, see the essays collected in *Political Shakespeare: New Essays in Cultural Materialism,* ed. Jonathan Dollimore and Alan Sinfield (Ithaca: Cornell Univ. Press, 1985).

28. For a theoretically informed history of the academic literary profession, see Gerald Graff, *Professing Literature: An Institutional History* (Chicago: Univ. of Chicago Press, 1987).

29. Boyd, "Metaphor and Theory Change," 362.

30. W. M. Leatherdale, *The Role of Analogy, Model and Metaphor in Science* (Amsterdam: North-Holland, 1974).

31. Ibid., 201.

32. Ibid., 204.

33. Ibid., 207.

34. Ibid.

35. I plan to treat these questions more fully in a section devoted to metaphor and science in a book I am writing, tentatively entitled *Literary Theory and the History of Science.*

36. See James J. Bono, "Medical Spirits and the Medieval Language of Life," *Traditio* 40 (1984): 91–130; Bono, "Reform and the Languages of Renaissance Theoretical Medicine," forthcoming in *Journal of the History of Biology;* P. M. Rattansi, "The Social Interpretation of Science in the Seventeenth Century," in *Science and Society, 1600–1900,* ed. Peter Mathias (Cambridge: Cambridge Univ. Press, 1972), 1–32; Steven Shapin, "Social Uses of Science," in *The Ferment of Knowledge: Studies in the Historiography of Eighteenth-Century Science,* ed. G. S. Rousseau and Roy Porter (Cambridge: Cambridge Univ. Press, 1980), 93–139; Evelyn Fox Keller, *Reflections on Gender and Science* (New Haven: Yale Univ. Press, 1985); Carolyn Merchant, *The Death of Nature: Women, Ecology, and the Scientific Revolution* (New York: Harper & Row, 1980). See also Stepan, cited below in note 53.

37. Leatherdale, *Role of Analogy,* 207; emphasis added.

38. Ibid., 211.

39. Ibid., 210.

40. Ibid., 211. Leatherdale's remarks here counter the notion of literary metaphor we have seen Boyd propose above.

41. Ibid., 212.

42. For example, see Mary Hesse, *Models and Analogies in Science* (Notre Dame: Notre Dame Univ. Press, 1966); and her "The Cognitive Claims of Metaphor," in *Metaphor and Religion,* Theolinguistics 2, ed. J. P. van Noppen (Brussels: Free Univ. of Brussels, 1984), 27–45.

43. Michael A. Arbib and Mary B. Hesse, *The Construction of Reality* (Cambridge: Cambridge Univ. Press, 1986), 147–70.

44. Ibid., 148.

45. Ibid., 150.

46. Ibid.

47. Ibid.

48. Ibid., 152.

49. Ibid., 155.

50. Ibid., 156.

51. Ibid.

52. Ibid., 157.

53. Nancy Leys Stepan, "Race and Gender: The Role of Analogy in Science," *ISIS* 77 (1986): 261–77.

54. Ibid., 268.

55. Ibid.

56. Ibid., 271–74.

57. Ibid., 275.

58. Ibid., 276.

59. See Derrida, "White Mythology."

60. See, for example, the works of Hesse cited above and those of Richard Rorty: *Philosophy and the Mirror of Nature* (Princeton: Princeton Univ. Press, 1979) and *Consequences of Pragmatism* (Minneapolis: Univ. of Minnesota Press, 1982).

61. Again, see the works of such theorists as de Man, Foucault, and Derrida.

62. Mark Johnson, "Introduction," suggests such a broad view of the function of metaphor. See also George Lakoff and Mark Johnson, *Metaphors We Live By* (Chicago: Univ. of Chicago Press, 1980).

63. I plan to discuss a third domain, the metascientific or methodological, in my *Literary Theory and the History of Science*. This third use of metaphor pertains to "styles" or "patterns" of scientific implication which are closely associated with the methods adopted by a particular scientific discourse. I see this use of metaphor as analogous to Hayden White's preoccupation with tropes and thought in his *Tropics of Discourse: Essays in Cultural Criticism* (Baltimore: Johns Hopkins Univ. Press, 1978).

64. William Harvey, *Exercitatio anatomica de motu cordis et sanguinis in animalibus* (Frankfurt, 1628).

65. Harvey, chap. 5. The English text is from William Harvey, *The Circulation of the Blood and Other Writings*, trans. Kenneth J. Franklin (London: Dent, 1966), 39.

66. See Bono, "Medical Spirits" and "Reform."

67. René Descartes, *Discours de la méthode* (1637), discusses the circulation of the blood in section 5. See also his *Treatise of Man*, French text with translation and commentary by Thomas Steele Hall (Cambridge, Mass.: Harvard Univ. Press, 1972).

68. The next several paragraphs draw upon my detailed study, "Medical Spirits and the Medieval Language of Life."

69. Stepan, "Race and Gender," 265.

70. Stepan, passim, and Stephen Jay Gould, *The Mismeasure of Man* (New York: Norton, 1981).

71. Stepan, "Race and Gender," 263.

72. Ibid.

73. Kuhn's theory of scientific change, in *The Structure of Scientific Revolutions,* 2d ed. (Chicago: Univ. of Chicago Press, 1970), unduly rejects the significance of interpretation, relying instead upon a model for change which privileges the special way of seeing of the scientific community. This almost necessarily limits the role that shifts of meaning occasioned by the interaction of different discourses can play in scientific "revolutions." Arbib and Hesse's redescription of Kuhn's theory in terms of metaphorical shifts represents something quite different and, I think, richer. See my "Literature, Literary Theory, and the History of Science." I plan to develop this perspective on scientific change in my *Literary Theory and the History of Science.*

74. In an important essay, Roy Porter challenges Kuhn's interpretation of Lyell as effecting "a revolution in geology." He suggests, instead, that "the image of revolution misdescribes what was in fact a complex dialogue of negotiation, persuasion and conviction" ("The Scientific Revolution: A Spoke in the Wheel?" in *Revolution in History,* ed. Roy Porter and Mikuláš Teich [Cambridge: Cambridge Univ. Press, 1986], 290–316, esp. 308). *Negotiation,* I think, captures aptly the dialogical and tension-filled interchanges within and among discourses in the process of scientific change.

Bibliography

AARSLEFF, HANS. *From Locke to Saussure: Essays on the Study of Language and Intellectual History.* Minneapolis: University of Minnesota Press, 1982.

ARBIB, MICHAEL A., and MARY B. HESSE. *The Construction of Reality.* Cambridge: Cambridge University Press, 1986.

BENJAMIN, ANDREW E., GEOFFREY N. CANTOR, and JOHN R. R. CHRISTIE, eds. *The Figural and the Literal: Problems in the History of Science and Philosophy, 1630–1800.* Manchester: Manchester University Press, 1987.

BENNINGTON, GEOFF. "The Perfect Cheat: Locke and Empiricism's Rhetoric." In *The Figural and the Literal: Problems in the History of Science and Philosophy, 1630–1800,* ed. A. E. Benjamin et al., pp. 103–23. Manchester: Manchester University Press, 1987.

BLACK, MAX. "Metaphor." *Proceedings of the Aristotelian Society* n.s. 55 (1954–55): 273–94.

———. *Models and Metaphors.* Ithaca: Cornell University Press, 1962.

———. "More about Metaphor." In *Metaphor and Thought,* ed. A. Ortony, pp. 19–43. Cambridge: Cambridge University Press, 1979.

BONO, JAMES J. "Literature, Literary Theory, and the History of Science." *Publication of the Society for Literature and Science* 2, 1 (November 1986): 5–9.

———. "Medical Spirits and the Medieval Language of Life." *Traditio* 40 (1984): 91–130.

———. "Reform and the Languages of Renaissance Theoretical Medicine: Harvey versus Fernel." Forthcoming in *Journal of the History of Biology.*

BOYD, RICHARD. "Metaphor and Theory Change: What Is 'Metaphor' a Metaphor For?" In *Metaphor and Thought,* ed. A. Ortony, pp. 356–408. Cambridge: Cambridge University Press, 1979.

DERRIDA, JACQUES. "The *Retrait* of Metaphor." Trans. F. Gasdner et al. *Enclitic* 2, 2 (1978): 5–33.

———. "White Mythology: Metaphor in the Text of Philosophy." In his *Margins of Philosophy.* Trans. Alan Bass, pp. 207–71. Chicago: University of Chicago Press, 1982.

DESCARTES, RENÉ. *Discours de la méthode.* Leiden, 1637.

———. *Treatise of Man.* French text with translation and commentary by Thomas Steele Hall. Cambridge, Mass.: Harvard University Press, 1972.

DOLLIMORE, JONATHAN, and ALAN SINFIELD, eds. *Political Shakespeare: New Essays in Cultural Materialism.* Ithaca: Cornell University Press, 1985.

FOUCAULT, MICHEL. "The Discourse on Language." In his *The Archaeology of Knowledge and the Discourse on Language.* New York: Pantheon, 1972.

———. "What Is an Author?" In *Language, Counter-Memory, Practice: Selected Essays and Interviews,* ed. Donald Bouchard, trans. Bouchard and Sherry Simon, pp. 113–38. Ithaca: Cornell University Press, 1977.

GASCHÉ, RODOLPHE. *The Tain of the Mirror: Derrida and the Philosophy of Reflection.* Cambridge, Mass.: Harvard University Press, 1986.

GOULD, STEPHEN JAY. *The Mismeasure of Man.* New York: Norton, 1981.

GRAFF, GERALD. *Professing Literature: An Institutional History.* Chicago: University of Chicago Press, 1987.

HARVEY, WILLIAM. *The Circulation of the Blood and Other Writings.* Trans. Kenneth J. Franklin. London: Dent, 1966.

———. *Exercitatio anatomica de motu cordis et sanguinis in animalibus.* Frankfurt, 1628.

HESSE, MARY. "The Cognitive Claims of Metaphor." In *Metaphor and Religion,* Theolinguistics 2, ed. J. P. van Noppen, pp. 27–45. Brussels: Free University of Brussels, 1984.

———. *Models and Analogies in Science.* Notre Dame: Notre Dame University Press, 1966.

JOHNSON, MARK. "Introduction: Metaphor in the Philosophical Tradition." In *Philosophical Perspectives on Metaphor,* ed. Mark Johnson, pp. 3–47. Minneapolis: University of Minnesota Press, 1981.

JOHNSON, MARK, ed. *Philosophical Perspectives on Metaphor.* Minneapolis: University of Minnesota Press, 1981.

JONES, ROGER S. *Physics as Metaphor.* Minneapolis: University of Minnesota Press, 1982.

KELLER, EVELYN FOX. *Reflections on Gender and Science.* New Haven: Yale University Press, 1985.

KUHN, THOMAS S. "Metaphor in Science." In *Metaphor and Thought,* ed. A. Ortony, pp. 409–19. Cambridge: Cambridge University Press, 1979.

———. *The Structure of Scientific Revolutions.* 2d ed. Chicago: University of Chicago Press, 1970.

LACAPRA, DOMINICK. "Who Rules Metaphor? Paul Ricoeur's Theory of Discourse." In his *Rethinking Intellectual History: Texts, Contexts, Language,* pp. 118–44. Ithaca: Cornell University Press, 1983.

LAKOFF, GEORGE, and MARK JOHNSON. *Metaphors We Live By.* Chicago: University of Chicago Press, 1980.

LEATHERDALE, W. M. *The Role of Analogy, Model and Metaphor in Science.* Amsterdam: North-Holland, 1974.

MATHIAS, PETER. *Science and Society, 1600–1900.* Cambridge: Cambridge University Press, 1972.

MERCHANT, CAROLYN. *The Death of Nature: Women, Ecology, and the Scientific Revolution.* New York: Harper & Row, 1980.

MIALL, DAVID S., ed. *Metaphor: Problems and Perspectives.* Atlantic Highlands, N. J.: Humanities Press, 1982.

NOPPEN, J. P. VAN, et al. *Metaphor: A Bibliography of Post-1970 Publications.* Amsterdam Studies in the Theory and History of Linguistic Science. Series V. Library and Information Sources in Linguistics. Amsterdam and Philadelphia: John Benjamins, 1985.

NOPPEN, J. P., VAN. *Metaphor and Religion.* Theolingustics 2. Brussels: Free University Press of Brussels, 1984.

OLSON, RICHARD, ed. *Science as Metaphor.* Belmont, Calif.: Wadsworth, 1971.

ORTONY, ANDREW, ed. *Metaphor and Thought.* Cambridge: Cambridge University Press, 1979.

PORTER, ROY. "The Scientific Revolution: A Spoke in the Wheel?" In *Revolution in History,* ed. Roy Porter and Mikuláš Teich, pp. 290–316. Cambridge: Cambridge University Press, 1986.

RATTANSI, P. M. "The Social Interpretation of Science in the Seventeenth Century." In *Science and Society, 1600–1900,* ed. Peter Mathias, pp. 1–32. Cambridge: Cambridge University Press, 1972.

RICHARDS, I. A. *The Philosophy of Rhetoric.* Oxford: Oxford University Press, 1936.

RICOEUR, PAUL. *The Rule of Metaphor.* Trans. Robert Czerny, with Kathleen McLaughlin and John Costello, S.J. Toronto: University of Toronto Press, 1977.

RORTY, RICHARD. *Consequences of Pragmatism.* Minneapolis: University of Minnesota Press, 1982.

———. *Philosophy and the Mirror of Nature.* Princeton: Princeton University Press, 1979.

SACKS, SHELDON, ed. *On Metaphor.* Chicago: University of Chicago Press, 1978.

SHAPIN, STEVEN. "Social Uses of Science." In *The Ferment of Knowledge: Studies in the Historiography of Eighteenth-Century Science,* ed. G. S. Rousseau and Roy Porter, pp. 93–139. Cambridge: Cambridge University Press, 1980.

SHIBLES, WARREN A. *Metaphor: An Annotated Bibliography and History.* Whitewater, Wis.: The Language Press, 1971.

STEPAN, NANCY LEYS. "Race and Gender: The Role of Analogy in Science." *ISIS* 77 (1986): 261–77.

TOULMIN, STEPHEN. "The Construal of Reality: Criticism in Modern and Postmodern Science." *Critical Inquiry* 9 (1982): 93–111.

TURBAYNE, COLIN. *The Myth of Metaphor.* 1962; Reprint. Columbia: University of South Carolina Press, 1970.

VICKERS, BRIAN. "Analogy versus Identity: The Rejection of Occult Symbolism, 1580–1680." In *Occult and Scientific Mentalities in the Renaissance,* ed. Brian Vickers, pp. 95–163. Cambridge: Cambridge University Press, 1984.

WHEELWRIGHT, PHILIP. *Metaphor and Reality.* Bloomington: Indiana University Press, 1962.

WHITE, HAYDEN. *Tropics of Discourse: Essays in Cultural Criticism.* Baltimore: Johns Hopkins University Press, 1978.

Contemporary Cosmology and Narrative Theory

ERIC CHARLES WHITE

HAYDEN WHITE CASTS DOUBT on the legitimacy of narrative as a way of making sense of human history when he says that the importance traditionally attached to "narrativity in the representation of real events arises out of a desire to have real events display the coherence, integrity, fullness, and closure of an image of life that is and can only be imaginary."[1] According to White, the desire to embrace the entire span of past events within a single, cohesive emplotment or Kantian "Universal History" evades a crucial recognition: "the conviction that one *can* make sense of history stands on the same level of epistemic plausibility as the conviction that it makes no sense whatsoever."[2] The great master narratives of history—myths of a providential design, of inevitable progress toward this or that Utopia—can best be understood, to borrow a phrase from Michel Foucault, as manifestations of a "unitary and totalizing paranoia."[3]

The belief that history constitutes a vast "untold story" is thus a dangerous illusion. If all knowledge is ideological, in the sense that it serves the interests of some particular individual or group or reflects a historically relative apprehension of the meaning of reality, this "is especially true," White says, "of historical knowledge . . . that appears in the form of a conventional narrative."[4] Historical master narratives provide the means for legitimating the domination of one group over another, or if one follows Foucault, the disciplining and normalization of whole populations. Inevitably, says Jean-François Lyotard, they do "violence to the heterogeneity of language games."[5] Master narratives embody totalizing visions that have as their practical consequence conformist demands for consensus and acquiescence. The narrativization of historical events consequently precludes, White argues, any "visionary politics."

Only a recognition of history's intrinsic meaninglessness—what White calls the "historical sublime"—"can goad the moral sense of living human beings . . . to endow their lives with a meaning for which they alone are fully responsible." White therefore looks forward to a form of history-writing that would refuse "to attempt a narrativist mode for the representation of its truth," that would not, in other words, discover in past events an untold story concerning the destiny of the human race.[6] Lyotard similarly celebrates the passing of the great political and historical teleologies of the nineteenth century and their succession in the twentieth by what he terms an ethos of "paralogical" experimentalism in which no narrative is ever accorded more than a strictly local or temporary validity.

White's suspicion of metanarratives extends even to the emancipatory master plot or "romance" of collective liberation that Fredric Jameson considers the most compelling way to view human history. Even that narrativization of the past according to which the mass of humanity struggles toward ever-greater freedom from hegemonic control is suspect in White's eyes. Though Jameson himself repudiates naive historicism by arguing that history itself "is *not* a text" and is, in fact, "fundamentally non-narrative and nonrepresentational"[7]—thereby implying that his own narrative should be received as a historically conditioned rhetorical construction—White counters that "the crucial problem, from the perspective of political struggle, is not whose story is the best or truest, but who has the *power* to make his story stick as the one that others will choose to live by or in." Impatient "with the stories that representatives of official culture are always invoking to justify the sacrifices and sufferings of the citizenry," White asserts anarchy as an alternative to "collective unity," an alternative that "becomes more attractive as an ideal, the more 'collective unity' is enforced upon us by a combination of 'master narratives' and instruments of control backed by weapons."[8]

Jameson shares White's suspicion of the ideological nature of historical narrative when he says that one task of any reflection upon history is to engage in a "negative hermeneutics" charged with uncovering just whose or what interests are served by particular versions of the past. But historical reflection must undertake a "positive hermeneutics" as well, must discover a Utopian affirmation of collective unity in even the most ideological of historical accounts. With Northrop Frye, Jameson holds that all literature should be read as a "symbolic meditation on the destiny of community." Indeed, "the unity of a single great collective story" recounting "the collective struggle to wrest a realm of Freedom from a realm of Necessity" provides an indispensable Utopian moment orienting social practice.[9]

White explains Jameson's view in this way: "Narrativity not only represents but justifies . . . a dream of how ideal community might be achieved. Not exactly a dream, rather more of a daydream, a wish-ful-filling fantasy which, like all such fantasies, is grounded in the *real* conditions of the dreamer's life but goes beyond these, to the imagining of how, in spite of these conditions, things *might* be otherwise."[10] Jameson thus asserts the imperative importance of affirming a master narrative. The "central function or *instance* of the human mind," an indispensable, indeed inescapable, semiotic practice, narrativity confers identity.[11] That is, it specifies the present location of the "subject of history" in the stream of time and charts a course toward a full realization of possibility. The narrativization of experience is thus an indispensable prelude to effective action. White would with this much agree: "story forms, or what Northrop Frye calls plot structures, represent an armory of relational models by which what would otherwise be nothing but chains of mechanical causes and effects can be translated into moral terms."[12] Storytelling is essential, then, if one would remain, in Jameson's phrase, "political and contestatory."[13] Without narrative history, no resistant or oppositional stand against hegemonic force might be taken.

Jameson here mounts a critique of those who claim no longer to require the legitimating agency of narrative history, those who, like Lyotard, assert that the "postmodern condition" entails dispensing with the great Hegelian and Marxist master narratives of the progress of knowledge and the emancipation of humanity. Modernism in the arts, Jameson says, was able to exercise a properly Utopian project of emancipation by attacking the various rigidities of nineteenth-century bourgeois culture. But postmodern artistic practice, which affirms the modernist creed of endless innovation during a period when modernism has been enshrined as official culture, is merely a fashion parade of styles, an ineffectual and ultimately nihilistic pastiche. As Paul Rabinow puts it,

Jameson enables us to see that postmodernism is blind to its "own situation and situatedness" because it "is committed to a doctrine of partiality and flux for which one's own situations are so unstable, so without identity, that they cannot serve as objects of sustained reflection." Postmodernism becomes a cultural hodgepodge that "has lost its normative moorings."[14]

In this connection, Jameson singles out the schizo-cultural ideal promoted by Gilles Deleuze and Felix Guattari. The "schizo's" plural, discontinuous, semantically anarchic, precisely non-narratival stance toward the world is not at all, Jameson says, "a revolutionary one, but a way of surviving under capitalism, producing fresh desires within the structural limits of the capitalist mode of production."[15] Such a decentered, purely occasional form of selfhood is vulnerable to manipulation within the totalizing purview of a late capitalist society of consumption. Deleuze and Guattari's "program for libidinal revolution is political only to the degree that it is itself the figure for social revolution."[16]

Certainly Deleuze and Guattari give the impression that their schizo-cultural "desiring machine" might be so polymorphously perverse, so psychically heterogeneous, so libidinally opportunistic that it would be vulnerable, as Jameson suggests, "to the dystopian prospect of a global private monopoly"[17] when they define the alternatives confronting contemporary thought as, respectively, "paranoid" and "schizophrenic." Where the former seeks unity, finality, a center that would rein in the productive mobility of desire, the latter affirms fragmentation, marginality, desiring heterogeneity. The alternatives would appear, then, to be the following: either a paranoid projection of structure and coherence onto the world—precisely Jameson's affirmation of a master narrative in history—or the destructured frenzy of schizophrenic desiring intensities—postmodern pastiche.

How could schizo-culture, which programmatically refuses narrativity, identity, the maintenance of any fixed position, provide a basis for resistance? Hubert Dreyfus and Paul Rabinow are evidently troubled by this problem when they pose a similar question to Michel Foucault: What is wrong, they ask, with a disciplinary, normalizing society? Foucauldian genealogy, a form of critique that refuses to legitimate itself with reference to a comprehensive master narrative, undermines a stance that opposes normalization "on the grounds of natural law or human dignity, both of which presuppose the assumptions of traditional philosophy." But if appeals to "natural law" and "human dignity" are ruled out, what "are the resources which enable us to sustain a critical stance?"[18] If one cannot legitimate a practical engagement with the world of affairs in terms of a comprehensive narrative shaping of the human situation, how can one maintain a consistently adversarial position?

We are thus confronted with a dilemma: on the one hand, narrativity provides an indispensable point of reference orienting our progress through the world. The ethical and aesthetic significance of life depends crucially on attributing a narrative shape to history's unfolding. On the other hand, the totalizing finality of comprehensive narrative history can only lead the mind into delusion. We are therefore enjoined to reject the all-encompassing "master narratives" of traditional society which effectively preclude cultural innovation by offering closed, definitive versions of the world.

This essay will attempt to mediate the dispute concerning the legitimacy of narrative history by turning to a particular case. That is, it will seek to resolve the present controversy in the course of reflecting on the narrative shape of *natural history* as given in contemporary cosmological theory. Cultural history transpires within the larger field of natural history. The vast spectacle of the universe provides the setting or determining ground of culture. Indeed, the history of civilization must ultimately be seen as one aspect of cosmic evolution. The story of nature should therefore contribute importantly to any comprehensive narrativization of the human situation. Is there, then, some way that narrative form might be conferred on cosmic evolution without imposing a purely imaginary closure? Can the moral of the story of nature be expressed in such a way as to avoid ideological mystification? The question this essay will address is, in fact, twofold: first, what contribution might contemporary cosmology make to resolving the present controversy over the legitimacy of narrative history? And alternatively, how should the concerns voiced by the respective opponents and proponents of narrativity affect lay reception of cosmological theory, the tales of cosmic evolution told by the physicists?

An answer to this question can be developed with reference to the traditional aesthetic categories of beauty and sublimity. Briefly, where the apprehension of beauty involves affirming a preexisting body of norms or harmony between perception and concept, tradition and the present, sublimity always exceeds the routine and predictable world of everyday life. According to Kant, "the Beautiful in nature is connected with the form of the object, which consists in having definite boundaries. The Sublime, on the other hand, is to be found in a formless object, so far as in it or by occasion of it *boundlessness* is represented." The sublime is thus paradoxical. As a "formless object," a representation of "boundlessness," sublimity tests the limits of intelligibility. It arises, that is, from a discrepancy between what can be "conceived" and what can be "imagined." Sublimity does violence to the "presentative faculty": no sensible intuition can contain it. Although we can conceive of infinity (as spatial extension or a numerical series), we cannot, strictly speaking, imaginatively grasp this concept. Infinity will never adequately be represented in an image. As Kant says, the feeling of the sublime arises "from the want of accordance between the aesthetical estimation of magnitude formed by the Imagination and the estimation of the same formed by the Reason."[19]

For Kant, this discrepancy proves the tremendous inventive power of the mind: *"the sublime is that, the mere ability to think which shows a faculty of the mind surpassing every standard of Sense."* When it entertains an idea for which no example can be found in the realm of the senses, when it conceives the unimaginable, the spirit is released from bondage. Thus, the prospect of an infinite universe "on which the Imagination fruitlessly spends its whole faculty of comprehension must carry our concept of nature to a supersensible substrate. . . . As this, however, is great beyond all standards of sense, it makes us judge as *sublime,* not so much the object, as our own state of mind in the estimation of it." Sublimity raises "the energies of the soul above their accustomed height" and causes the soul to feel "the proper sublimity of its destination" in a world beyond this one.[20] The predominant feeling associated with sublimity is, then, one of spiritual exultation.

Following Kant, Lyotard has suggested that the paralogical experimentalism characteristic of postmodern art can be understood with reference to an aesthetic of sublimity in which pleasure derives from the "shock of the new," from the experience of going beyond the limits of received understanding. Contemporary artistic practice affirms not the "logical," or what conforms to a tradition of representational expectations, but the "paralogical," which paradoxically goes beyond the *doxa,* the realm of custom, habit, tradition. It seeks constantly "to present the fact that the unpresentable exists," the fact that inventive thought can transcend the mundane, the taken-for-granted, the putative finality of common sense.[21]

The aesthetic category of the sublime provides an equally appropriate frame of reference for apprehending key elements in modern physics. The physical view of nature offers preeminently an experience of sublimity. Nature remains sublimely irreducible, forever confounding the desire to contain natural history within a beautifully cohesive representation. Physical theory fails to provide a finished representation of reality in which ambiguous and conflicting elements have fully been resolved. In fact, natural history as depicted by modern physics is frequently counterintuitive or paradoxical from the perspective of common sense. If the principal concepts of classical physics, as N. Katherine Hayles remarks, "are simply the experiences of everyday life cast into more exact and rigorous terms," in relativity theory neither the time dilation effect as velocity approaches the speed of light nor the curvature of space around massive celestial bodies can readily be understood from the standpoint of common sense. Relativity theory introduces a sublime discontinuity between what can be visualized in the imagination and what is theoretically conceivable. As Hayles suggests, although relativity theory "permits a more general formulation of the laws of physics . . . at the same time any perspective from which we might actually view the world is made partial and contingent."[22]

The complementarity principle in quantum mechanics similarly introduces a discontinuity between sensible intuition and theoretical conception. As Heisenberg puts it, for some experiments, "the Bohr atom can be described as a small-scale planetary system, having a central atomic nucleus about which the central electrons revolve. For other experiments, however, it might be more convenient to imagine that the atomic nucleus is surrounded by a system of stationary waves whose frequency is characteristic of the radiation emanating from the atom."[23] Instead of the beautifully resolved imagery of classical physics (matter is granular, energy is wavelike), we are now obliged to entertain mutually exclusive perspectives at the subatomic level (electrons behave like waves, light is particulate). The wave/particle duality thus verges on paradox. A subatomic entity that can appear as both a wave and a particle is irresolvably ambiguous.

The recognition that fundamental reality is sublimely remote from everyday experience carries with it an important implication. In modern physics, the world of classical science, understood as a fully comprehensible totality, has been replaced by a nontotalizable field of relations, what Hayles calls "the cosmic web." Ilya Prigogine and Isabelle Stengers remark that "the irreducible plurality of perspectives on the same reality expresses the impossibility of a divine point of view from which the whole of reality is visible." Quantum mechanics thus obliges us to give up classical expectations of representational closure or "objectivity." In other words, there exist multiple, equally valid representations of reality that cannot be assimilated into a comprehensive vision. As Prigogine and Stengers suggest, the crucial disclosure of quantum mechanics lies in "emphasizing the wealth of reality, which overflows any single language, any single logical structure."[24] Representations of the world are situated: each can claim to encompass only a limited domain.

There no longer is, then, a "big picture" we might contemplate with detachment. Despite persistent efforts to restore one-to-one correspondence between theory and reality, quantum mechanics, in Evelyn Fox Keller's words, "makes it extremely difficult, if not impossible," to regard "the state of a system as simultaneously and equally an attribute of the theoretical description and of the system itself."[25] The modern scientific "picture" of nature, Heisenberg says, is a *"picture of our relationships with nature."*[26] The traditional view that the world exists as a discrete, well-defined object, and that scientific representations effectively mirror the world as object, can no longer be maintained. The paradoxical "reality" of modern physics is inseparable from the manner in which the physicist experimentally interacts with phenomena: "What we observe is not nature in itself, but nature exposed to our method of questioning. . . . In this way quantum theory reminds us, as Bohr has put it . . . that in the drama of existence we are ourselves both players and spectators."[27] According to Heisenberg, it makes no sense to ask whether subatomic particles "exist in space and time objectively, since the only processes we can refer to as taking place are those which represent the interplay of particles with some other physical system, e.g., a measuring instrument."[28] Although he was himself unhappy with the quantum mechanical view of nature, Einstein agrees on this point: physical representations of natural fact are, precisely, "free creations of the human mind, and are not, however it may seem, uniquely determined by the external world."[29]

From the standpoint of a Kantian aesthetic of the sublime, our uncertainty concerning how we ought to imagine the fundamental constituents of matter/energy at the quantum level is more than offset by this new revelation of the sublimely inventive power of thought. Physical theory has broken decisively with sensible intuition and the desire for representational closure. *The modern physicist must conceive the unimaginable*. In fact, although Niels Bohr himself held that the two complementary images of subatomic phenomena "can be regarded as different aspects of observable events" (thus preserving at least an attenuated continuity between perception and concept), many physicists, Mary Hesse reports, prefer to approach the natural world solely by means of a mathematical formalism so that the wave and particle pictures are merely "crutches for thought and not descriptions of reality."[30]

The sentiment of sublimity is perhaps nowhere more profoundly evoked than when physicists theorize the origin of the universe. According to the most imaginatively accessible version of the origin, in the beginning was the big bang, a cosmic fireball that, Heinz Pagels argues, should *not* be visualized as an explosion that originates at a point in space and expands outward. A better way of visualizing the big bang is to imagine that the space of the universe is closed and is just the two-dimensional surface of a sphere. On the surface of that sphere is the homogeneous gas of quantum particles at a definite temperature which interacts according to the laws of statistical mechanics. The expansion or contraction of the universe is visualized as the expanding or contracting of the sphere. As the sphere contracts in time the gas on its surface gets hotter, and if it expands it gets cooler. Of course, if one assumes the universe is open, then instead of the closed surface of a sphere one has to imagine an infinite surface. The main point, however, is that the big bang is spatially homogeneous and isotropic—it happens everywhere at once, all over the universe.[31]

The origin of material reality in the big bang can be "visualized," then, as the surface of an expanding sphere, a perfectly imaginable picture of the universe at the moment of its birth *except* that this sphere has neither an inside nor an outside, neither a center nor a circumference.

But the quest for the origin of the universe does not end with the theory of the big bang. The origin retreats through a succession of contingent beginnings—a sequence of developmental stages recently theorized as preceding the big bang itself—until we arrive at the most remote and clearly most sublime moment conceivable in cosmic evolution, that instant when "something" came from "nothing": "the nothingness 'before' the creation of the universe is the most complete void we can imagine—no space, time, or matter exists. It is a world without place, without duration or eternity, without number—it is what the mathematicians call 'the empty set.' Yet this unthinkable void converts itself into the plenum of existence."[32] The quest for the origin here touches its limit when thought runs up against an ungraspable absolute, an incomprehensible void "outside" and "before" our universe from which space and time, matter and energy, Being and Becoming emerged. Like the concept of infinity in the eighteenth century, this theory of a void that gave birth to the universe expresses the ultimate sublime.

Indeed, reality here exceeds not only the imagination but the power of conceptualization as well. To this question—"What 'tells' the void that it is pregnant with a possible universe?"—Pagels answers as follows: even the originary void must be "subject to a law, a logic that exists prior to space and time."[33] The void that produced the plenum of existence is not, then, "nothing" after all. Although the categories of space and time are inappropriate in this context, one might nevertheless observe that, figuratively speaking, a "structure" is inscribed in the pure nothingness of the originary void, a structure sufficiently dynamic and unstable to "cause" a certain "event," namely, the emergence of the spacetime continuum. The void thus loses its originary status: it is itself a phenomenon in "history," derivative or dependent on something "prior" that endowed it, precisely, with its characteristic prior-to-space-and-time logic. In this connection, Pagels reports the exasperation of a colleague who insists that in any truly satisfying account of the origin of reality nothing would really be nothing. The effort to theorize an origin, in Jacques Derrida's phrase, as "simple, intact, pure, standard, self-identical, in order *then* to conceive of derivation, complication, deterioration, accident" has once more been confounded.[34] The "origin," one is tempted to say, is always discovered to be already in relation to a determining "other" that defines the origin as merely a contingent beginning. The quest for the *origin* of the universe, in the strong sense of that term, unfolds in effect as an infinite regress.

Such a recognition suggests that the Kantian conception of sublimity as an experience of spiritual transcendence needs to be qualified in one crucial respect. When he suggests that sublimity "does not reside in anything of nature, but only in our mind, insofar as we can become conscious that we are superior to nature within us, and therefore also to nature without us," Kant verges on a denial of human historicity, a solipsistic indifference to the intractable suchness of the world.[35] Alluding to Kant, Harold Bloom challenges this conception of sublimity when he observes that the pleasure of transcendence is equivalent to "narcissistic freedom, freedom in the shape of that wildness that Freud dubbed 'the omnipotence of thought,' the greatest of all narcissistic illusions."[36] To understand sublimity exclusively in terms of the mind's inventive power involves wishful thinking. As a radical departure from expectation and habit, the sublime pertains not only to those moments when thought transcends itself but to those other times when reality takes the self by surprise, traumatically disrupting an existing system of meanings.

Since sublimity for Edmund Burke is an attribute of the external world rather than a subjective effect, his views may be pertinent at this juncture. When we regard nature tamed in the form of a garden, our mood may appropriately be one of restful contemplation. But the wildness of volcanoes, thunderstorms, chasms, gorges, hurricanes, and waterfalls—or nature in its sublime aspect—evokes very different feelings. According to Burke, the idea of beauty is founded on pleasure, that of sublimity on pain. The sublime provokes a condition of psychic distress, albeit "delightful horror": "Whatever is fitted in any sort to excite the ideas of pain, and danger, that is to say, whatever is in any sort terrible, or is conversant about terrible objects, or operates in a manner analogous to terror, is a source of the *sublime;* that is, it is productive of the strongest emotion which the mind is capable of feeling."[37] For Burke, then, to reflect upon the sublime spatial and temporal vastness of the cosmos is truly frightening. If the all-surpassing greatness of nature evokes feelings of awe, wonder, and astonishment, the perceiver is filled with terror as well when reduced to insignificance in the face of incomprehensible natural force. Kant describes the sublime in similar terms: in the presence of a sublime object the mind "is not merely attracted by the object but is ever being alternately repelled" so that the satisfaction produced by the sublime is best characterized as a form of "negative pleasure."[38]

As a form of consolation and renewal, beauty therefore emerges as an indispensable complement to the sublime in the aesthetic apprehension of nature. If the recognition of a fundamentally sublime universe provides a skeptical safeguard against the totalizing delusion of a single, overarching "master narrative," the terrors of sublimity, when the sublime is understood in its Burkean formulation, argue the advisability of recourse to beautifully comprehensible narrative form as we encounter what would otherwise be a demoralizingly incomprehensible flux, the raw stuff of history—"unclassified and unclassifiable"—that White describes pointedly as "grotesque."[39] In this sense, the terrifying character of sublimity regarded as an objective attribute of cosmic evolution redeems narrative consciousness. An authorizing center of meaning, precisely, a narrative shaping of natural history, remains necessary. Is there, then, some way to tell the story of nature which would provide a point of reference without occulting Nature's sublimely nonrepresentational character?

Considering the taxonomy of narrative forms developed by Northrop Frye—a taxonomy that Hayden White claims is fundamental to historical understanding—one may define four primary forms of emplotment: tragedy, comedy, romance, and farce. First of all, the comic vision of reality involves a reconciliation of opposing forces, a resolution of conflict, the perfect gratification of desire symbolized by the weddings and other festive occasions with which comedies often conclude. According to Frye, the establishment of a new social order free from constraint and frustration is the archetypal theme of comedy. Every comedy aims at a happy ending. Tragedy, on the other hand, achieves a contrary effect, not reconciliation but a revelation of the forces in the world opposing humanity. Though the tragic hero has "an extraordinary, nearly divine destiny almost within his grasp," the audience witnesses finally "the supremacy of impersonal power and . . . the limitation of human effort." Tragedy "seems to lead up to an epiphany of law, of that which is and must be," an epiphany of the implacable fate that determines human existence.[40]

The "radical of romance," Frye observes, "is a sequence of marvellous adventures," adventures that center on the hero's continually renewed struggle with an enemy frequently identified as an incarnation of chaos. The romantic knight-errant's struggle with confusion and sterility may well be a perpetual task. His endless succession of heroic labors only ceases when romance borrows from the conventions of comedy in order to contrive a conclusion. Adventure is, then, the essence of a romantic emplotment of reality, "which means that romance is naturally a sequential or processional form." Farce or satire is also a processional form, but one in which chaos reigns supreme over reality. Farce proclaims that "heroism and effective action are absent, disorganized or foredoomed to defeat."[41] A parody of romance, it reminds its audience, White says, "of the ultimate inadequacy of consciousness to live in the world or to comprehend it fully."[42] Skepticism is typical of the satiric outlook. The rogue protagonist of a picaresque novel, Frye remarks, "makes society look foolish without setting up any positive standard." The world is revealed to be "bigger than any set of beliefs about it," so that if the farceur has a position, it is "the preference of practice to theory, experience to metaphysics."[43]

Comedy and tragedy share an important characteristic. Comedy, which emphasizes the *resolution* of conflict, and tragedy, in which there is a *revelation* of the limiting parameters of existence, are both modes of emplotment in which closure is a principal aesthetic objective. Each intends a conclusive framing of the human situation. They contrast in this respect with romance and farce, in which the audience remains in a state of suspense, uncertain from one incident to another what direction the narrative will next take. In the case of romance, the hero's adventures are theoretically limitless. In farce, the characters never rise above immediate circumstance to achieve a comprehensive vision. Both romance and farce depict reality as an endless sequence of events: history's unfolding is eternal. If the universe can accurately be characterized as a sublimely nontotalizable field, then one would expect, contradicting the traditional hierarchy of literary forms in which comedy and tragedy have priority, that romance and farce will henceforth prove to be privileged modes of emplotment.

According to Prigogine and Stengers, contemporary research in nonequilibrium thermodynamics and, more generally, in chaos theory or complex dynamics emphasizes the "multiple, the temporal, and the complex" in nature. Such a view of nature does not permit the attainment of a totalizing representation of the whole. Prigogine and Stengers are frankly skeptical of every attempt to construct a "big picture," from the clockwork universe of Newtonian physics to modern efforts beginning with Einstein to achieve a grand "unified field theory" or ultimate "theory of everything." This "rediscovery of time" constitutes a major departure from classical science, which had no place for "spontaneous, unattended developments." The denial of time and complexity, they say, "was central to the cultural issues raised by the scientific enterprise in its classical definition." From Aristotle to Newton, western science pursued a "quest for an eternal truth behind changing phenomena." Classical physics can in fact be traced back to the ancient Greek belief in "a divine and immutable heaven" from which "becoming" and "natural diversity" have been banished.[44]

Newton thus sought "a vision of nature that would be universal, deterministic, and objective inasmuch as it contains no reference to the observer, complete inasmuch as it attains a level of description that escapes the clutches of time."[45] The full import of Newton's insistence on the time-independent character of natural law can be appreciated when one considers Laplace's demon, that creature of Newtonian science who, once apprised of the position and motion of all masses in the universe, could both predict the future and retrodict the past. Laplace describes this demon in these terms: "Such an intelligence would embrace in the same formula the movements of the greatest bodies of the universe and those of the lightest atom; for it, nothing would be uncertain and the future, as the past, would be present to its eyes."[46] The totality of existence, all of the future and all of the past, would thus constitute a simultaneity in the mind of this entity.

In such a vision of natural history, the specification of any single state enables an exhaustive definition of the entire system: "At every instant, therefore, everything is given." And if everything is given, then, so to speak, nothing ever happens. The description of nature was thus "nearly reduced to a static picture." Prigogine and Stengers suggest that the deterministic universe of classical physics, in which past and future are merely attributes of a theoretically graspable present totality, offers spiritual consolation and relief from anxiety by discovering an imaginatively satisfying design in nature. That is to say, Newtonian mechanics supports an essentially comic vision of the universe as an ordered, harmonious whole. Nature would be "law-abiding, docile, and predictable, instead of being chaotic, unruly, and stochastic." Even Einstein shares this aversion to temporality, regarding the phenomenological time of lived experience as an illusion. For Einstein, who in this respect might be characterized as the last classical physicist, "the intelligible was identified with the immutable."[47]

But by an irony of fate, this comedy of nature was converted into a tragedy at the beginning of the nineteenth century with the emergence of thermodynamics. According to the second law of thermodynamics, natural processes retain their deterministic character but temporal direction is now introduced in the form of an "irreversible" tendency to disorder in nature. Entropy, the measure of disorder in a physical system, never decreases. If for classical mechanics "the symbol of nature was the clock; for the Industrial Age, it became a reservoir of energy that is always threatened with exhaustion."[48] Although the evolution of life as theorized by Darwin apparently revealed a steady increase in complexity, the consequent future of the material world would nevertheless seem to be the following: as energy steadily dissipates, matter will disintegrate until the universe reaches a terminal state of undifferentiated chaos and frigid stillness.

If rising entropy is truly irreversible, then tragedy would appear to be the most compelling narrative perspective on natural history. Human striving would thus be undone by implacable thermodynamic law, by the entropic "heat death" of the cosmos. Among contemporary cosmologists, a tragic emplotment is evidently favored by Steven Weinberg when he suggests that the future of the universe will be either entropic heat death or gravitational collapse, a likelihood motivating his pessimistic assertion that "the more the universe seems comprehensible, the more it also seems pointless." For Weinberg, only the heroic effort to comprehend the universe endows human life with "some of the grace of tragedy."[49]

Prigogine and Stengers's account of the history of physical speculation about the universe might thus be summarized: eighteenth-century Newtonian physics seeks to transcend the vicissitudes of history by proposing a comic vision of the cosmos as a knowable, at least conceptually masterable whole. But if nineteenth-century physics accepts the historical character of physical process, it does so in a mood of pessimism and anxiety. With the emergence of thermodynamics, the Newtonian comedy of Nature and its successor, a romantic emplotment of natural history as progressive, are transformed into tragedy when entropy, an irreversible tendency to disorder, appears to govern cosmic evolution.

Prigogine and Stengers intervene here with their own theory of thermodynamic process: "In far-from-equilibrium conditions we may have transformation from disorder, from thermal chaos, into order. New dynamic states of matter may originate, states that reflect the interaction of a given system with its surroundings." Contemporary thermodynamics thus effects a rapprochement with Darwinian theory: the evolution of life on earth bears witness to the self-organizing properties of all complex dynamical systems. According to this view, near a "bifurcation point," a small cause, a purely chance fluctuation, may have large effects. What chaos theorists call "sensitive dependence on initial conditions" entails that small inputs have unpredictably large outputs. In highly unstable dynamic systems, macroscopic consequences follow from microscopic stochastic occurrences. The amplification of a minute chance fluctuation can radically redefine an entire system. The notion of a deterministic trajectory, and hence of a universe that could be completely known, is therefore of limited utility. Knowledge is always local rather than global: there can be no omniscient perspective outside of time, outside of a particular historically contingent situation. In a world in which "reversibility and determinism apply only to limiting, simple cases, while irreversibility and randomness are the rules," the observer remains in a permanent state of suspense.[50]

The universe does not, then, follow a predictable trajectory or line of development. The fact that small fluctuations may result in systemic reorganization and an increase in complexity means that only the unexpected can legitimately be expected in cosmic evolution. Passing beyond both the determinism of classical mechanics and the nineteenth-century conception of inevitable thermodynamic decay, Prigogine and Stengers effect at least a partial recovery of a comic vision of nature.

The unpredictable emergence of order from disorder justifies skepticism, Prigogine and Stengers claim, toward predictions of cosmic doom. They take no position themselves on the future fate of the cosmos. For them, present knowledge in astrophysics is "scanty and very problematic." Scenarios envisioning universal catastrophe are less scientifically warranted than reflections of anxiety occasioned by the "social and economic upheavals" of industrialization.[51] The tragic is only an attribute of reality. And a comic emplotment of the world remains feasible, as Victor Weisskopf evidently believes when he observes that the story of evolution

> is a development from the simple to the complicated, from unordered chaos to highly differentiated units, from the unorganized to the organized. . . . The spots at which matter acquires more differentiated shape are very few and selected. They must be considered as the most developed and most outstanding parts of the universe, the parts where matter was able to make fuller use of its potentialities. We find ourselves, therefore, in a very privileged and central position, since our Earth is one of these spots.[52]

But comedy is a possibility only. Prigogine and Stengers's vision of stochastic self-organization "leads both to hope and a threat: hope, since even small fluctuations may grow and change the overall structure. As a result, individual activity is not doomed to insignificance. On the other hand, this is also a threat, since in our universe, the security of stable, permanent rules seems gone forever." The favored emplotment for Prigogine and Stengers is, then, that of romance. As in the archetype of this narrative form described by Frye, the hero of the tale— Humanity—is locked in mortal combat with a representative of chaos, precisely, Entropy as a possible direction of natural history. Though the outcome is in doubt, Prigogine and Stengers evidently intend to communicate an optimistic mood of hopeful striving when they thus quote Freeman Dyson: "Life may succeed against all the odds in molding the universe to its own purpose."[53] Sentient matter may influence the course of cosmic evolution. Though a happy ending is not fated, humanity is nevertheless free to create one.

But this qualified hope—Prigogine and Stengers's *decision* to ratify a romantic emplotment—underestimates, in Hubert Reeves's view, the ineluctability of entropy. When he reflects on the same developments that Prigogine and Stengers cite in support of their romance of cosmic evolution, Reeves comes to a different conclusion. According to Reeves, the emergence of local order actually contributes to disorder in the cosmos as a whole: "In the great universal disorder, islands of orderliness spontaneously appear. The acquisition of this organization is costly. It is accompanied by a further increase in the cosmic entropy."[54] Entropy and negentropy thus exist in a reciprocal relationship. As Michel Serres puts it, the universe is "globally entropic, but negatively entropic in certain swirling pockets."[55] Romance, in which the hero progresses toward final triumph, must therefore give way before farce.

Existence unfolds essentially as farce precisely because order and chaos are co-present contraries: as states of chaotic flux provoke the emergence of orderly systems, so the creation of negentropic complexity contributes to entropic homogeneity. In such a tale, any agent would therefore resemble less a romantic figure of heroic stature, who makes steady progress toward final triumph, than a character out of picaresque literature, whose every success entails unforeseen consequences and further complications. In other words, if the knight-errant of courtly romance looks forward with confidence to a future resolution of conflict in a comic denouement, the farceur—trickster and improvisational artist—lives from one escapade to another with no expectation of achieving a consummating satisfaction. The farcical vision is one of gaiety in the face of disaster. Among contemporary physicists, Richard Feynman has perhaps most famously articulated this point of view. To the

Nietzschean question—"Can we remove the idea of a goal from the process and then affirm the process in spite of this?"[56]—Feynman answers: "There are many things I don't know anything about, such as whether it even means anything to ask why we are here. But I don't have to have an answer. I don't feel frightened by not knowing things, by being lost in a mysterious universe without any purpose, which is the way it really is, so far as I can tell." Concerning his own motives as a scientist, his sense of mission in life, Feynman offers this explanation: "One day I thought to myself: I haven't done anything important, and I'm never going to do anything important. But I used to enjoy physics and mathematical things. It was never very important, but I used to do things for the fun of it. So I decided: I'm going to do things only for the fun of it."[57] Though his manner is amiably ingenuous, as befits a farceur, Feynman would no doubt concur with Nietzsche's insistence that the ideal way of being in the world is to be oneself an incarnation of universal "becoming."

Contemporary cosmology—according to which the emergence of "order out of chaos" is an unpredictable, stochastic process accompanied by an increase in overall cosmic entropy—proposes a view of cosmic evolution radically discrepant with tragic, comic, and romantic forms of narrative emplotment. Comedy and romance, both of which look forward to the achievement of lasting perfection, are contradicted by rising entropy that possibly (if not certainly) dooms the universe to a terminal state of frigid stillness and chaos. Similarly, a tragic emplotment predicated on a revelation of the laws that determine existence seems an unlikely prospect given the sublime incomprehensibility of the universe: Being exceeds Knowledge. The most appropriate way to tell the story of nature is, then, a satiric emplotment of cosmic evolution as farce or picaresque. Alone among the traditional armory of narrative forms, farce offers a vision of history that remains cognizant of the sublime unrepresentability of cosmic evolution, a form of narrativity consistent with relativity theory (there is no privileged frame of reference), quantum mechanics ("reality" is inseparable from specific representational strategies), and chaos theory (the historical unfolding of the universe is unpredictably "open").

This recourse to picaresque constitutes a form of narrative legitimation qualitatively distinct from the romantic vision to which Prigogine and Stengers, like Fredric Jameson, evince a lingering attachment. If a romantic emplotment of history as progressive descends directly from traditional myths of world salvation in which reality attains a state of culminating perfection, the farcical vision is poised midway between the sinister beauty of totalizing master narratives and the terrifying sublimity of history's intrinsic incomprehensibility. The respective positions of the ostensive opponents of narrative history—the schizo-culture of Deleuze and Guattari, the paralogical game-playing of Lyotard, Foucault's genealogical critique of a normalizing society—are not incompatible with such an emplotment. Certainly Hayden White appears to privilege it when he remarks that historical situations "are not inherently tragic, comic, or romantic. [But they] may all be inherently ironic."[58] A picaresque emplotment enables the assumption, as Paul Rabinow puts it, of an "oppositional stance . . . suspicious of sovereign powers" and "universal truths."[59] But it does so without plotting the history of reality, in Richard Rorty's words, as "one in which a pre-existent goal is triumphantly reached or tragically not reached."[60] Forsaking the comprehensive perspective of Universal History to remain *in* the world rather than above or beyond it, neither deterministically constrained by a privileged beginning nor eschatologically oriented toward an apocalyptic end, the farcical vision conceives of history as a process without a *telos* or goal in which promise and possibility oscillate interminably with the prospect of devolution.

Notes

1. Hayden White, "The Value of Narrativity in the Representation of Real Events," in *On Narrative,* ed. W. J. T. Mitchell (Chicago: Univ. of Chicago Press, 1981), 23.

2. Hayden White, "The Politics of Historical Interpretation: Discipline and De-sublimation," in *The Politics of Interpretation,* ed. W. J. T. Mitchell (Chicago: Univ. of Chicago Press, 1983), 129.

3. Michel Foucault, Preface to Gilles Deleuze and Felix Guattari, *Anti-Oedipus: Capitalism and Schizophrenia,* trans. Robert Hurley, Mark Seem, and Helen R. Lane (New York: Viking, 1977), xiii.

4. White, "Historical Interpretation," 136.

5. Jean-François Lyotard, *The Postmodern Condition: A Report on Knowledge,* trans. Geoff Bennington and Brian Massumi, Foreword by Fredric Jameson (Minneapolis: Univ. of Minnesota Press, 1984), xxv.

6. White, "Historical Interpretation, 128, 136.

7. Fredric Jameson, *The Political Unconscious: Narrative as a Socially Symbolic Act* (Ithaca: Cornell Univ. Press, 1981), 82.

8. Hayden White, "Getting Out of History," review of *The Political Unconscious,* by Fredric Jameson, *Diacritics* 12,3 (1982): 12–13.

9. Jameson, *Political Unconscious,* 70, 19.

10. White, "Getting Out of History," 8.

11. Jameson, *Political Unconscious,* 13.

12. Hayden White, "The Narrativization of Real Events," in *On Narrative,* ed. Mitchell, 253.

13. Jameson, Foreword to Lyotard, *The Postmodern Condition,* xx.

14. Paul Rabinow, "Representations Are Social Facts: Modernity and Post-

Modernity in Anthropology," in *Writing Culture: The Poetics and Politics of Ethnography,* ed. James Clifford and George E. Marcus (Berkeley: Univ. of California Press, 1986), 252, 249.

15. Jameson, Foreword to Lyotard, *The Postmodern Condition,* xviii.

16. Jameson, *Political Unconscious,* 73.

17. Jameson, Foreword to Lyotard, *The Postmodern Condition,* xx.

18. Hubert Dreyfus and Paul Rabinow, *Michel Foucault: Beyond Structuralism and Hermeneutics,* 2d ed. (Chicago: Univ. of Chicago Press, 1983), 206.

19. Immanuel Kant, *Critique of Judgment,* trans. J. H. Bernard, 2d ed. (London: Macmillan, 1914), 102, 119.

20. Ibid., 110, 117, 125, 126.

21. Lyotard, *The Postmodern Condition,* 78.

22. N. Katherine Hayles, *The Cosmic Web: Scientific Field Models and Literary Strategies in the Twentieth Century* (Ithaca: Cornell Univ. Press, 1984), 44, 49.

23. Werner Heisenberg, *The Physicist's Conception of Nature,* trans. Arnold J. Pomerans (London: Hutchinson, 1958), 40.

24. Ilya Prigogine and Isabelle Stengers, *Order Out of Chaos: Man's New Dialogue with Nature* (New York: Bantam, 1984), 225.

25. Evelyn Fox Keller, *Reflections on Gender and Science* (New Haven: Yale Univ. Press, 1985), 143.

26. Heisenberg, *The Physicist's Conception of Nature,* 29.

27. Werner Heisenberg, *Physics and Philosophy: The Revolution in Modern Science* (New York: Harper & Row, 1958), 58.

28. Heisenberg, *The Physicist's Conception of Nature,* 15.

29. Albert Einstein and Leopold Infeld, *The Evolution of Physics: The Growth of Ideas from Early Concepts to Relativity and Quanta* (New York: Simon & Schuster, 1938), 33.

30. Mary Hesse, "Models and Matter," in *Quanta and Reality: A Symposium* (London: Hutchinson, 1962), 54.

31. Heinz Pagels, *Perfect Symmetry: The Search for the Beginning of Time* (New York: Simon & Schuster, 1985), 239.

32. Ibid., 347.

33. Ibid.

34. Jacques Derrida, "Limited Inc.," *Glyph* 2 (1977): 236.

35. Kant, *Critique,* trans. Bernard, 129.

36. Harold Bloom, *Agon: Towards a Theory of Revisionism* (New York: Oxford Univ. Press, 1982), 101.

37. Edmund Burke, *A Philosophical Enquiry into the Origin of Our Ideas of the Sublime and the Beautiful,* ed. J. T. Boulton (London: Routledge & Kegan Paul, 1958), 39.

38. Kant, *Critique,* trans. Bernard, 102.

39. Hayden White, "The Historical Text as Literary Artifact," in *The Writing of History: Literary Form and Historical Understanding,* ed. Robert H. Canary and Henry Kozicki (Madison: Univ. of Wisconsin Press, 1978), 58.

40. Northrop Frye, *Anatomy of Criticism: Four Essays* (Princeton: Princeton Univ. Press, 1957), 209, 208, 210.

41. Ibid., 40, 186, 192.

42. Hayden White, *Metahistory: The Historical Imagination in Nineteenth Century Europe* (Baltimore: Johns Hopkins Univ. Press, 1973), 10.

43. Frye, *Anatomy*, 229, 230.

44. Prigogine and Stengers, *Order Out of Chaos*, 2, 8, 3, 305.

45. Ibid., 213.

46. Quoted in James Gleick, *Chaos: The Making of a New Science* (New York: Viking, 1987), 14.

47. Prigogine and Stengers, *Order Out of Chaos*, 60, 72, 63, 294.

48. Ibid., 111.

49. Steven Weinberg, *The First Three Minutes: A Modern View of the Origin of the Universe* (New York: Basic Books, 1977), 144.

50. Prigogine and Stengers, *Order Out of Chaos*, 12, 8.

51. Ibid., 116.

52. Victor Weisskopf, *Knowledge and Wonder: The Universe as Man Knows It,* 2d ed. (Cambridge, Mass.: MIT Press, 1984), 168.

53. Prigogine and Stengers, *Order Out of Chaos*, 313, 117.

54. Hubert Reeves, *Atoms of Silence: An Exploration of Cosmic Evolution,* trans. Ruth and John Lewis (Cambridge, Mass.: MIT Press, 1984), 168.

55. Michel Serres, *Hermes: Literature, Science, Philosophy,* ed. Josué Harari and David Bell (Baltimore: Johns Hopkins Univ. Press, 1982), 116.

56. Friedrich Nietzsche, *The Will to Power,* trans. Walter Kaufmann and R. J. Hollingdale (New York: Random House, 1967), 36.

57. Quoted in Pagels, *Perfect Symmetry,* 369, 367–68.

58. White, "The Historical Text as Literary Artifact," 48.

59. Rabinow, "Representations," 258.

60. Richard Rorty, "The Contingency of Selfhood," *London Review of Books* 8,8 (8 May 1986): 12.

Bibliography

BLOOM, HAROLD. *Agon: Towards a Theory of Revisionism.* New York: Oxford University Press, 1982.

BURKE, EDMUND. *A Philosophical Enquiry into the Origin of Our Ideas of the Sublime and the Beautiful.* Ed. J. T. Boulton. London: Routledge & Kegan Paul, 1958.

DELEUZE, GILLES, and FELIX GUATTARI. *Anti-Oedipus: Capitalism and Schizophrenia.* Trans. Robert Hurley, Mark Seem, and Helen R. Lane. New York: Viking, 1977.

DERRIDA, JACQUES. "Limited Inc." *Glyph* 2 (1977): 162–254.

DREYFUS, HUBERT, and PAUL RABINOW. *Michel Foucault: Beyond Structuralism and Hermeneutics.* 2d ed. Chicago: University of Chicago Press, 1983.

EINSTEIN, ALBERT, and LEOPOLD INFELD. *The Evolution of Physics: The Growth of Ideas from Early Concepts to Relativity and Quanta.* New York: Simon & Schuster, 1938.

FRYE, NORTHROP. *Anatomy of Criticism: Four Essays.* Princeton: Princeton University Press, 1957.

GLEICK, JAMES. *Chaos: The Making of a New Science.* New York: Viking, 1987.

HAYLES, N. KATHERINE. *The Cosmic Web: Scientific Field Models and Literary Strategies in the Twentieth Century.* Ithaca: Cornell University Press, 1984.

HEISENBERG, WERNER. *The Physicist's Conception of Nature.* Trans. Arnold J. Pomerans. London: Hutchinson, 1958.

————. *Physics and Philosophy: The Revolution in Modern Science.* New York: Harper & Row, 1958.

HESSE, MARY. "Models and Reality." In *Quanta and Reality: A Symposium.* London: Hutchinson, 1962.

JAMESON, FREDRIC. *The Political Unconscious: Narrative as a Socially Symbolic Act.* Ithaca: Cornell University Press, 1981.

KANT, IMMANUEL. *Critique of Judgment.* Trans. J. H. Bernard. 2d ed. London: Macmillan, 1914.

KELLER, EVELYN FOX. *Reflections on Gender and Science.* New Haven: Yale University Press, 1985.

LYOTARD, JEAN-FRANÇOIS. *The Postmodern Condition: A Report on Knowledge.* Trans. Geoff Bennington and Brian Massumi. Minneapolis: University of Minnesota Press, 1984.

NIETZSCHE, FRIEDRICH. *The Will to Power.* Trans. Walter Kaufmann and R. J. Hollingdale. New York: Random House, 1967.

PAGELS, HEINZ. *Perfect Symmetry: The Search for the Beginning of Time.* New York: Simon & Schuster, 1985.

PRIGOGINE, ILYA, and ISABELLE STENGERS. *Order Out of Chaos: Man's New Dialogue with Nature.* New York: Bantam, 1984.

RABINOW, PAUL. "Representations Are Social Facts: Modernity and Post-Modernity in Anthropology." In *Writing Culture: The Poetics and Politics of Ethnography,* ed. James Clifford and George E. Marcus, pp. 234–61. Berkeley: University of California Press, 1986.

REEVES, HUBERT. *Atoms of Silence: An Exploration of Cosmic Evolution.* Trans. Ruth and John Lewis. Cambridge, Mass.: MIT Press, 1984.

RORTY, RICHARD. "The Contingency of Selfhood." *London Review of Books* 8,8 (8 May 1986): 11–15.

SERRES, MICHEL. *Hermes: Literature, Science, Philosophy.* Ed. Josué Harari and David Bell. Baltimore: Johns Hopkins University Press, 1982.

WEINBERG, STEVEN. *The First Three Minutes: A Modern View of the Origin of the Universe.* New York: Basic Books, 1977.

WEISSKOPF, VICTOR. *Knowledge and Wonder: The Universe as Man Knows It.* 2d ed. Cambridge, Mass.: MIT Press, 1979.

WHITE, HAYDEN. "Getting Out of History." Review of *The Political Unconscious,* by Fredric Jameson. *Diacritics* 12,3 (1982): 2–13.

————. "The Historical Text as Literary Artifact." In *The Writing of History: Literary Form and Historical Understanding,* ed. Robert H. Canary and Henry Kozicki; pp. 41–62. Madison: University of Wisconsin Press, 1978.

————. *Metahistory: The Historical Imagination in Nineteenth Century Europe.* Baltimore: Johns Hopkins University Press, 1973.

————. "The Narrativization of Real Events." In *On Narrative,* ed. W. J. T. Mitchell, pp. 249–54. Chicago: University of Chicago Press, 1981.

————. "The Politics of Historical Interpretation: Discipline and De-sublimation." In *The Politics of Interpretation,* ed. W. J. T. Mitchell, pp. 113–37. Chicago: University of Chicago Press, 1983.

————. "The Value of Narrativity in the Representation of Real Events." In *On Narrative,* ed. W. J. T. Mitchell, pp. 1–24. Chicago: University of Chicago Press, 1981.

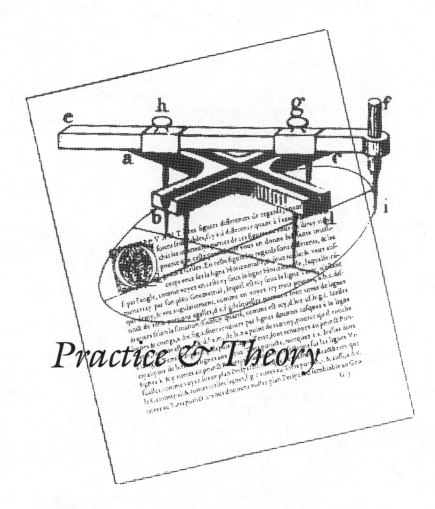

Practice & Theory

Eighteenth-Century Poetry Represents Moments of Scientific Discovery
Appropriation and Generic Transformation

MARK L. GREENBERG

> *Facts. And what are they?*
> *He admired accidents, because governed by laws,*
> *Representing them (since the illusion was not his end)*
> *As governed by feeling. The end is our approval*
> *Freely accorded, the illusion persuading us*
> *That it exists as a human image. . . .*
> > *Art is itself*
> *Once we accept it.* —Charles Tomlinson, "A Meditation on John Constable"

AN OLD BUT STILL PREVAILING VIEW among students of the relations between "literature" and "science" during the eighteenth century holds that poets generally thought of themselves as integral members of the unified and mutually supporting culture of their age. That culture was compounded of natural philosophers and men of letters alike, gentlemen who often considered themselves equally adept in the laboratory or at the writing desk and who saw few fundamental distinctions between experimenting with gases or light and composing poetry. William Powell Jones, for example, declares unequivocally that the "conflict between the visionary power of the artist and the analytical method of the scientist," characteristic of the nineteenth century and its aftermath, "did not exist . . . in the late seventeenth and early eighteenth centuries, when poets greeted the advancements of Science with enthusiasm."[1] Even a skeptical critic refers to a "momentary and perhaps somewhat fanciful and superficial marriage between Newtonian mechanistic . . . [and] experimentalist emphases and the poetic imagination of Thomson, Pope, and many other writers."[2] Thomas L. Hankins, in his excellent 1985 study, *Science and the Enlightenment,* offers

115

merely the most recent version of an argument whose contours are by
now quite familiar: "The classical and humanistic traditions had placed
natural philosophy in the category of letters, or literature. By the nineteenth century the separation of science from literature was almost
complete, but the Enlightenment still retained the emphasis on literature. . . . The ideology of the Enlightenment tended to make natural
philosophers into heroes, and in France the greatest hero of all was
Newton. . . ."[3] A number of influential studies treat eighteenth-century poets' deification of natural philosophers and especially of Newton; few, however, have been written since ideas about science and literature as social constructions have become generally accepted.[4]

In perhaps the definitive studies of the self-conscious dissociation of
imaginative writers from society at large, *Culture and Society, 1780–
1950* and *Keywords,* Raymond Williams maintains that this separation
"is itself in part a product of the nature of the Romantic" movement
and that the "lifetime of Blake, 1757–1827, is, in general, the decisive
period"[5] when the rise of democracy, of capitalism, and of indus-
trialism fueled fundamental changes in how poets viewed themselves,
the production of their art, the ideology and value of that art, and the
relation of that art to the "reading public." The full developments that
Williams treats were not experienced until Blake's lifetime. Yet poets
writing early in the eighteenth century anticipated in their responses
to scientific discoveries and discoverers a deep sense of the fundamental
differences between scientists and poets, of the diminishing role of poetry in a society dominated by revolutionary scientific and technological achievements, even a sense of isolation in a culture increasingly hostile to poetry—attitudes and ideas we have associated
most closely with romanticism.[6] For the increasing social importance
of science, along with its rapid institutionalization, occurred at precisely the same time as literature was also becoming institutionalized
and professionalized and, in an irony experienced most profoundly by
professional writers, increasingly marginalized.

A distinguished body of scholarship, including works by Alvin B.
Kernan, Marilyn Butler, and Hans Eichner, has originated ways of discussing literature and science as social institutions, and these new, historically centered approaches suggest that the rift between literature
and science began during the early decades of the eighteenth century
rather than with the romantics.[7] The eighteenth century is, in fact,
rapidly emerging as the pivotal period for what deepens into an on-
going antipathy between the two socially constructed institutions.
Works written during this period ostensibly to celebrate Newton's
achievements record instead a fierce (if muted and often encoded)

struggle between science, or natural philosophy, and literature as competing (though hardly equally matched) social institutions. The particular forms this struggle takes reveal something about the precise nature of the threat that scientific and technological advances posed for poets and also something about poets' modes of engaging this perceived threat. By tracing poetic representations of moments of scientific discovery in representative works by Thomson, Hughes, Glover, Halley, and Akenside, important writers during the height of Newtonianism, we can see quite specifically a process of appropriation and transformation operating in even the most overtly sympathetic, often encomiastic, renditions of the great scientist and his work.

The language of many eighteenth-century poems devoted to science tropes for poetry and the poet—captures for writing—key instances of scientific discovery while it struggles to represent linguistically that which equations or other purely rational systems can never communicate. Significantly, eighteenth-century poets figure such moments in terms of the body, with prosopopoeia the dominant trope. The body becomes the field upon which the competition is waged between the competing social institutions of science and literature. By humanizing moments of natural discovery, poets spatially represent and enhance such discoveries, thereby capturing them for poetry; simultaneously, of course, the poems also communicate the unique power of poets to accomplish such spectacular imaginative feats. Thomson, Hughes, Glover, and Akenside present themselves as voyagers or voyeurs, observing charged instances of discovery, while their language reaches toward expressing intensely lyrical moments of heightened emotional and imaginative activity. These lyrical moments are often embedded in long narrative poems. Almost completely framed "quanta," these scenes, with their heightened rhetoric and dramatic form, tell us more about the poets' emotions and anxieties than about the actual processes of scientific discovery (however one understands such a process).

"Ther are some com'd from London here lately that teach natural Philosophy by way of show by the beat of drum," James Thomson remarks casually and without elaboration to his friend William Cranstoun on December 11, 1724, breaking off the subject by promising "but more of that afterwards."[8] One could hardly predict the pervasive influence developments in natural philosophy would have on Thomson from this brief observation. The fact that natural philosophy, with its panoply of equipment and tangible, profitable displays of power, was very much in the air during the early eighteenth century figures importantly not only in the professionalization of science but also in the social reception of science, especially its reception in literature, the subject of this essay.

It is worth recalling that the popularization of science during the lifetimes of poets I am treating included a variety of activities and projects beyond the well-known books by Newtonians written for non-specialists in the public (including children and "the Ladies"). Larry Stewart and Margaret C. Jacob have detailed popularizations of science and its powers, mostly undertaken for profit, as important components in the institutionalization of science. Traveling demonstrations of new technologies and laboratory equipment, lectures, pamphlets, and brief traveling courses of instruction offered by legitimate authorities and charlatans alike helped establish scientific developments as newsworthy, scientific knowledge as momentous, and science itself as fact.[9] These messages, as Thomson's remark indicates, were not lost on the period's writers: men (almost exclusively) of letters and especially poets, whose own professionalization was just now underway, writers who, for the first time in history, were able to earn their living with their pens.

A number of important studies urge us to view both science and literature as undergoing their crucial formative periods from the late seventeenth to the mid-eighteenth centuries, emerging at roughly this time as self-consciously competing social institutions. In two recent books that draw upon and extend the work of Marshall McLuhan, Walter Ong, and especially Elizabeth Eisenstein, Alvin Kernan has offered both a theory of the social construction of literature and a detailed study of how Samuel Johnson emerges paradigmatically as the professional author in the new age of print. "Literature," explains Kernan, "reveals the culture-making activity more overtly than more stable institutions because of a historical vulnerability to change consequent on its failure . . . ever to achieve more than a semblance of objective existence and coherence. . . . 'Weak' institutions, we could say, provide better sources for understanding the dynamics of culture than do 'strong' institutions that more successfully manage to make themselves look like eternal facts of nature or the everlasting values of culture." The consequences of the changing social system of literature during the eighteenth century, according to Kernan, rendered the poet "a hard-pressed human being finding ways to earn a living and, at the same time, to give himself some dignity and his work some value, in the midst of a radical change in English society and its system of letters."[10] Ironically, as Eisenstein and Kernan argue, both institutions were made possible by the innovations and progress of print technology, as were the needs of both scientists and poets for developing modes of self-identification and self-protection within this new system.

Advances in printing and papermaking during the eighteenth century made literature available to increasingly large portions of the reading public (whose insatiable demand for printed materials technology fostered) and quite literally created within the extensive printing industry the profession of "author." Surviving as a professional poet during the early eighteenth century often depended upon securing the approval and support of a network of interconnecting institutions and powerful persons: critics, wealthy subscribers to his work, publishers, booksellers, and, as the century wore on, readers in sufficient numbers to justify expensive publication. When reimagining the impulses that moved poets to compose poems on science, it is worth recalling that associating one's poetry intimately with the prevailing philosophy of the day was simply good business.

A number of key insights developed in the second chapter of Eisenstein's *The Printing Press as an Agent of Change* emphasize features of books that, beginning in the early decades of the eighteenth century, also helped make poets possible: the logical structuring of book production along commercial lines and of the books themselves, what Eisenstein terms their *"esprit de système,"* represented by title pages, tables of contents, indexes, running heads, chapter divisions, varied typefaces and printing styles, pagination, and the creation of neat columns and other graphic organizing devices, all of which enforce the internal logic of the book, convey a sense of order and authority, and facilitate the classification of books in libraries; the "typographical fixity" that preserves words and ideas materially and durably while enhancing the status of the printed text; and reproduction, with its effects of spreading ideas and authors' identities abroad while amplifying and legitimizing the contents of printed materials.[11] The technological and commercial system of printing framed the world in which poets lived, moved, and enjoyed their professional being. Its power was extensive and pervasive, as we can see by glancing ahead to the romantics. In these poets, whom we typically associate with rejection of industrial technology and ideology and the social and economic system they served, there developed a sophisticated consciousness of how to use the features of the printed book in fashioning a body of work and a poetic identity in a culture created by printing technology: "On a wider scale than ever before . . . [romantic poets were] now self-conscious about their contextural practice, and their fear of critics played a significant role in establishing this awareness."[12]

As Kernan works from "within" literature to reach his conclusions, so Steven Shapin and Simon Schaffer, employing a historical and theoretical approach that complements that of Kernan, operate from "within" science of the late seventeenth century to reach theirs. Shapin's and Schaffer's findings regarding Hobbes, Boyle, and their historical context are remarkably similar to Kernan's: "As we come to recognize the conventional and artifactual status of our forms of knowing," they conclude a richly complex book, "we put ourselves in a position to realize that it is ourselves and not reality that is responsible for what we know."[13] Science and literature were, then, being formed in much the same way at about the same time.

The broad idea that science and literature are alike embedded in culture and have taken shape as the result of particular historical, economic, social, religious, and gender determinants is now accepted as fact, at least by the majority of scholars writing on the history and philosophy of science and on relations between literature and science. As George Levine shrewdly observes, each of the essays in his 1987 collection, *One Culture: Essays in Science and Literature*, assumes "that the positivist model of history of science and of scientific method cannot hold."[14] Having achieved this considerable plateau in our understanding, we may now move beyond it. In particular, the overall direction of study in science and literature encourages us to consider to what degree authors before the nineteenth century sensed at least on some level that theirs was the weaker of the two emerging institutions, that their authority as poets was, because socially constructed, threatened by the ascendancy of science and the scientist: sensed, in short, at least some of the ramifications of Blake's profound understanding in *The Marriage of Heaven and Hell* that "What is now proved was once only imagin'd"—and that what is imagined is in large measure determined by a network of forces and pressures which eighteenth-century writers experienced intellectually and viscerally. It is, I believe, at this formative period in the "lives" of both institutions that one can best witness the friction and incommensurabilities as well as the complementarities between literature and science—witness poets embracing Newton, for example—in order to appropriate for themselves a portion of his vast power. What follows, then, is a preliminary attempt to study, from *within* selected poetic responses to scientific discovery and scientists written during the eighteenth century, how ambitious human beings responded in poetry to the paradox of their simultaneous liberation from the patronage system and increasing marginalization by achievements in science and technology. What emerges is a more complicated picture of poetry "about" science and scientists during the crucial early period of rapid scientific change than we have seen before.

The advertisement of a raucous and extravagant "natural Philosophy . . . show" impressed young James Thomson, as did the ideas advanced by Newton and his followers. After making his way to London from Edinburgh in 1725 in order to seek fame and fortune as a poet, Thomson did not wait long before embodying in elegiac verse, "To the Memory of Sir Isaac Newton" (1727), the most noted theorist of natural philosophy of his age. We can understand Thomson paradigmatically as a member of the new class of poets emerging during the early eighteenth century who actually entered into the *profession* of letters hoping to forge reputations that would enable them to earn a living from their writing. Technology made such careers possible, even created the profession of "Poet" to which Thomson aspired. A keen sense of market conditions, popular taste, and the prevailing "philosophical" (or scientific) ideology rightly observed in verse could serve the young poet's needs well. And the poet attuned to the drumbeat of popular interest in Newton and his achievements could secure for himself a habitation in the pantheon of poetry, a name, and a handsome income.

Circumstances affecting Thomson's life in the mid-1720s help underscore the reading of the elegy to Newton which follows. They reinforce an understanding of the poem as primarily an exercise in poetic self-making in which the poet appropriates for poetry—and for himself as aspiring poet—a portion of the power and authority Newton had accrued at the time of his death in 1727. Lawrence Lipking writes that, if the "lives of the poets tend to be peripheral to the insides of poems, the life of the poet is often the life of the poem."[15] James Thomson's "To the Memory of Sir Isaac Newton" is very much concerned with the young poet's recontextualizing moments of scientific discovery in order to fashion a legitimate poetic persona and, concomitantly, professional standing for himself.

Three years before composing the elegy to Newton, Thomson decided to leave divinity school at Edinburgh University for London and, if he could, become a poet. Samuel Johnson, who had himself embarked on precisely this kind of life, characterizes Thomson's precarious existence at this time: "His first want was a pair of shoes. For the supply of all his necessities, his whole fund was his *Winter,* which for a time could find no purchaser; till, at last, Mr. Millan was persuaded to buy it at a low price."[16] Millan was himself new to the business of bookselling and could hardly offer a great deal of money to the unknown poet. *Summer,* also published by Millan, appeared in February 1727; it was dedicated to George Bubb Dodington, a member of Walpole's government described by one modern historian as having "raised toadyism to almost sublime proportions." Dodington also became Thomson's chief patron, subscribed to twenty copies of the *Seasons* in 1730, and offered Thomson valuable introductions to other members of Walpole's government. Thomson's attachment to this man, which he later regretted, indicates his almost desperate sense of need for financial and personal support at this time.[17] In late March 1727, hard at work on *Spring,* Thomson abruptly postponed completion of this composition. He had good reason to believe that its publication would serve him well, as earlier published segments of the long poem that would come to be called *The Seasons* had already attracted attention to him. Yet he evidently felt that there was more pressing work to do, for Newton had died on March 20, and James Thomson seized the moment to write in honor of his memory.

Published by Millan on 8 May, Thomson's 209-line elegy was, quite deliberately and significantly, the first of many such poems on Newton to be written by various poets. In the new age of print, being first and being original mattered. The poem's dedication (perhaps at Dodington's suggestion) to "that most illustrious *Patriot* Sir Robert Walpole" represented an act of self-abasement that, although failing to achieve its end, demonstrates the young poet's continuing sense of need for financial and social support: Thomson, it turned out, slighted Walpole later that year in *Britannia* and attacked him vehemently by 1730. Thomson's urgency to publish the first elegy to Newton, along with the other details of his professional life sketched above, suggests that Newton's death offered a propitious opportunity for the poet, and he seized it. The resulting poem stands mostly as a memorial to the poet's ingenuity and ambition, a sophisticated exercise in poetic self-fashioning and, to borrow Jonathan Freedman's recent phrase, in "autocanonization," in which the poet tropes his poem and himself into being.[18]

Writing within days or, at most, weeks after Newton's death, the twenty-six-year-old aspiring poet begins "To the Memory of Sir Isaac Newton" with a question one might expect only after an inordinately long period of time had passed without fit memorial recognition for the great scientist:

> Shall the great soul of Newton Quit this earth
> To mingle with his stars, and every Muse,
> Astonished into silence, shun the weight
> Of honours due to his illustrious name?[19]

Thomson's pose in this opening passage, that of dedicated poet determined that poetry perform its social obligation, poised to chastise those who, despite the mighty efforts involved, remain silent, contrasts sharply with his actual professional status at this time. Who is James Thomson, we might ask, to challenge poets? He is, I maintain, the poet in the act of forging, in the several senses of the term, an identity for himself.

This act of forging requires courage and ambition, as well as cheeky opportunism. Pausing momentarily, self-consciously, in his challenge to "every Muse" in order to reflect upon human limitations, he asks, "But what can man?" Thomson's first question to the Muses, followed by this slight bow in the direction of human frailty, creates and then intensifies the urgent, morally sanctioned "need" for the poem that follows. This merely rhetorical gesture, the sentiment of which is repeated, again rhetorically, in lines 132–36, opens the way for the stalwart poet to declare himself ready for the grand commitment to this high task:

> *Yet am not I deterred, though high the theme,*
> *And sung to harps of angels, for with you,*
> *Ethereal flames! ambitious, I aspire*
> *In Nature's general symphony to join.*
> (8–11)

The attentive reader has by now anticipated my analysis of this remarkable passage. The fact that by 1727 the greatest hero of the European Enlightenment, Sir Isaac Newton, needed no memorial accolades from the virtually unknown James Thomson does not matter to the poet, for it cannot. Here he tropes himself into harmony with Nature and into a central position within his culture. Newton's death occasions the poet's ambitious ascent, a momentary linguistic reversal of the predominant social vectors that had already resulted in the displacement of poetry and the poet's authority by logical mathematical systems, pure reason, and prose discourse. Newton's death thus figures as the instrument that allows the poet not only to join the "general symphony" but, for a time at least, to conduct it.

Almost immediately in the poem Thomson fashions himself into attentive watcher, reader, and interpreter of Newton's invisible intellect during charged moments of discovery. He is able to assert at once that Newton "Could trace the secret hand of Providence . . . All-piercing sage!" (15; 23). And the poet alone images the moment when, "bidding his amazing mind attend, / And with heroic patience years on years / Deep-searching" Newton "saw at last the system dawn, / And shine, of all his race, on him alone" (26–29). By so imaging this privileged moment, Thomson appropriates for poetry and the poet that which only art can express. And he renders the scene, significantly, in specific images of light, which for eighteenth-century readers would evoke Newton's well-known work in optics: Thomson weds admittedly conventional poetic imagery to the scientist's work, accomplishing a complex "double appropriation" for the poem and its author.

As the passage continues, Thomson extends and intensifies the poet's

power. The poet evokes in language the heightened mental state he
imagines Newton achieved when, in a single charged moment, he realized the laws of celestial mechanics: "What were his raptures then! how
pure! how strong!" (30), the poet begins rhapsodizing. In an extraordinary poetic effort, Thomson then attempts to recapitulate the moment
in verse. Depiction yields to imaginative transport as the poet's mental
action becomes the subject of the poem:

> *instead*
> *Of shattered parcels of this earth usurped*
> *By violence unmanly, and sore deeds*
> *Of cruelty and blood, Nature herself*
> *Stood all subdued by him, and open laid*
> *Her every latent glory to his view.*
>   (33–38)

Perhaps the most striking feature of this passage for its eighteenth-century audience was the dynamically increasing process of excitation exhibited by the poet, culminating in the personification of a subdued
Nature yielding herself rather enticingly to Newton (who, ironically, is
thought to have lived a celibate life). In a classic article on personification in the eighteenth century, Earl Wasserman shows that achieving a
high degree of emotional intensity in poetry was taken by contemporary readers as one important indicator of a poet's abilities: "only great
boldness and intense emotional force could create effective personification . . . the artistic use of this figure effectively conveyed to the reader
the passionate transport of the author."[20] In the passage just cited,
Thomson's palpable sexualizing of the charged moment of discovery
extends the power of his prosopopoeia by further investing the scene
with the force of desire. The result is a humanizing and ordering of the
chaos of experience. The passage also affirms the poet's special status:
who but an initiate into the workings of the great scientist's mind and
the secret ways of nature could depict such a scene? It is worth noting
that twice more in the poem (lines 72–75 and 96–102), in passages I
have analyzed in a previous study, Thomson represents metaphoric sex-
ual encounters between Newton and Nature which signify along the
lines I am developing here.[21]

Having achieved the personified moment, Thomson proceeds to describe in other terms how Newton envisioned the cosmos. Confidently,
the poet becomes compositor of the scientist's mental processes, in-
forming us what the scientist "saw":

> *All intellectual eye, our solar round*
> *First gazing through, he, by the blended power*

Of gravitation and projection, saw
The whole in silent harmony revolve.
                     (39–42)

Thomson proceeds to particularize and interpret Newton's achievements in a dazzling passage that moves, significantly, from a terrestrial
point of view up to the heavens. At first figuring the scientist on earth as
he "fixed our wandering Queen of Night" (46), Newton (and necessarily his poetic interpreter "with" him, though this point remains un-
stated), "breaking hence" as mental voyager, "took . . . ardent flight /
Through the blue infinite" (57–58) where "every star"

          at his approach
    Blazed into suns, the living centre each
    Of an harmonious system—all combined,
    And ruled unerring by that single power
    Which draws the stone projected to the ground.
                     (63–67)

The ascent figured here and the mastery over nature is the poet's. The
passage stands as tribute to the author's ability to imagine a figurative
journey and energize it as if he were present at the scene.

In the most recent full-length study of this poem, Michael G. Ketcham writes that "Thomson takes the elegy for Newton as an occasion
to define the scientific imagination poetically, and, through the definition of science, to define implicitly the potentials of the poetic imagination."[22] I read the poem as appropriating the authority of scientist,
whom it imaginatively transfigures, and the power of his works, which
it transvalues. In perhaps the most famous passage in the poem, the
lines on light and "the refractive law" (96–124), Thomson metaphorically depicts both Newton's mind as it "Untwisted all the shining
robe of day" and each color of light analyzed by the prism. He thereby
recontextualizes radically the scientist and his experimental findings,
which are now, transformed by the poet, made lovely: "infinite
source / Of beauty, ever flushing, ever new" (117–18). Having just
aestheticized Newton's optical discoveries, Thomson asks somewhat
wistfully,

    Did ever poet image aught so fair,
    Dreaming in whispering groves by the hoarse brook?
    Or prophet, to whose rapture heaven descends?
                     (119–21)

Such questions recall an age of poetic prophecy long past, though by
doing so they associate this poet with the age of prophetic bards and

suggest powers no longer invested in poets by society. The answer to the two questions just posed is, of course, yes: James Thomson has just imaged this scene of optical discovery. By doing so, he joins in that ancient company of poets and prophets he has just invoked. Through his intimate association with the mythologized Newton embodied in his poem, the young poet carves out a privileged place for himself close to the exemplary scientist he has animated and transformed.

"To the Memory of Sir Isaac Newton" was immediately popular, read with admiration by ordinary citizens of eighteenth-century Europe and poets alike. When in 1730 Thomson collected for publication in a single volume the four separate seasonal poems that form his masterpiece, *The Seasons,* he also included "A Hymn on the Seasons" (as one might expect) and "To the Memory of Sir Isaac Newton." Following publication of that volume, Thomson's reputation, already rising, was secure. Although still not wealthy, he no longer wanted a pair of shoes.

Selected passages from a number of poems produced during the first half of the eighteenth century exemplify the remarkable ingenuity writers exhibit as they attempt to partake of the power science had only recently achieved. A few years before Thomson attempted in his poem on the scientist to capture the high ground for poetry, poets desired to join Newton as coeval mental travelers. In 1720, for example, John Hughes, in his visionary poem "The Ecstasy,"[23] concocted a voyage whose figurative excesses overwhelm even the magisterial presence of Newton's ecstatic soul. Hughes, figuring himself as leaving "Mortality's low sphere" (60), defying Newtonian gravity, encounters Newton's soul during its regular heavenly transport:

> 'Tis he—as I approach more near,
> The great Columbus of the skies I know!
> 'Tis Newton's soul, that daily travels here
> In search of knowledge for mankind below.
>
> (61)

This scene of recognition, voiced by Hughes from an already exalted position, elevates the poet to the figurative high plane occupied by Newton's soul. Simultaneously, it exalts poetry, with its unique ability to operate beyond the limitations of Newtonian physics in representing this "encounter." Hughes, emboldened by his recognition, proceeds to beg Newton's soul become his "Sibyl" (61), while allowing him to be the soul's "companion," wandering from "orb to orb" (62). Now "rais'd sublime on Contemplation's wings" (and leaving any mention of the mediating Newton-Sibyl behind), the poet, in visionary rapture, becomes "An inmate of the Heavens, adopted into light!" (62).

The poem ultimately yields to the apotheosis of the poet, for which achievement, it turns out, the scientist offered but temporary and subordinate assistance. Newton's presence in the poem helps the poet liberate himself from constraints of time and space and gravity; it also helps him intensify his previous supernatural psychic state as he beholds comets and learns "how sun-born colours rise / In rays distinct" (62), an unmistakable reference to Newton's discussion of refraction in the *Opticks* (1704). Key moments of discovery depicted by Hughes in the poem, however, are generated by the ecstatic speaker to whom, ultimately, they refer and signify. Despite Newton's singular prominence in "The Ecstasy," the poet's bold self-presentation and the tropes that figure it elevate the vatic bard beyond his Sibyl.

It is hard for us not to read Richard Glover's "Poem on Sir Isaac Newton" as an extravagant display of eighteenth-century poetic conventions that, like Hughes's ecstatic speaker, seem to dwarf the putative subject of Glover's poem. In some 830 lines, Newton's name appears but fourteen times, mostly at the poem's beginning and end.[24] And though Glover may have drawn upon Hughes when he begs "Newton, let me soar with thee" (*L*, 14), by comparison Glover's poem seems to lack lyrical intensity. The central sections of the work embody a long hymn to the "Majestic Ruler Of The Skies . . . He taught great Newton the all potent laws / Of gravitation" (*R*, 14), and extended prayers by the poet to the "great Dispenser of the world / Propitious" (*L*, 14) for poetic inspiration. The poet's desire for divine aid, though conventional, is especially pertinent here. Prefixed to Henry Pemberton's *A View of Sir Isaac Newton's Philosophy* (London, 1728), Glover's poem was composed in the poet's sixteenth year by a virtually self-tutored youth with serious poetic ambitions. Not surprisingly, this poetic tour de force exemplifies the ephebe who is trying to establish his poetic credentials far more than it concerns Newton or his discoveries.

Two features of the poem support this reading: its thick texture of allusions and poetic devices and the poet's dramatic posturing. Glover overwhelms "Newton" with a vast array of conventional poetic elements which has the effect of absorbing and almost eradicating the scientist. Invocations of the Muse and of figures from classical and biblical literature and characters and events from history or legend, epic metaphors (often extending for twenty lines or more), conventional personifications of nature, Latinisms and Latinate sentence structure, Miltonic blank verse and imagery, appeals to ancient authors—all of these elements render the poem a virtual compendium of early eighteenth-century poetic practice. One representative example, appearing some 150 lines into a passage that has little to do with Newton or his contributions, should suffice:

> Here rest awhile, and humble homage pay,
> Here, where the sacred genius, that inspir'd
> Sublime Maeonides, and Pindar's breast,
> His habitation once was famed to hold
> Here, thou, O Homer, offer'dst up thy vows;
> Thee, the kind Muse Calliopaea heard.
>   (L. 15)

Repeatedly in Glover's poem such passages last for several hundred lines without referring to Newton or his achievements. The subject of much of this poem is the young poet's remarkable ability to imitate authors he has read, and in this sense the poem is "about" poetic tradition and, by absorbing and reconfiguring tradition, the poet's desire to display his individual talent. But about that talent, the young poet is, understandably, somewhat unsure.

Early in the poem Glover declares, "Newton demands the Muse; his sacred hand / Shall raise her to the Heliconian height" (*L*, 13). By figuring Newton as "demanding" the poem that follows, the young Glover creates an urgent need for his composition, and by investing the resultant poem with Newton's "sacred" authority, Glover elevates this verse "on" him. In addition, "Newton," figured in the poem as having supplanted all previous wisdom, now supplants the previously unquestioned power of poetry: "his sacred hand" alone (as Glover figures it) will "raise" the poem to "Heliconian" heights, which poetry formerly achieved without the scientist's sanctioning. Having extolled the virtues of Newton's discovery of the laws of gravitation, Glover next wonders "How . . . the Muse" shall represent the moment of Newton's discovery of refraction. He seizes the occasion to share the scientist's exalted moment. Becoming light's inquisitor, Glover poses to the sun alternative explanatory scenarios, asking it

> How Newton dar'd advent'rous to unbraid
> The yellow tresses of thy shining hair.
> Or didst thou gracious leave thy radiant sphere,
> And to his hand thy lucid spendours give,
> T'unweave the light-diffusing wreath, and part
> The blended glories of thy golden plumes?
>   (R, 14)

Although this passage has been the subject of some commentary, scholars have not noticed that by positing alternative depictions of Newton's moment of discovery the poet suggests both the problematic nature of imagining discovery itself and his ability to reduce to two the potential chaos of possible "explanations."[25] Whereas science strives for direct relations between causes and effects expressed univocally, the poet, analyzing the moment of Newton's analysis of light, weaves a rich linguistic texture that expresses the variety and also the limits of his ability to represent this charged moment.

Glover achieves through the instrument of his verse the self-conscious stature of a Poet who has just written a long work "on" the greatest intellect of his age. Near the conclusion of his poem, Glover wills himself into the posture of prophet and sage. First, the sixteen-year-old bard laments the fact that "Ev'n Newton left unknown" the "hidden power" that causes sound to travel through the air (*L*, 16). Then he fashions himself into mature Spokesperson for his age, calling for the continued advancement of learning's "empire," the only fitting memorial to Newton: "Let him not see Philosophy in tears," Glover implores, "So may he see another sage arise, / That shall maintain her empire" (*L*, 16). The prophet concludes his composition wisely, with an eye toward futurity. Glover thus succeeds in forging of himself the Muse that, he declared at the outset of his poem, Newton demands.

The poem assumed by most commentators on the scientific verse of the eighteenth century to be Glover's immediate precursor—and indeed a model for all panegyrics on Newton—is Edmund Halley's "Ode to Newton," prefixed to the first edition of Newton's *Principia* (1687). It is worth noting at this juncture that Halley's poem resists efforts to read it as "about" anything other than its titular subject. It alone of all the poems from this period on science or Newton which I have studied reveals little about poetry or the poet and does not attempt to appropriate for letters the scientist or his work. In this sense, at least, it represents a "model" from which most of the poems believed to be its descendants depart. Written in Latin (like the work it precedes), it was inaccessible to all but educated readers, its author deliberately refining the social class and gender of those who could comprehend his verse. Newton is conceived in the poem as necessarily prior to readers' understanding of Nature. Throughout, Halley focuses exclusively upon Newton's signal achievements for his culture. The first person pronoun never appears in the poem. The lyrical experiences of the poet, forming the fabric of Newtonian verse by Hughes, Thomson, Glover, and Akenside, among others, play no part in this poem, and Halley never represents himself dramatically. The poet makes no effort to envision moments of discovery. And the few personifications evoked are highly conventional and spare. Halley, we should recall, was an astronomer and chief sponsor of the publication of Newton's *Principia*. Unlike the other poets I treat, Halley did not aspire to a career as poet, and, significantly, his verse communicates a sense of where his professional interests lie. Although I know that, based upon this single example, I cannot elaborate a convincing theory of difference between practicing scientists who write poetry and professional poets who write about science during the eighteenth century, the perceptible differences are striking.

Striking, too, is the persistence into midcentury of poetic strategies for swerving from Halley's model. In Mark Akenside's "Hymn to Science" (1740), "science" again figures importantly, not for its own sake but as a means by which the poet achieves at first a heightened state of mind and ultimately psychic peace. The poem is structured dynamically according a pattern of vertical descent, ascent, and return downward designed to express the poet's transformation under the "influence" of science. Througout the poem, however, the poet commands, directs, and defines the limitations of science, orders it according to his own needs and desires. "Science! thou fair effusive ray / From the great source of mental day," the poet demands at the poem's outset,

> *Descend with all thy treasures fraught,*
> *Illumine each bewilder'd thought,*
>   *And bless my labouring mind.*[26]

Akenside thus begins his poem by taming a potent "science," not only demanding that it "Descend," but immediately transvaluing and reducing it, by synecdoche, to a "ray" from the already metaphorical (and quite conventional) representation of its source as "mental day." The subject of this "Hymn to Science" thus becomes the poet's mental journey, seemingly generated by the poet's command, at the conclusion of the first stanza, that science "bless my labouring mind."

Akenside energizes the remainder of the poem with a series of forceful directional cues delivered to the personified agent of his mental renewal. Throughout the poem, the bewildered, laboring mind of the poet remains in control, sponsoring the visionary journey to his own psychic redemption through a series of specific commands: "Descend . . . bless . . . Disperse those phantoms [of earlier learning] from my sight . . . Give me to learn . . . Let Number's, Figure's, Motion's laws / Reveal'd before me stand . . . Disclose [Nature] . . . Next . . . Detect Perception . . . Say [from whence ambition springs] . . ." (150–51). And as the poet exhausts available terrestrial learning, he next commands the poem's figurative ascent and its moment of greatest emotional intensity as he cries, "Dive through the infinity of space . . ." (151). At precisely the center of the poem, the poet directs his own apotheosis: "Then launch through Being's wide extent . . . To

Instinct, Reason, God" (151). Following this charged moment, the poet urges a return "downwards" and deep within his moral being:

Then downwards take thy flight again

. . . . .

Teach me to cool my passion's fires
Make me the judge of my desires,
The master of my heart.
(151–52)

Imagistically as well as structurally, the poem ends where it began, down now from the heavenly heights and back to the scene of the poet's self-conscious depiction of his own state of mind. Yet we are not exactly back to where we began, as psychic change has occurred. Now the "effusive ray" has become tamed, humanized, focused on its principal object, the poet himself: "Sun of the soul! thy beams unveil." And what they "unveil" is the poet's new-found ability to achieve a measure of peace, as he intones quietly to science,

happier I
From the vain tumult timely fly
And sit in peace with thee.
(152)

Science in Akenside's poem becomes the instrument by which the poet achieves psychic harmony as "bewilder'd thought" and "labouring mind" yield to "peace." The poem's mental dynamics inform the poem's subject and structure its action. Akenside thus anticipates developments in lyric poetry which would occur during the romantic age as the movements of the poet's mind rather than the achievements of science take center stage.[27]

Akenside, a physician by professional training, was intrigued throughout his life by the ability of language to transform science even as science had transformed the culture in which he lived. A passage in his long didactic poem, *Pleasures of the Imagination* (1744),[28] exemplifies how fundamentally polysemous tropes strain not only against the fictional idea, advocated during the early eighteenth century by Sprat, Locke, and others, of a spare, rational discourse "unadorned" by figures of speech, but also against the poet's best intentions to refrain from sensual excess and its embodiment in language.[29] Akenside declares the rational, univocal nature of truth:

For Man loves knowledge, and the beams of Truth
More welcome touch his understanding's eye
Than all the blandishments of sound his ear,
Than all of taste his tongue.
(2, 100–103)

Yet immediately thereafter, as if overcome by the moment of his own poetic awakening, he launches into a description astonishingly rich in tropes and word sounds that appeal to the corporeal ear and eye, palpably to the sense of touch. Indeed, in the following passage, the poet's obvious aesthetic delight in transfiguring the scientific explanation for the phenomenon overcomes and thereby reduces the claim that Newton's purely rational description of how a rainbow forms intensifies the poet's pleasure in witnessing the natural phenomenon:

> Nor ever yet
> The melting rainbow's vernal-tinctured hues
> To me have shown so pleasing, as when first
> The hand of science pointed out the path
> In which the sun-beams gleaming from the west
> Fall on the watery cloud, whose darksome veil
> Involves the orient; and that trickling shower
> Piercing through every crystalline convex
> Of clustering dew-drops to their flight oppos'd,
> Recoil at length where concave all behind
> The internal surface on each glassy orb
> Repells their forward passage into air;
> That thence direct they seek the radiant goal
> From which their course began; and, as they strike
> In different lines the gazer's obvious eye,
> Assume a different lustre. . . .
>   (2, 103–18)

The end of refraction for Akenside, it seems, is human perception; the "gazer's obvious eye" completes the Newtonian process of refraction. Refracted light, Akenside suggests, may be realized only by the responsive observer. In this passage, the poet effectively spatializes and personifies the invisible refractive process. He elaborates in language, thus in time, a series of movements which actually occurs in an instant. Despite the claim that the "hand of science pointed out the path" of light's refractive action and thus improved the experience derived from viewing the spectrum, the passage itself actually recontextualizes and radically transforms the science upon which it is based. A particularized, figurative rendering of Newton's discussion of refraction in the *Opticks*, the passage concerns the poet's enhanced experience of his own linguistic creation as well as his emergence as a man of "feeling." This element of the persona Akenside develops is marked by his extraordinary sensitivity to even the most minute nuances of natural phenomena, which his verse renders effortlessly.

This personified and sensually appealing passage thus has the effect of emphasizing the poet's abilities to engage and transform natural phenomena and to transcend the science to which his description refers. It also implicates the perceiver fundamentally and intimately in realizing a natural phenomenon, an important aesthetic consideration that also carries with it commercial implications. Poets were especially mindful of appealing to readers, a group they were also actively trying to shape during this new age of commercial authorship. Presumably, the community of readers created by Akenside's poem was meant to marvel at what Newton's interpreter had wrought.

Notes

1. *The Rhetoric of Science* (Berkeley and Los Angeles: Univ. of California Press, 1966), 1.

2. Gerd Buchdahl, *The Image of Newton and Locke in the Age of Reason* (London: Sheed & Ward, 1961), 2–3.

3. (Cambridge: Cambridge Univ. Press, 1985), 8–9. One may find similar expressions in Marjorie Hope Nicolson, *Newton Demands the Muse: Newton's Opticks and the Eighteenth Century Poets* (Princeton: Princeton Univ. Press, 1946), chap. 1, in which poets merely "answer the supposed 'demand' for the Muse, and express Newtonian theories in verse" (18).

4. The most influential studies have been those, previously cited, by Nicolson, Jones, and Buchdahl, to which I would add chapter 11 of M. H. Abrams, *The Mirror and the Lamp: Romantic Theory and the Critical Tradition* (New York: Oxford Univ. Press, 1953).

5. *Culture and Society, 1780–1950* (New York, Columbia Univ. Press, 1958), 31; *Keywords: A Vocabulary of Culture and Society* (New York: Oxford Univ. Press, 1976).

6. For a fascinating discussion of writers' sense of isolation during the eighteenth century, see John Sitter, *Literary Loneliness in Mid-Eighteenth Century England* (Ithaca: Cornell Univ. Press, 1982).

7. Alvin B. Kernan, *The Imaginary Library: An Essay on Literature and Society* (Princeton: Princeton Univ. Press, 1982), and *Printing Technology, Letters and Samuel Johnson* (Princeton: Princeton Univ. Press, 1987); Hans Eichner, "The Rise of Modern Science and the Genesis of Romanticism," *PMLA* 97 (1982): 8–30; and Marilyn Butler, *Romantics, Rebels, and Reactionaries: English Literature and Its Background, 1760–1830* (Oxford: Oxford Univ. Press, 1982), esp. chap. 1. Readers may also wish to consult Julia L. Epstein and Mark L. Greenberg, "Decomposing Newton's Rainbow," *Journal of the History of Ideas* 45 (1984): 115–40, in which we treat poetic appropriations of cultural and scientific ideas concerning rainbows; and my "Blake's 'Science,'" *Studies in Eighteenth-Century Culture* 12 (1983): 115–30, which traces Blake's appropriation and transformations of the word *science* and the meanings it commonly designates.

8. *James Thomson (1700–1748): Letters and Documents,* ed. Alan Dugald McKillop (Lawrence: Univ. of Kansas Press, 1958), 2. McKillop then quotes

from an advertisement in the *Edinburgh Evening Courant* of 4 January 1725 in order to help explain Thomson's reference; it also illustrates the point I am about to make: "The Course of Natural and Experimental PHILOSOPHY, lately advertised in this Paper, will begin on Wednesday the 6th of January at five of the Clock in the Afternoon, at Skinners Hall in Edinburgh; where the Apparatus may be seen, and Subscriptions taken in" (3).

9. Larry Stewart, "The Selling of Newton: Science and Technology in Early Eighteenth-Century England," *Journal of British Studies* 25 (1986): 178–92; Margaret C. Jacob, "Scientific Culture in the Early English Enlightenment: Mechanisms, Industry, and Gentlemanly Facts," in *Anticipations of the Enlightenment in England, France, and Germany*, ed. Alan Charles Kors and Paul J. Korshin (Philadelphia: Univ. of Pennsylvania Press, 1987), 134–64. On popularizations of Newton, see also Hankins, *Science and the Enlightenment*, 9–10, and Epstein and Greenberg, "Decomposing Newton's Rainbow," 118–21.

10. Kernan, *Printing Technology*, 6–7, 19.

11. Elizabeth Eisenstein, *The Printing Press as an Agent of Change: Communications and Cultural Transformation in Early Modern Europe*, 2 vols. (Cambridge: Cambridge Univ. Press, 1979), 43–159.

12. Neil Fraistat, *The Poem and the Book: Interpreting Collections of Romantic Poetry* (Chapel Hill: Univ. of North Carolina Press, 1985), 25.

13. Steven Shapin and Simon Schaffer, *Leviathan and the Air Pump: Hobbes, Boyle and the Experimental Life* (Princeton: Princeton Univ. Press, 1985), 344. For a recent historical study of one important controversy involving the clash between two different ways of figuring the world and the "reality" each discovers, see Dennis L. Sepper, *Goethe Contra Newton: Polemics and the Project for a New Science of Color* (Cambridge: Cambridge Univ. Press, 1988).

14. George Levine, ed., *One Culture: Essays in Science and Literature* (Madison: Univ. of Wisconsin Press, 1987), 340. Of course, Levine's astute critique is applicable to the current, prevailing system of belief developed during the twentieth century as a result of work by distinguished scholars, including Karl Popper, Thomas S. Kuhn, Paul Feyerabend, John Searle, Evelyn Fox Keller, Marilyn Butler, and Margaret C. Jacob, to list names instantly familiar to most readers of this book.

15. Lawrence Lipking, *The Life of the Poet: Beginning and Ending Poetic Careers* (Chicago: Univ. of Chicago Press, 1981), viii.

16. "Life of Thomson," in *The Lives of the Poets*, 2 vols. (London: Oxford Univ. Press, 1952), 2:349.

17. Basil Williams voiced this judgment about Dodington in his *Whig Supremacy, 1714–1760*, 2d ed. rev. by C. H. Stewart (Oxford: Clarendon Press, 1962), 107. I derive the facts concerning Thomson's life in this section of my essay from Hilbert H. Campbell, *James Thomson* (Boston: Twayne, 1979), 26–27 and 96–98.

18. See "Autocanonization: Tropes of Self-Legitimation in 'Popular Culture,'" *Yale Journal of Criticism* 1 (1987): 203–17.

19. For my text of Thomson I am using *James Thomson: Poetical Works*, ed. J. Logie Robertson (London: Oxford Univ. Press, 1908; rpt. 1970), 436–42. I

indicate line numbers parenthetically in the text. Ralph Cohen's *The Unfolding of* The Seasons (Baltimore: Johns Hopkins Univ. Press, 1970) details Thomson's debt to Newtonian science throughout his long poem. Readers interested in passages whose dynamics recapitulate or complement those elaborated in my reading of the elegy to Newton will find them throughout *The Seasons,* though they are especially strong in *Spring* (see lines 203–12, for example).

20. Earl Wasserman, "The Inherent Values of Eighteenth-Century Personification," *PMLA* 65 (1950): 441; on the widespread belief during the eighteenth century that the congruence between the mind and the created world justified our projecting human desires onto nature, see Hans Eichner, "The Rise of Modern Science," 9–11.

21. See Epstein and Greenberg, "Decomposing Newton's Rainbow," 130–32.

22. "Scientific and Poetic Imagination in James Thomson's 'Poem Sacred to the Memory of Sir Isaac Newton,'" *Philological Quarterly* 61 (1982): 33.

23. My text for Hughes is Alexander Chalmers, ed., *The Works of the English Poets, From Chaucer to Cowper,* 21 vols. (London: J. Johnson, et al., 1810), vol. 10. Since no line numbers are supplied, parenthetical references for Hughes refer to page numbers.

24. My text for Glover is Chalmers's *English Poets,* 17: 13–16; parenthetical references in the text indicate column (R = right, L = left), as lines are not numbered, and page number. For details concerning Glover's life, see pp. 3–12.

25. See Nicolson, *Newton Demands,* 13–14, and Epstein and Greenberg, "Decomposing Newton's Rainbow," 134.

26. Akenside's poem is available in his *Works* (London, 1772), in Chalmers's *English Poets,* 14: 132, and, perhaps more conveniently, in *Poems of Science,* ed. John Heath-Stubbs and Phillips Salman (Harmondsworth: Penguin Books, 1984), 150–52, the text to which I refer and whose page numbers I cite parenthetically; this citation: 150.

27. I am referring specifically to the development of what M. H. Abrams, in a justly famous essay, calls the Greater Romantic Lyric: see "Structure and Style in the Greater Romantic Lyric," in *From Sensibility to Romanticism: Essays Presented to Frederick A. Pottle,* ed. Frederick W. Hilles and Harold Bloom (New York: Oxford Univ. Press, 1965), 527–60.

28. My text for *Pleasures* is Chalmers's *English Poets,* 14: 65–71; I indicate book and line numbers parenthetically.

29. For eighteenth-century theories of language, see Murray Cohen, *Sensible Words: Linguistic Practice in England, 1640–1785* (Baltimore: Johns Hopkins Univ. Press, 1977), esp. chap. 1; Hans Aarsleff, *The Study of Language in England, 1780–1860* (Princeton: Princeton Univ. Press, 1967); and Stanley E. Fish, *Surprised by Sin: The Reader in* Paradise Lost (1967; rpt. Berkeley and Los Angeles: Univ. of California Press, 1971), 22–37 and 107–30.

Bibliography

AARSLEFF, HANS. *The Study of Language in England, 1780–1860.* Princeton: Princeton University Press, 1967.

ABRAMS, M. H. *The Mirror and the Lamp: Romantic Theory and the Critical Tradition*. New York: Oxford University Press, 1953.

————. "Structure and Style in the Greater Romantic Lyric." In *From Sensibility to Romanticism: Essays Presented to Frederick A. Pottle*, ed. Frederick W. Hilles and Harold Bloom, pp. 527–60. New York: Oxford University Press, 1965.

AKENSIDE, MARK. *Works*. London, 1772.

BUCHDAHL, GERD. *The Image of Newton and Locke in the Age of Reason*. London and New York: Sheed & Ward, 1961.

BUTLER, MARILYN. *Romantics, Rebels, and Reactionaries: English Literature and Its Background, 1760–1830*. Oxford: Oxford University Press, 1982.

CAMPBELL, HILBERT H. *James Thomson*. Boston: Twayne, 1979.

CHALMERS, ALEXANDER, ed. *The Works of the English Poets, From Chaucer to Cowper*. 21 vols. London: J. Johnson et al., 1810.

COHEN, MURRAY. *Sensible Words: Linguistic Practice in England, 1640–1785.* Baltimore: Johns Hopkins University Press, 1977.

COHEN, RALPH. *The Art of Discrimination: Thomson's* The Seasons *and the Language of Criticism*. London: Routledge & Kegan Paul, 1964.

————. *The Unfolding of* The Seasons. Baltimore: Johns Hopkins University Press, 1970.

EICHNER, HANS. "The Rise of Modern Science and the Genesis of Romanticism." *PMLA* 97 (1982): 8–30.

EISENSTEIN, ELIZABETH. *The Printing Press as an Agent of Change: Communications and Cultural Transformation in Early Modern Europe*. 2 vols. Cambridge: Cambridge University Press, 1979.

EPSTEIN, JULIA L., and MARK L. GREENBERG. "Decomposing Newton's Rainbow." *Journal of the History of Ideas* 45 (1984): 115–40.

FISH, STANLEY E. *Surprised by Sin: The Reader in* Paradise Lost. 1967. Reprint. Berkeley and Los Angeles: University of California Press, 1971.

FRAISTAT, NEIL. *The Poem and the Book: Interpreting Collections of Romantic Poetry*. Chapel Hill: University of North Carolina Press, 1985.

FREEDMAN, JONATHAN. "Autocanonization: Tropes of Self-Legitimation in 'Popular Culture.'" *Yale Journal of Criticism* 1 (1987): 203–17.

GREENBERG, MARK L. "Blake's 'Science.'" *Studies in Eighteenth-Century Culture* 12 (1983): 115–30.

HALLEY, EDMUND. "To the Illustrious Man Isaac Newton and this His Work Done in Fields of the Mathematics and Physics a Signal Distinction of Our Time and Race." Trans. Leon J. Richardson. In *Sir Isaac Newton's Mathematical Principles of Natural Philosophy and His System of the World*, 2 vols., trans. Andrew Motte, ed. Florian Cajori, 1: xiii–xv. Berkeley: University of California Press, 1966.

HANKINS, THOMAS L. *Science and the Enlightenment*. Cambridge: Cambridge University Press, 1985.

HEATH-STUBBS, JOHN, and PHILLIPS SALMAN, eds. *Poems of Science*. Harmondsworth: Penguin Books, 1984.

JACOB, MARGARET C. "Scientific Culture in the Early English Enlightenment: Mechanisms, Industry, and Gentlemanly Facts." In *Anticipations of the En-*

lightenment in England, France, and Germany, ed. Alan Charles Kors and Paul J. Korshin, pp. 134–64. Philadelphia: University of Pennsylvania Press, 1987.

JOHNSON, SAMUEL. *The Lives of the Poets.* 2 vols. Introduction by Arthur Waugh. London: Oxford University Press, 1952.

JONES, WILLIAM POWELL. *The Rhetoric of Science: A Study of Scientific Ideas and Imagery in Eighteenth-Century English Poetry.* Berkeley and Los Angeles: University of California Press, 1966.

KERNAN, ALVIN B. *The Imaginary Library: An Essay on Literature and Society.* Princeton: Princeton University Press, 1982.

———. *Printing Technology, Letters and Samuel Johnson.* Princeton: Princeton University Press, 1987.

KETCHAM, MICHAEL G. "Scientific and Poetic Imagination in James Thomson's 'Poem Sacred to the Memory of Sir Isaac Newton.'" *Philological Quarterly* 61 (1982): 33–50.

LEVINE, GEORGE, ed. *One Culture: Essays in Science and Literature.* Madison: University of Wisconsin Press, 1987.

LIPKING, LAWRENCE. *The Life of the Poet: Beginning and Ending Poetic Careers.* Chicago: University of Chicago Press, 1981.

NICOLSON, MARJORIE HOPE. *Newton Demands the Muse: Newton's* Opticks *and the Eighteenth Century Poets.* Princeton: Princeton University Press, 1946.

SEPPER, DENNIS L. *Goethe Contra Newton: Polemics and the Project for a New Science of Color.* Cambridge: Cambridge University Press, 1988.

SHAPIN, STEVEN, and SIMON SCHAFFER. *Leviathan and the Air Pump: Hobbes, Boyle and the Experimental Life.* Princeton: Princeton University Press, 1985.

SITTER, JOHN. *Literary Loneliness in Mid-Eighteenth Century England.* Ithaca: Cornell University Press, 1982.

STEWART, LARRY. "The Selling of Newton: Science and Technology in Early Eighteenth-Century England." *Journal of British Studies* 25 (1986): 179–92.

THOMSON, JAMES. *James Thomson (1700–1748): Letters and Documents.* Ed. Alan Dugald McKillop. Lawrence: University of Kansas Press, 1958.

———. *James Thomson: Poetical Works.* Ed. J. Logie Robertson. Oxford: Oxford University Press, 1908. Reprint. 1970.

TOMLINSON, CHARLES. "A Meditation on John Constable." In *Poems of Science,* ed. John Heath-Stubbs and Phillips Salman, pp. 304–5. Harmondsworth: Penguin Books, 1984.

WASSERMAN, EARL. "The Inherent Values of Eighteenth-Century Personification." *PMLA* 65 (1950): 435–63.

WILLIAMS, BASIL. *The Whig Supremacy, 1714–1760.* 2d ed. rev. by C. H. Stewart. Oxford: Clarendon Press, 1962.

WILLIAMS, RAYMOND. *Culture and Society, 1780–1950.* New York: Columbia University Press, 1958.

———. *Keywords: A Vocabulary of Culture and Society.* New York: Oxford University Press, 1976.

Blake, Priestley, and the "Gnostic Moment"

STUART PETERFREUND

The "Gnostic Moment" as a Critique of Reification

ONE STUBBORN, DEEPLY LATENT OBSTACLE to understanding the relationship of literature and science has been the distinction, maintained until recently, between the methods and objects held to be characteristic of the two discourses. Originating with Bacon, ratified for the modern era by the likes of Horkheimer and Adorno, and promulgated in the present age by the likes of Gadamer and Habermas, the distinction, drawn and valorized as essential and fundamental, is between science (*Naturwissenschaft*) and other discourses in general and the human sciences (*Geisteswissenschaft*) in particular. With specific reference to literature and science, Hans Eichner expounds a position very much like the one set down above, distinguishing between a science immune to social and historical contingency, purely objective in its operations, and driven to the end of discovering the timeless laws of external nature, and other discourses (such as philosophy and literature) that are ineluctably dependent upon social and historical contingency, subjective to the point of partial nescience in their operations as the result

of such contingency, and driven to the end of discovering the enduring
truths of human nature, as those truths are accessible in a given time, in
a given place. In his conclusion, Eichner ventures "a brief statement,
which admittedly is an oversimplification," distinguishing, after Dilthey, "between *Naturwissenschaft* and *Geisteswissenschaft*. The former
studies nature, assumes determinacy, reasons ahistorically, and aims to
establish timeless universal laws. The latter studies human creations,
assumes free will, takes a basically historicist approach, and focuses on
the individual, unique, timebound, and unrepeatable."[1]

To hold a position such as Eichner's is also to believe that one may
propose that the sociology of knowledge applies to the human sciences,
but not to the natural sciences. The position also implies a belief that
the only good history of science is an "internalist" history that views
the development of scientific ideas as being somehow removed from the
social developments, transitions, and revolutions that serve to shape the
rest of the culture and its discourse. The arguments against this position
have been around for more than half a century, although extreme examples of the kind such as Boris Hessen's Marxist analysis of the so-
cioeconomic context of Newton's *Principia* have not helped to advance
the premise that science is a socially conditioned (and socially constructed) discourse, no different in this regard from all other discourses.[2]

One article of faith that has sustained the *Naturwissenschaft-
Geisteswissenschaft* distinction is the belief in the mind's ability to transcend questions of ideology and social contingency, in order to become
what Richard Rorty, with a little help from Shakespeare's *Measure for
Measure* (II.iii.120), terms "the glassy essence" of the object-world.[3]
However, the very project of epistemology underwritten by this belief—more specifically, the concern, central to philosophy from Plato to
Russell and Husserl, "to keep philosophy [and its way of knowing]
'rigorous' and 'scientific'"[4]—has been questioned by Rorty, who argues for the inevitable transition from epistemology to hermeneutics,
the "idealistic" way of knowing adopted originally by the human sciences.[5] As a consequence of disenfranchising epistemology, one cannot
fail to understand that its motivation is a Platonic or Baconian will to
the sort of totalized knowledge that is power. The ideal of such knowl-
edge/power depends for its part on the assumption of a correspondence
theory of knowledge (and language) that emphasizes clarity both as an
end in itself and as the means of attaining dominion over the life-world
and its creatures. Such clarity is only possible if one feature of language
is an essentialist, totalizing metonymy capable of perfect and complete
substitutive "naming" to attain those ends. Cases in point are the super-

human "legislators" who, according to Cratylus, gave things their first and true names[6] and Bacon's unfallen Adam, himself only a little lower than the angels, naming the animals.[7] The person or institution that operates on the assumption that it speaks the language that possesses such metonymic power as its attribute feels empowered in turn to practice a totalizing form of reification to the end of establishing clarity. Moreover, that person or institution privileges clearly defined—one is tempted to say self-evident—structures of authority, be they civil, religious, scientific (or, in an age before "disciplines," some combination of these).

Metonymy is a figural strategy—indeed, a tropological engine—that makes a totalizing form of reification possible. In so doing, however, it supplants metaphor, which is by its nature relational rather than substitutive, leaving both terms and their respective frames of reference intact rather than allowing one term to possess and supplant the other through "naming" its essence. The resultant presence of the metonym testifies to the enactment of a process, described by Fredric Jameson,

> in which "natural" unities, social forms, human relations, cultural events, even religious systems, are systematically broken up to be reconstructed more efficiently, in the form of new post-natural processes or mechanisms; but in which, at the same time, these now isolated broken bits and pieces of the older unities acquire a certain autonomy of their own, a semi-autonomous coherence which . . . serves to compensate for the dehumanization of experience reification brings with it, and to rectify the otherwise intolerable effects of the new process.[8]

As Jameson elsewhere suggests, the process in question betokens class struggle,[9] and the force of the reification is to silence the dialogical discourse of that struggle, in the process reducing what Bakhtin calls "heteroglossia" and Todorov after him calls "heterology" to "a common language" intended to serve the ends of the victorious and dominant ideology.[10]

If the relationship of a figural process such as metonymy and a cultural process such as reification to questions having to do with literature, science, and, as the presence of the concept of gnosticism suggests, religion, is not yet clear, it is now appropriate to attempt a clarification. It is reification, driven by substitutive tropes generally and metonymy in particular, that leads to the creation of literary "truths," scientific "laws," and religious and political "establishments" sanctioned by a dominant ideology.

For example, the authorial subject, seeking a suitable object of contemplation (a "subject," that is), is enjoined to "follow nature," transformed by metonymy into the reified and generally passive, feminized forms—tulips the streaks of which one should refrain from number-ing—that constitute the proper object of literary scrutiny. Matter metonymized as "corpuscles" entirely uniform and without immanent potential or interiority leads to Newtonian laws and the ideological construction of a fully reified universe consisting entirely of matter, mo-tion, and force set into being and motion by a transcendent but since absconded first cause. God, metonymized by the creed "I believe in one God, Father Almighty, Maker of heaven and earth," leads within the Church to a reified structure of patriarchal authority.[11] That patriarchy in its turn sanctions the prerogatives of a monarch who, more often than not, is not only God's vice-gerent but a member of a patrilineal succession in his own right. As a logical consequence, the ecclesiastical patriarchy arrogates to itself exclusive license, by dint of the apostolic succession, to dispense *ex cathedra* truths and sacraments alike, includ-ing the sacramental viaticum of "daily bread" mentioned in a prayer canonized by the Church Fathers and now held by Catholic and Protes-tant scholars alike to be the words not of the originally ascribed author but of someone else—perhaps a disciple. The monarchical patriarchy dispenses civil truths and more nearly temporal forms of sustenance—preferments, patents, places at court, and so on. Although it is anachro-nistic and hopelessly secular and democratic, the common metonym "go fight city hall"[12] does a serviceable job of capturing the sense of frustration, even oppression, that the average person feels in confront-ing any such avatar of absolute power, the acts of which may well sug-gest questionable judgment and authority and perhaps a hint of cor-ruption as well.

The examples adduced above in support of the argument about the relationship between metonymy, reification, and the establishment of structures of authority in the name of a dominant ideology have a dis-tinctly late-seventeenth- or eighteenth-century resonance that is not co-incidental. In the second half of the eighteenth century, the age of Blake, Priestley, and, if the title of the essay is aptly descriptive, some-where in the midst of a "gnostic moment," the use by those subscribing to the dominant ideology of substitutive tropes—personification, syn-ecdoche, and above all metonymy—rather than tropes demonstrating the relational alternative was in an ascendancy perhaps unequaled be-fore or since.

However, the second half of the eighteenth century was hardly the first historical instance of someone's using the metonymic move as a means of appropriating and sustaining authority "in the name of" an untotalizable totality—God[13]—whose substitutive likeness bears a strikingly close resemblance to an empowered segment of society that wishes, naturally enough, to remain in power. Other instances of note are those of early Christian Rome (from the second century A.D. to the council of Nicea [A.D. 325]), sixteenth- and early-seventeenth-century Italy, and early-seventeenth-century England.[14]

The gnostic texts themselves demonstrate how early and how astute gnosis in general, and gnosticism in particular,[15] were in responding to the metonymic move. *Allogenes,* for example, is one of the texts in the Nag Hammadi Library which was buried by the gnostic faithful circa A.D. 400, when the post-Nicene intolerance epitomized by the likes of Athanasius was condemning the gnostics and their texts, respectively, as "heretics and . . . 'apocryphal books to which they attribute antiquity and give the name of saints.'"[16] Commenting on "the Unknown God," "the powers of the Luminaries" speak to the author of *Allogenes,* leaving little doubt that one tropes God by relational rather than substitutive means and must resist the delusion of totalization as a means of self-authorization or empowerment to speak for God or command others in his name.

> Now he ⟨i.e., God⟩ is reified insofar as he exists in that he either exists and becomes, or acts and knows, although he lives without Mind or Life or Existence or Non-Existence, incomprehensibly. And he is reified among his attributes. He is not left over in some way, as if he yields something that is assayed or purified or that he receives and gives. And he is not diminished in some way, [whether] by his own desire or whether he gives or receives through another—it does not affect him. Rather, neither does he give anything by himself lest he become diminished in another way, nor for this reason does he need Mind, or Life, or indeed anything at all. He is indeed better than the Totalities in his privation and unknowability, that is, the non-being Existence, since he is endowed with silence and stillness lest he be diminished by those who are not diminished. (XI, 3: *61,* 24–*62,* 28)[17]

Seen in historical perspective, the "gnostic moment" is symptomatic of a particular set of circumstances, in its turn the occasion for the production of an exemplar of the genre that Amos Funkenstein calls "counter-history."[18] To return, however, to the "gnostic moment" being played out in the second half of the eighteenth century in England and elsewhere, such as Germany:[19] one of the things that is distinctive about that particular "gnostic moment" is both the discursive breadth of the authority claimed by those basing their empowerment on the dominant ideology and the breadth of the response. Prior to the eighteenth century, claims of authority and the gnostic responses to them were played out almost exclusively in the discourses of eccle-siastical and civil authority, the two discourses more often than not being virtually indistinguishable. Literature, if it had a discursive role in the struggle, assumed that role only as the expression of one of the two contending theological or political positions—here Bruno's *De umbris idearum* (1582) and Campanella's *Citta del Sole* (1623) serve as exam-ples. And scientists, although no strangers to hermetic lore, did not make that lore the basis of the discourse of science, however else they might have put it to use, the one weakly conjectural possible exception being Galileo.[20]

As the fates of these three Italian "heretics" suggest, the temporal power of church and state, especially the former, was such that there were, up to a certain point, clear winners and losers in the interpretive struggle of the "gnostic moment." Bruno was burned at the stake, Cam-panella and Galileo recanted their "heresies," and Rome, its Jesuits, and the Inquisition remained in the ascendant. So, too, with the early Christian gnostics, who had to choose either to go underground, in the several senses of that phrase, or to risk persecution for their beliefs. Thus the history of the "gnostic moment" up to the late seventeenth and eighteenth centuries has been, in large measure, obscured, and both the basis and the point of its critique have, for the most part, been lost or obscured. There were winners and losers, that is to say, in a game of winner-take-all.

Another distinction between the "gnostic moment" of the late seven-teenth and eighteenth centuries and its predecessors in the context of western culture, a distinction perhaps owing to the very discursive breadth noted above, is that for the first time there were no clear win-ners and losers. Thus the "gnostic moment" of that time and all pre-vious "gnostic moments" to which that moment referred, as well as the critique that all of these moments, with some variation, mounted, came to the attention of those seeking alternatives to a hegemonic western culture and provided them with an alternative cultural position even as the gnostic viewpoint itself began gradually to become assimilated into a pluralized "mainstream" (if not hegemonic) modern western culture. Whether the "gnostic moment" is responsible for "such movements as progressivism, positivism, Marxism, psychoanalysis, communism, fas-cism, and national socialism," as Eric Voegelin claims,[21] is debatable. That one particular "gnostic moment" had a good deal to do with es-tablishing a dissenting position from which to mount a powerful cri-tique of the dominant ideology of the moment and the power relations underwritten by that ideology seems certain.

Toward Blake and Priestley's "Gnostic Moment"

In assessing the impact of the first "gnostic moment," Elaine Pagels speculates on what Christianity might have become if the gnostic doctrines embodied in the Nag Hammadi codices had not, as it were, gone underground. But their very submersion, as she concludes, underscores the truism that

> it is the winners who write history—their way. No wonder, then, that the viewpoint of the successful majority has dominated all traditional accounts of the origin of Christianity. Ecclesiastical Christians first defined the terms (naming themselves "orthodox" and their opponents "heretics"); then they proceeded to demonstrate—at least to their own satisfaction—that this triumph was historically inevitable, or, in religious terms, "guided by the Holy Spirit."

Nevertheless, as Pagels observes, "the concerns of gnostic Christians survived," if "only as a suppressed current."[22] In the late sixteenth and seventeenth centuries and, more importantly for the present discussion, in the late seventeenth and eighteenth centuries, the current surfaced, giving rise to the "gnostic moment" that is here the subject of discussion. It was a moment in which the history and ideology of the winners were problematized in the attempt to recover and reconsider those of the losers. The antiheretical position that originated with such Christian ideologues and propagandists (*propaganda fidei,* "propagation of the faith") as Irenaeus (*Adversus haereses* [ca. 180–92]), Tertullian (*De praescriptione haereticorum* [ca. 200]), Origen (*Contra Celsum* [before 254]), and Epiphanius of Salamis (*Panarion* [374–77]) and was ratified by the Church at the Council of Nicea (325) was no longer conceded the last word in the debate. The time had come to reassess the heretical position that originated with gnostics such as Marcion, Valentinus, and Menander and was energized by dissent. This is the nature of the reassessment undertaken by Protestant revisionists such as the Pietist Gottfried Arnold.

Arnold's *Unparteiischen Kirchen- und Ketzerhistorie* (*Impartial History of Churches and Heresies* [1699; 1729]), the product of "the disdain of history and the sharpening of critical faculties" symptomatic of a distinctively Protestant "critical-polemical" approach to history,[23] did not take the winners at their word, arguing forcefully instead "for a new view of church history which could seek the true Christianity among the outlaws and the heretics."[24] To use Funkenstein's term, Arnold's text is, generically speaking, a "counter-history": "It consists of the systematic exploitation of the adversary's most trusted sources against their own intent: in the fortunate phrase of Walter Benjamin, counter-histories 'comb the sources against the grain,' as Marxist historiography indeed does to reconstruct the history of the victim rather than that of the victors."

Not that Arnold originated the genre: Funkenstein allows that counter-histories had been written "since antiquity."[25] Far more important than the characteristics of the genre itself is its revival at a particular moment in the history of Protestant dissent. Other works in the genre followed closely upon Arnold's—for example, the Reformed theologian Isaac de Beausobre's *Critique de Manichée et Manichéisme* (1734; 1739) and the Lutheran theologian Johann Lorenz von Mosheim's *Ecclesiastical History* (1739; 1758; trans. 1764). Although "modern research into Gnosis" did not begin until the 1820s, Arnold's counter-history and the studies of Beausobre and Mosheim after it served notice, in Kurt Rudolph's words, that "the ground was prepared for an independent consideration of the gnostics, and in the first place in particular with the sources relating to them."[26]

If anything, the ground in England was both more fertile and earlier prepared than it was in Germany or France, owing to the vitality of radical English Protestantism and the use to which English commentators put hermetic thought in defense of that position.[27] Keith Thomas may be correct in characterizing English hermeticism as "largely a derivative affair, stimulated by continental writings, but adding little of its own," but it soon took on a distinctly English character. Notwithstanding scholarly challenges—for example, "Isaac Casaubon's scholarship [which] deprived the Hermetic books of their claim to be pre-Christian as early as 1614" (in a "polemic against the Counter Reformation historian Baronius," it should be noted)—"[Robert] Fludd wrote prolifically during the following decades . . . and John Everard's English translation of the hermetic *Pymander* (1649) disseminated the tradition more widely. The preface unrepentantly asserted that the work had been written 'some hundreds of years before Moses.'"[28]

Both Fludd and Everard are important to any consideration of the "gnostic moment" in England. As Betty Jo Teeter Dobbs notes, Fludd took Comenian pansophy, which is based on the assumption that immanentist chemical essences are responsible for the full range of intelligible phenomena,[29] and applied it to the account of the creation in Genesis, fully mindful of the significance of such an application.

> If the act of creation was to be understood chemically, then all of nature was to be understood similarly. In short, chemistry was the key to all nature, the key to all the macrocosmic-microcosmic relationships sought by Robert Fludd and others. A study of chemistry was a study of God as He had

Himself written out His word in the Book of Nature. Such a study could only lead one closer to God and was conceived as having moral value as well as contributing to the better grasp of the workings of nature.[30]

Everard was one of the principal importers of gnostic thought into the England of Blake and Priestley, although other possible sources include the Codex Brucianus and the Codex Askewianus, as well as Priestley's own *Disquisitions Relating to Matter and Spirit* (1777). Priestley discusses and quotes at length from Beausobre and Mosheim, especially the latter, who was also available in a 1764 English translation.[31]

But these other possibilities should not cause one to lose sight of the importance of Everard, especially when considered in the context of political and religious radicalism. What Michael Ferber "find[s] interesting" about Everard, in addition to his plausibility as "one source of gnostic ideas in Blake," is both his politics—Everard "was a radical Protestant troublemaker, frequently in jail for heresy (King James said his name should be 'Never-out')"—and, as the religious dimension of those politics suggests, his theology. Everard "preached to the lowest classes that God was immanent in nature, though preeminently in man, and that heaven and hell were in our hearts. The social implications of his teachings, not very different from Gerrard Winstanley's, were clear to the bishops, who continually persecuted him. . . . In 1650, and perhaps again in 1790, the thrust of gnostic speculation seems to have been subversive, radical, and democratic."[32]

A brief glance at Everard's *Divine Pymander* suggests how readily the immanentist metaphysics of the *Corpus Hermeticum* lends itself to a radical program of social reform, even leveling, as well as to an immanentist science of divinely engendered powers and essences. As Ferber's comments on heaven and hell suggest, one of established religion's chief claims to authority is its propounding and interpretation of a doctrine of the afterlife that stipulates rewards for "good" behavior (following the commandments of church and state) and sanctions for "bad" behavior (breaking the commandments of church and state). Any doctrine of the afterlife depends in its turn on the assumption that death is real and irrevocable—at least until the Apocalypse. If death is not real and irrevocable, then there is nothing to be gained by being "good" and nothing to be lost by being "bad," at least not in the senses of "good" and "bad" set forth above. One simply is and acts on the inner "motion" that is his or her vital energy. Such, at least, is one of the implications that might be drawn from the following exchange between Hermes Trismegistus and his son Tat (i.e., Thoth, Theuth):

TAT.   Therefore, O Father, do not the living things in the World die,
         though they be parts thereof.
HERM.   Be wary in thy Speech, O Son, and do not be deceived by the
         names of things.
         For they do not die, O son, but as compound Bodies they are
         dissolved.
            But dissolution is not death; and they are dissolved, not that they
         may be destroyed, but that they may be made new.
TAT.   What then is the operation of life? Is it not Motion?
HERM.   And what is there in the World unmoveable? Nothing at all, O
         Son.[33]

The vital energy in question is a pervasive form of immanence, and as
such it exercises a leveling influence. Acting on the authority of Genesis
2:7 and other texts, the Church sets itself up as the institution best able
to deal with the concerns of the soul, that immortal and immaterial
entity and emblem of divine afflatus characteristic of human beings
alone of all the living creatures in the world. But what if vital energy is
everywhere and ensoulment is universal rather than particularly characteristic of humanity alone? As Hermes tells Tat, "the parts of the World
are Heaven, and Earth, and Water, and Air, after the same manner the
members of God are Life, and Immortality, and Eternity, and Spirit,
and Necessity, and Providence, and Nature, and Soul, and Mind, and
the Continuance or perseverance of all these which is called Good."
These "members" are at work everywhere within the world of matter in
which one lives. "If it [i.e., matter] be actuated, by whom is it actuated?
for we have said, that Acts and Operations, are the parts of God."[34]

Both Fludd and Everard acted on the gnostic imperative to frame a
counter-history, up to and including a counter-cosmology, and both
endorsed the notion of immanent causation essential to that counter-
cosmology and its revision of orthodox notions of good and evil, although whether they are on the basis of these positions properly regarded as gnostics is neither entirely clear nor necessarily relevant.[35]

Blake and Priestley's "Gnostic Moment"

Blake, for his part, publicly embraced gnosticism—at least on the report of Henry Crabb Robinson. His *Reminiscences* (1852) includes a
report of a discussion with Blake in which the latter reiterates "the
doctrine of the Gnostics" that the creation of the material world is a fall
into error "with sufficient consistency to silence one so unlearned as
myself."[36] Blake's understanding of creation-as-fall comports well with
the gnostic understanding of that phenomenon and will be discussed at
some length below.

Priestley, for his part, repudiated a number of gnostic doctrines—for example, "the doctrine of *pre-existence*, or that of all human souls having been lapsed angels, which was the source of *Gnosticism*, and most of the early corruptions of Christianity," and the doctrines that "the Supreme Mind [is] the author of all good, and *matter* [is] the source of all evil, that all inferior intelligences are *emanations* from *the Supreme Mind*."[37] But this repudiation is partial. Although Priestley rejects the preexistence of souls and particular immanence, it does not follow that he accepts Newtonian materialism as the alternative. He questions its understanding of matter, noting especially "the difficulty which attends the supposition of *the creation of it out of nothing*, and also the continual moving of it by a being which has hitherto been supposed to have no common property with it" (*DMS*, 18). Something more closely akin to such matter than the God of Genesis 1 must preexist it and relate to it as pervasive immanent cause to general effect. Discussing solidity, one of the five irreducible properties of Newtonian matter, Priestley takes a position reminiscent of Comenius and Fludd after him, endorsing the preexistence of powers if not of souls and arguing that this property "is possessed only in consequence of being endued with certain *powers*, and together with this *cause*, solidity, being no more than an *effect*, must cease, if there be any foundation to the plainest and best established rules of reasoning in philosophy" (*DMS*, 7).

Whatever their particular doctrinal accommodations with "orthodox" gnosticism may have been, Blake and Priestley were critical of and resistant to the metonymic move. Blake, although troubled by the idea of nature—particularly Wordsworthian nature—nevertheless took as his article of faith that the world of natural objects is permeated by an immanent principle that originates with God and is attributable only to him. Blake's view of nature, whether metonymized as feminized and passive by Johnson or by Wordsworth, threatens by its very substitutive presence to preempt and extinguish the imagination's ability to forge the individual's relationship to the life-world around him or her by dint of strong metaphor. In the introduction to *Europe* (1794), for example, "a Fairy mocking as he sat on a streak'd Tulip" describes the plight of a reified humanity in a reified world.

Five windows light the cavern'd Man; thro' one he breathes the air;
Thro' one, hears music of the spheres; thro' one, the eternal vine
Flourishes, that he may receive the grapes; thro' one, look.
And see small portions of the eternal world that groweth;
Thro' one, himself pass out what time he please, but he will not;
For stolen joys are sweet, & bread eaten in secret, pleasant.[38]

And in his "Annotations to Wordsworth's *Poems*" (1815), Blake writes,

"Natural Objects always did & now do Weaken deaden & obliterate Imagination in me[.] Wordsworth must know that what he Writes Valuable is not to be found in Nature" (*Poetry,* p. 665).

The problem with a metonymized nature for Blake is that it locks humanity ineluctably into a solipsistic materialism without the hope or possibility of transcendence. In his first engraved text, *There Is No Natural Relligion [a]* (1788), Blake makes the point that if "Man" were "only a natural organ subject to Sense," and if "from a perception of only 3 senses or 3 elements none could deduce a fourth or fifth," humanity would be limited to nothing "other than natural or organic thoughts." However, Blake posits the existence of an immanence that helps to break the circle. "If it were not for the Poetic or Prophetic character the Philosophic & Experimental would soon be at the ratio of all things, & stand still unable to do other than repeat the same dull round over again" (*Poetry,* p. 1).

Priestley's lifelong search for underlying, immanent principles, both electrical and chemical, in nature made him leery of the metonymic move and its tendency toward easy reification. In his first scientific text, Priestley suggests by way of preface that Newtonian corpuscles, rather than being the irreducible units of a universe of matter, force, and motion, are themselves the result of a prior, immanent constitutive cause.

> Hitherto philosophy has been chiefly conversant about the more sensible properties of bodies; electricity, together with chymistry, and the doctrine of light and colours, seems to be giving us an inlet into their internal structure, on which their sensible properties depend. By pursuing this new light therefore, the bounds of natural science may possibly be extended, beyond what we can now form an idea of. New worlds may open to our view, and the glory of the great Sir Isaac Newton himself, and all of his contemporaries be eclipsed [*sic*], by a new set of philosophers, in a quite new field of speculation.[39]

The search for immanentist models also helps to explain Priestley's advocacy of the phlogiston theory in opposition to Lavoisier and his admiration for Boscovich, who, according to Priestley's letter of 7 March 1773 to Reverend Joseph Bretland, "seems to suppose that matter consists of *powers* only, without any substance." According to Robert E. Schofield, the "concepts of Boscovich (so influential with Davy, Faraday, Kelvin, and Maxwell in the nineteenth century)" were "introduced to the serious attention of British scientists" by Priestley.[40] As was seen above, Priestley argues in *Disquisitions* not that powers exist without substance, but that powers are a necessary principle prior to substance, a position pointedly at odds with Newton's corpuscular view.

Blake's belief in God as an immanent principle dates from no later than *There Is No Natural Religion [b]*: "He who sees the Infinite in all things sees God" (*Poetry*, pl. 3).[41] That Blake intends a principle rather than a personification is clear from Isaiah's observation in the second "Memorable Fancy" of *The Marriage of Heaven and Hell* (1790–93): "I saw no God. nor heard any, in a finite organical perception; but my senses discovered the infinite in every thing, and as I was then perswaded. & remain confirm'd; that the voice of honest indignation is the voice of God, I cared not for consequences but wrote" (*Poetry*, pl. 12).

Priestley's belief in God as an immanent principle, apparent no later than 1767, received perhaps its fullest articulation a decade later in *Disquisitions*. Discussing the mechanical philosophy's telling inability to account satisfactorily for consciousness and the relationship of mind to body,[42] Priestley begins by considering perhaps the strongest evidence for the existence of an immanent principle such as *pneuma*: the soul. He argues contra Newton that, "if we suffer ourselves to be guided in our inquiries by the universally acknowledged *rules of philosophizing*, we shall find ourselves intirely unauthorized to admit anything in man besides that *body* which is the object of our senses." (*DMS*, xiv–xv). To acknowledge such a limitation would be, for Priestley, to beg the question of how one comes to perceive the body itself, let alone to possess the intelligence necessary to posit the existence of a unitive soul that is the ground of the senses. Thus Priestley asserts "that the soul of man cannot be material and divisible, because the *principle of consciousness*, which comprehends the whole of the thinking power, is necessarily simple and indivisible" (*DMS*, 86). As with the principle, so with its origin: "IT will be said, that if the principle of thought in *man* may be a property of material substance, the *divine Being* himself may be material also; whereas, it is now almost universally believed to be the Doctrine of Revelation, that the Deity is, in the strictest sense of the word, an *immaterial substance*, incapable of local preference" (*DMS*, 103).

Both Blake and Priestley were aware of the importance of reconsidering the canonical biblical account of the creation in articulating their respective cosmologies. Given the importance of that account for natural as well as ecclesiastical history, the very act of reconsideration cast the two as counter-historians, although in Blake's case the counter-historical texts of record were poetic histories, not chronicles. For example, in *The Marriage*, Blake calls into question the "history [that] has been adopted by both parties" (*Poetry*, pl. 5), the satanic as well as the messianic, regarding reasons for and significance of the fall. And he questions the delusions arising from the strategies of argument from design and reification employed by orthodoxy, the "system [of] which some took advantage of & enslav'd the vulgar by attempting to realize or abstract the mental deities from their objects: thus began Priesthood." Such an orthodoxy, in using the material world to validate its claims to authority and correctness, denies the primacy of such immanent principles as the gnostic *pneuma*. "Thus men forgot that all deities reside in the human breast" (*Poetry*, pl. 11).

The story that Blake tells, like that of Everard's *Pymander*, is supposed to antedate the Mosaic account by a considerable span of time. In fact, Blake's account makes the origin of priesthood connate with the creation of the material world by Urizen, Blake's rendering of the gnostic demiurge.[43] Blake's tale "Of the primeval Priests assum'd power" (*Poetry*, pl. 2:1) in *The Book of Urizen* (1794) begins with Urizen's denial of the primacy of *pneuma* as the manifestation testifying to the existence of the gnostic Protennoia.[44] Prior to Urizen's advent,

> 1. *Earth was not: nor globes of attraction*
> *The will of the Immortal expanded*
> *Or contracted his all flexible senses.*
> *Death was not, but eternal life sprung.*
>   (*Poetry*, pl. 3:46–49)

But when Urizen comes on the scene, he brings with him judgment, death, and above all, matter.

> 2. *The sound of a trumpet the heavens*
> *Awoke & vast clouds of blood roll'd*
> *Round the dim rocks of Urizen, so nam'd*
> *That solitary one in Immensity.*
>   (*Poetry*, pl. 3:50–53)

This is a very different cosmology, or history of the creation, than the "official" reificatory version found in Genesis 1.

Priestley's counter-history is an attempt to defend the Unitarian view of Christ, which he ascribes to "the ancient Jewish church," against the orthodox view on the one hand and the gnostic view on the other. However, Priestley's disagreements with the gnostic view are actually not so profound as they might at first appear to be. The argument of *An History of the Corruptions of Christianity* (1782) is "that Christ was simply a *man,* and not either *God Almighty,* or a *super angelic being.*"[45] This denial of the orthodox trinitarian doctrine of *homoousia* (consubstantiality) and the gnostic doctrine of Christ's superangelic origins and nature is not a denial of the proposition that God works immanently and miraculously in the world and in at least some of its creatures, however.

Priestley does debunk the belief of "the Carpocratians, Valentinians, and others who were generally termed Gnostics . . . that Christ had a pre-existence and was a man only in appearance" (*History,* 1:8). His notion of what a man is and may do when God works in him, however, suggests that the quarrel is less about the efficacy of divine immanence than about whether it is pervasive or particular. Priestley's Unitarian Christ may have been "simply a *man,*" but he is the man "whose history answers to the description given of the Messiah by the prophets," the man who "made no other pretensions; referring all his extraordinary power to God, his father, who, he expressly says, spake and acted by him, and who raised him from the dead; and it is most evident that the apostles, and all those who conversed with our Lord, before and after his resurrection, considered him in no other light than simply as *a man approved by God, by signs and wonders which God did by him*. Acts ii. 22" (*History,* 1:2).

Priestley's Christ is finally the best of men, but his relationship with God, if it does differ from the relationships of others "approved by God," differs in degree rather than in kind, and the divine immanence that "spake and acted by him" may speak and act by others similarly approved, if not in fact by all. The Church's unwillingness to accept this view, with its disastrously subversive implications for any structure of hierarchy and the consequent need for proprietary control of governance, doctrine, and liturgy,[46] is grounded on a willful misunderstanding of and tendency to reify the doctrine of the *Logos*—a move that Priestley identifies as "the personification of the *Logos*" (*History,* 1:30)—by platonizing Jews such as Philo Judaeus and Christians such as Justin Martyr. The former "calls this divine word *a second God*" (ibid.); the latter inaugurates the doctrine of applying the divinity explicitly to Christ (*History,* 1:32–35).

The main chance seized by Justin and his successors, according to Priestley, is the beginning of the Gospel According to John ("In the beginning was the word [*Logos*], and the Word was with God, and the word was God" [1:1]).

> The christian philosophers having once got the idea that the *Logos* might be interpreted as Christ, proceeded to explain what John says of the *Logos* in the introduction of his gospel, to mean the same person, in direct opposition to what he really meant, which was that the *Logos* by which all things were made was not a being distinct from God, but God himself, being his attribute, his wisdom and power, dwelling in Christ, speaking and acting by him. (*History,* 1:31)

Logos, in other words, is an indwelling or immanent power that originates with God and pervades the world rather than being localized in one person or the church founded upon his life, words, and acts.

Priestley refers to the precedent of the Septuagint in his argument for dissevering the concept of *Logos* from the person of Christ: "there is one particular passage in the book of Psalms in which they imagined that the origin of the *Logos,* by way of emanation from the divine mind, is most clearly expressed, which is what we render, *My heart is inditing good matter. Psalm* xlv. 1, this *matter* being *Logos* in the Seventy [Septuagint], and the verb *ereugomenou*[,] *throwing out*" (*History,* 1:30).

Despite their insistence on the superangelic nature of Christ, the gnostics, like Priestley's early Unitarians, likewise believed in at least a partially pervasive rather than a particular immanence. Those "initi-ates" able to see the creation of the material world for the fall it was were "'released' from the demiurge's power" and from the claims of established ecclesiastical authority by dint of the workings of this per-vasive immanence. "Every initiate was assumed to have received, through the initiation ritual, the charismatic gift of direct inspiration [*pneuma*] through the Holy Spirit."[47]

Conclusion: The "Gnostic Moment" as Cultural Symptom

Limitations of scope and space prevent much further elaboration at present. Yet this discussion of the "gnostic moment"—"gnostic mo-ments," actually, since Rome before the Council of Nicea, with its Val-entinians and Marcionites, and the England of circa 1650, with its her-metics, Anabaptists, Ranters, Muggletonians, and other radical "inner light" sects, are as deserving of the designation as the England of circa 1790, with its dissenting sects—does bring one back to the question of whether there are any predisposing conditions for or defining charac-teristics of each.

The short answer is that there are such conditions and characteristics and that they are evident from the first "gnostic moment" onward. From the beginning of the dispute, in the days of the gnostic "heretic" Marcion and his "orthodox" antagonist Irenaeus (ca. 180–92), orthodoxy has deployed a strategy of metonymic repetition leading to reification, to the end of creating an object-world that may be used to demonstrate the presumed originary truth of those reifications, to the exclusion of pluralism, and in celebration of the absolute priority of the status quo of the material universe as that status quo is constructed by the ideology of the empowered as the ground of all meaning and the evidence for any valorization of dogma.

Pagels begins her discussion of "the politics of monotheism" by not-ing the importance of the beginning of the Christian Creed: "I believe in one God, Father Almighty, Maker of heaven and earth."[48] Learned by rote repetition, often by those too young or otherwise unable to read and reflect, such a creed demonstrates what Shelley, in a discussion of much the same problem, aptly terms "the abuse of a metaphorical expression to a literal purpose"—an abuse, it might be added, that has the precise effect of reducing the "vitally metaphorical" language of the imagination to a condition in which "words . . . become . . . signs for portions or classes of thoughts instead of pictures of integral thoughts"[49] (metonymy, in other words). The vehicles "Father Almighty" and "Maker of heaven and earth" tend to overwhelm the tenor "one God," with the result that God comes to be understood in terms of earthly authority figures (fathers) and the object-world of a "made" heaven and earth *and justified with reference to those authority figures and that object-world.*

Thus a principled objection by "the heretic Marcion," who "was struck by what he saw as the contrast between the creator-God of the Old Testament who demands justice and punishes every violation of the law, and the Father whom Jesus proclaims—the New Testament God of forgiveness and love"[50]—is rejected for its dualistic (and ultimately pluralistic) implications. The process is the perfect illustration of how Bakhtin's "heteroglossia" or Todorov's "heterology" is reduced to ideology when what "arises spontaneously from social diversity" is subjected to "the aspiration, correlative to all power, to institute a common language (or rather a speech)."[51]

The reification in question results from viewing God as—actually, reducing him to—a father and an artisanal maker and from viewing the material world as both the ground and the divinely designed result of God's fatherly and artisanal acts, the culmination of which is the creation of humanity in his own image. If God is the maker of heaven and earth, then the perceived properties *heaven* and *earth* must somehow reveal the mark of divine agency. Thus long before the rise of natural theology in the seventeenth century, some version of the argument from design was being used to justify a particular view of God and the authority structures of an orthodoxy committed to indoctrinating the laity in that particular view. The particular view intended is suggested by the credal phrase "Maker of heaven and earth," which strongly echoes the first verse of Genesis 1 ("In the beginning God created the heaven and the earth"). Implicit in both the credal phrase and its biblical source is the decision to privilege the account of material origins over that of immaterial origins (*pneuma*) that is narrated in Genesis 2,[52] to privilege an externalist metaphysics over the immanentist alternative, and to extend the tyranny of the bodily eye to social control

based on the manipulation by the empowered of an ideologically constructed visible world encompassing all that one "sees," from the icons
and images of orthodoxy to "nature" itself. Being created in God's image becomes the pretext for speaking for him and ruling in his stead.

The gnostic response of the second century adumbrates what was to
follow in the 1650s and 1790s. As Pagels suggests, the gnostics believed neither in the substance of the Christian Creed nor in the metaphysics underwriting it:

> while the Valentinians publicly confessed faith in one God, in their own
> private meetings they insisted on discriminating between the popular image
> of God—as master, king, lord, creator, and judge—and what that image
> represented—God understood as the ultimate source of all being. Valen-
> tinus calls that source "the depth"; his followers describe it as an invisible,
> incomprehensible primal principle. But most Christians, they say, mistake
> mere images of God for that reality.[53]

To believe in such a principle, whether it is manifested as poetic inspiration up to and including prophetic power, electrical powers of attrac-
tion and repulsion, phlogiston, or what have you, is to disavow the
reification of authority—"God . . . as master, king, lord, creator, and
judge"—and those who rule in the name of such reification. To believe
in such a principle is the first step toward the "gnostic moment."

Notes

1. Hans Eichner, "The Rise of Modern Science and the Genesis of Romanticism," *PMLA* 97, 1 (1982): 8–30, esp. 25.

2. See Boris Hessen, *The Economic Roots of Newton's* Principia (1931; rpt.
New York: Howard Fertig, 1971). For more balanced social analysis of approx-
imately the same vintage, see Robert Merton, *Science, Technology, and Society in
Seventeenth-Century England* (New York: Columbia Univ. Press, 1938); J. D.
Bernal, *The Social Foundations of Science* (New York: Macmillan, 1939); or
Edgar Zilsel, "The Sociological Roots of Science," *American Journal of So-
ciology* 47 (1942): 544–62. A good and more recent collection dealing with the
social construction of scientific discourse is *The Social Production of Scientific
Knowledge,* ed. Everett Mendelsohn, Peter Weingart, and Richard Whitley
(Dordrecht: Reidel, 1977).

3. Richard Rorty, *Philosophy and the Mirror of Nature* (Princeton: Princeton
Univ. Press, 1979), 42, 346. Citing Book II of Bacon's *Advancement of Learning*
as well as Shakespeare, Rorty observes, "Our Glassy Essence—the 'intellectual
soul' of the scholastics—is also Bacon's 'mind of man' which 'far from the
nature of a clear and equal glass, wherein the beams of things should reflect
according to their true incidence . . . is rather like an enchanted glass, full of
superstition and imposture if it be not delivered and reduced.'" Rorty prob-
lematizes "the distinction between the *Geistes-* and *Naturwissenschaften,*" stat-

ing in the process that "this . . . distinction is supposedly coextensive with the distinction between hermeneutical and other methods."

4. Ibid., 4.

5. Ibid., 315, 346. Rorty does not see hermeneutics as a successor to epistemology. On the contrary: he characterizes hermeneutics as "an expression of hope that the cultural space left by the demise of epistemology will not be filled." But "the demise of epistemology" does not automatically entail the onset of a warm and fuzzy aquarian age. Rorty undertakes to debunk "the claim that hermeneutics is particularly suited to the 'spirit' or to 'the sciences of man,' whereas some other method (that of 'objectivizing' and 'positive' sciences) is appropriate to 'nature.' "

6. See *Cratylus* 438c, in *Plato, with an English Translation*, rev. ed., trans. H. N. Fowler, vol. 6 (1939; rpt. Cambridge, Mass.: Harvard Univ. Press, 1953), 182, 183. Speaking to Socrates, Cratylus states his opinion that "the truest theory of the matter . . . is that the power which gave the first names to things is more than human, and therefore the names must necessarily be correct."

7. See *Valerius Terminus*, in *The Works of Francis Bacon*, ed. James Spedding, Robert Leslie Ellis, and Douglas Denon Heath, 2d ed., 7 vols. (London: Longmans, 1870), 3:222: "the true end . . . of knowledge is a restitution and reinvesting (in great part) of man to the sovereignty and power (for whensoever he shall be able to call the creatures by their true names he shall again command them) which he had in his first state of creation."

8. Fredric Jameson, *The Political Unconscious: Narrative as a Socially Symbolic Act* (1981; rpt. Ithaca: Cornell Univ. Press, 1986), 63.

9. Ibid., 84.

10. See Tzvetan Todorov, *Mikhail Bakhtin: The Dialogical Principle*, trans. Wlad Gozich, Theory and History of Literature, vol. 13 (Minneapolis: Univ. of Minnesota Press, 1984), 57.

11. For a discussion of the politics of this creed, see Elaine Pagels, *The Gnostic Gospels* (New York: Random House, 1979), 28.

12. So common, in fact, that it is the example for metonymy given in Sylvan Barnet, Morton Berman, and William Burto, *Introduction to Literature: Fiction, Poetry, Drama*, 7th ed. (Boston: Little, Brown, 1981), 428.

13. Consider Newton's characterization of the "Lord God Pantokrator" in the "General Scholium" of the *Principia:* "In him are all things contained and mooved. . . ." See Isaac Newton, *Mathematical Principles of Natural Philosophy*, trans. Andrew Motte, rev. Florian Cajori (1934; rpt. Berkeley and Los Angeles: Univ. of California Press, 1966), 545.

14. Early Christian Rome is discussed in Pagels, *Gnostic Gospels*. Sixteenth- and early-seventeenth-century Italy is discussed in Frances Yates, *Giordano Bruno and the Hermetic Tradition* (1964; rpt. New York: Vintage, 1969). Early-seventeenth-century England is discussed in Christopher Hill, *The Intellectual Origins of the Puritan Revolution* (Oxford: Oxford Univ. Press, 1965), and *The World Turned Upside Down* (New York: Viking, 1972). According to Eric Voegelin, in *Science, Politics, and Gnosticism* (Chicago: Henry Regnery, 1968),

83, the late nineteenth and early twentieth centuries have also been a "gnostic moment" of sorts, during which the practice of self-validating interpretation originated by Spinoza has given rise to a plethora of oppressive and reductive -isms, including Marxism, Freudianism, and Nazism!

15. Kurt Rudolph, *Gnosis: The Nature and History of Gnosticism,* trans. Robert McLachlan Wilson (San Francisco: Harper & Row, 1983), 56–57. I take my understanding of these terms from Rudolph, and he takes his in turn from the Congress on the Origins of Gnosticism, held in Messina in 1966. "According to this view we should understand by 'Gnosis' a 'knowledge of divine secrets which is reserved for an elite' (and thus has an esoteric character), but 'Gnosticism' should be used in the above-mentioned sense for the gnostic systems of the second and third centuries." Obviously, my use of the term "gnostic moment" is an attempt to remain true to the letter of these definitions while quarreling with the spirit of the latter one. The quarrel is in some measure sanctioned by another of the pronouncements of the Congress of Messina, concerning gnosticism's centering myth:

> the idea of the presence in man of a divine "spark" . . . , which has proceeded from the divine world and has fallen into this world of destiny, birth and death and which must be reawakened through its own divine counterpart in order to be finally restored. This idea . . . is ontologically based on the conception of a downward development of the divine whose periphery (often called *Sophia* or *Ennoia*) has fatally fallen victim to a crisis and must—even if only indirectly—produce this world, in which it cannot be disinterested, in that it must once again recover the divine spark (often designated as *pneuma,* "spirit").

It seems clear that this same myth pervades and informs, with some variation, the "gnostic moments" discussed in this essay.

16. James M. Robinson, "Introduction," *The Nag Hammadi Library in English,* trans. members of the Coptic Gnostic Library Research Project of the Institute for Antiquity and Christianity, ed. Marvin W. Meyer (San Francisco: Harper & Row, 1977), 2, 19.

17. Ibid., 450. All further citings of the Nag Hammadi codices themselves will be parenthetical, by codex number, binding order, chapter, and verse.

18. See Amos Funkenstein, *Theology and the Scientific Imagination from the Middle Ages to the Seventeenth Century* (Princeton: Princeton Univ. Press, 1986), 273.

19. See Alan P. Cottrell, *Goethe's View of Evil and the Search for a New Image of Man in Our Time* (Edinburgh: Floris, 1982), 26. Cottrell documents convincingly the argument that Goethe's response to the problem of evil has a good deal to do with his early reading in esoterica, including "Gnostic, Hermetic, cabalistic, Neoplatonic and other esoterical literature of the pansophical stream."

20. Yates, *Giordano Bruno,* 358–59, speculates that the dialogical form of Galileo's *Dialogo* (1632) owes something to the similarly dialogical form of Bruno's *Cena de la ceneri* (1584), but the case rests on the fact that both Bruno and Galileo were in Padua at nearly the same time in 1592 and that Galileo used the library of Vincenzo Pinelli, an associate of Bruno's and a collector of her-

metica. However, Galileo was no gnostic. If anything, his advocacy of a corpuscular model of matter, which implicitly denied the principle of consubstantiality and thereby caused his problems with the Jesuits and the Inquisition, was opposed to the immanentist concept of *pneuma* central to gnosticism. See Pietro Redondi, *Galileo Heretic,* trans. Raymond Rosenthal (Princeton: Princeton Univ. Press, 1987).

Newton's fascination with hermetic lore, chiefly in the context of his fascination with alchemy, is well documented in Betty Jo Teeter Dobbs, *The Foundations of Newton's Alchemy, or "The Huntyng of the Greene Lyon"* (1975; rpt. New York: Cambridge Univ. Press, 1984). Once again, however, Newton's heresies, such as they are, are inimical to gnosticism. Richard S. Westfall, *Never at Rest: A Biography of Isaac Newton* (New York: Cambridge Univ. Press, 1980), 292, 524–25, corroborates Dobbs's identification of the significance of hermetica for Newton's alchemical studies in the mid-1670s. But Westfall (pp. 313–14) notes that, during virtually the same period, Newton was hard at work refuting the doctrine of *homoousia* (consubstantiality) because of its implications both for his corpuscular model of light and for his attempt to reconcile his optics with the cosmogony depicted in the *P* account in Genesis (1: 1–2:4a). That account implicitly denies the concept of *pneuma*, which is central to the *J* account (2:4b–2:25).

21. See note 14 above.

22. Pagels, *The Gnostic Gospels,* 142, 150.

23. Funkenstein, *Scientific Imagination,* 273.

24. Rudolph, *Gnosis,* 30.

25. Funkenstein, *Scientific Imagination,* 273. Cottrell, *Goethe's View of Evil,* 26, notes the influence of counter-history in general and of Arnold's account in particular on the young Goethe's understanding of the problem of evil.

> Through the ministrations of an intimate of Goethe's mother, the Pietist Fräulein Susanne Katharina von Kletterberg (1723–1774), the young man was introduced to an array of mystical, alchemical, theosophical books from the Gnostic, Hermetic, cabalistic, Neoplatonic and other esoterical literature of the pansophical stream. In his father's library he found the second edition (1729) of the *Kirchen- und Ketzergeschichte* (History of the Church and of Heretics) by Gottfried Arnold (1666–1714), whose discussion of church history from the time of the Apostles to Pietism convinced Goethe that those figures condemned as heretical might be viewed in a more positive light.

26. Rudolph, *Gnosis,* 30.

27. Pagels, *Gnostic Gospels,* 150, observes that "radical visionaries like George Fox, themselves unfamiliar, in all probability, with gnostic tradition, nevertheless articulated analogous interpretations of religious experience." Although Pagels's speculation that such visionaries were not familiar with gnostic tradition is questionable, she is correct in understanding the ready compatibility of gnosticism with a radical political and religious position. In this last regard, see Stephen Shapin, "History of Science and Its Sociological Reconstructions," *History of Science* 20 (1982): 157–211, esp. 82. Speaking of the Digger Gerrard Winstanley, whose "inner light" metaphysics and politics were very close

to those of the overtly gnostic John Everard, Shapin correctly notes the importance of immanentism for that metaphysics and politics.

> His argument was founded upon a vision of God's relationship to the universe in which divinity was immanent in material nature just as it was immanent within each believer. Divine power was thus accessible to all; revelation was democratized and the hierarchical order which made nature dependent upon an external spiritual Deity, the believer dependent upon an external spiritual intermediary, and civil society dependent upon supervision by a divine-right monarch was collapsed and rejected.

28. Keith Thomas, *Religion and the Decline of Magic* (New York: Scribners, 1971), 225. The imprint date on the supposedly reprinted first edition of Everard that I cite in note 33 below is 1650, not 1649 as Thomas has it. Yates, *Giordano Bruno*, 398–99, concurs with Thomas's assessment of the effect Casaubon's dating had on the decline of Renaissance magic. Rudolph, *Gnosis*, 26, notes that the tractate "which bears the name 'Poimandres' ('shepherd of men') . . . which for the first time gave its name to the whole work [i.e., the *Corpus Hermeticum*]" was first translated into Latin by Ficino in 1463, then published under the patronage and protection of Cosimo de Medici in 1471, after which date "it exercised a great influence on Renaissance philosophy in Italy. Several editions appeared in the course of the sixteenth and seventeenth centuries, of which that of 1554 offered the Greek text for the first time." Patrizi's *New Philosophy* (1591) "even attempted to supplant the Catholic school philosophy of Aristotle, since he saw in the teachings of Hermes something that was in conformity with Christian thought." Rudolph does not even begin to take into account the writings of Pico della Mirandola, Cornelius Agrippa, Giordano Bruno, and Tommaso Campanella, all of whom are discussed by Yates, *Giordano Bruno*, passim. Clearly, then, Everard's *Pymander*, although its heretical implications are no less than those of Patrizi's *New Philosophy*, has its place in a long line of Renaissance philosophical humanism that is profoundly at odds with the line of Christian orthodoxy.

29. See, for example, *A Reformation of Schools* (1642), 47–48, as cited in Dobbs, *The Foundations of Newton's Alchemy*, 61: "Also the practise of the Chymists came into my mind, who have found out a way so to cleare, and unburden the essences, and spirits of things from the surcharge of matter, that one drop extracted out of Mineralls, or Vegetables containes more strength, and vertue in it, and is used with better successe, and efficacy than can be hoped for from the whole, and entire lumpe."

30. Ibid., 60–61. Yates, *Giordano Bruno*, 432–55, esp. 443, comments on Fludd's controversies with the likes of Mersenne and Kepler, calling into question Fludd's grasp of the mathematical rudiments necessary to pursue his scientific program. "Fludd's mathematics are really 'mathesis' and 'vana geometria' which he utterly confuses with 'Chymia' and with 'Hermes.' Kepler is concerned not with 'Pythagorean intentions' but with reality (*res ipsa*). He uses mathematics as a mathematician, while Fludd uses them 'more Hermetico.'"

31. On the Codex Brucianus, see Pagels, *Gnostic Gospels*, xxiv: "in 1769 . . . a Scottish tourist named James Bruce bought a Coptic manuscript near Thebes

(modern Luxor) in upper Egypt" and brought it back to England, where he deposited it in the Bodleian Library at Oxford as the Codex Brucianus no later than 1778. On the Codex Brucianus and the Codex Askewianus, see Rudolph, *Gnosis*, 27. A certain Dr. Askew deposited in the British Museum Library another manuscript, known as the Codex Askewianus, also no later than 1778. Both codices "were first brought to the attention of scholars by C. G. Woide in 1778."

Morton D. Paley, *Energy and the Imagination: The Development of Blake's Thought* (Oxford: Clarendon, 1970), 66, suggests that in his use of the concept of creation-as-fall, "Blake need not have gone to esoteric sources of this and other Gnostic doctrines, for they are summarized in J. L. Mosheim's *Ecclesiastical History,* first published in English translation in 1764. He could also have found a succinct exposition of Gnostic theology reprinted from Mosheim in Priestley's *Matter and Spirit."*

32. Michael Ferber, *The Social Vision of William Blake* (Princeton: Princeton Univ. Press, 1985), 93.

33. "The Eleventh Book of Hermes Trismegistus. Of the Common Mind to Tat," in [John Everard], *The Divine Pymander of Hermes Mercurius Trismegistus in XVII Books,* vol. 2 of *Collectanea Hermetica,* ed. W. Wynn Westcott (1650; rpt. London: Theosophical Publishing Society, 1894), 86.

That "the operation of life" is an immanent, vital energy is clear from the authoritative version of the text. See *Corpus Hermeticum,* ed. A. D. Nock, trans. A. J. Festugière, 4 vols. (1945–54; rpt. Paris: Société d'Edition "Les Belles Lettres," 1960), 1:180–81. In his translation of what is, in this edition, the twelfth rather than the eleventh book, Festugière renders "the operation of life" as "l'énergie de la vie," taking his lead from Nock's Greek original, where the term is *energeia.*

34. Everard, *Pymander,* 88–89. See also *Corpus Hermeticum,* 1:183. Festugière renders the passage last quoted as follows: "Et si elle est mise en oeuvre, par qui l'est elle? Car ses énergies qui opérent, nous l'avons dit, sont parties de Dieu." Nock's original reads *tinos energeitai* for "mise en oeuvre," and *energeias* for "énergies."

35. See note 2 above.

36. *Blake Records,* ed. G. E. Bentley, Jr. (London: Oxford Univ. Press, 1969), 545.

A number of others have commented on Blake's gnostic proclivities, including Paley (see note 31 above); Ferber (see note 32 above); Stuart Curran, "Blake and the Gnostic Hyle: A Double Negative," *Blake Studies* 4 (Spring 1972): 117–33; and Leslie Tannenbaum, "Blake's Art of Crypsis: *The Book of Urizen* and Genesis," *Blake Studies* 5 (Fall 1972): 141–64. Tannenbaum further elaborates Blake's relation to gnosticism in *Biblical Tradition in Blake's Early Prophecies* (Princeton: Princeton Univ. Press, 1982), 4, 6, 15, 202, 257–58.

37. Joseph Priestley, *Disquisitions Relating to Matter and Spirit* (London: Joseph Johnson, 1777), 50, xxxix. Subsequent parenthetical page references will be to *DMS.*

38. William Blake, *Complete Poetry and Prose,* rev. ed., David V. Erdman

(Garden City: Anchor, 1982), pl. iii, ll. 1–7. Subsequent parenthetical references to Blake's writings by line, plate and line, or page will be to *Poetry*.

See also Everard, *Pymander,* 37. The predicament that Blake describes shows some striking affinities with the account of "the wickedness of the Soul" given by Trismegistus [i.e., Hermes] in "The Fourth Book Called 'The Key'": "And the wickedness of the Soul is ignorance; for the Soul that knows nothing of the things that are, neither the nature of them, nor that which is good, but is blinded, rusheth and dasheth against the bodily Passions, and unhappy as it is, not knowing itself, it serveth strange Bodies, and evil ones, carrying the Body as a burden, and not ruling, but ruled. And this is the mischief of the Soul."

39. *The History and Present State of Electricity* (1767), xiii, as cited in Joseph Priestley, *Autobiography,* ed. Jack Lindsay (Teaneck: Fairleigh Dickinson Univ. Press, 1971), 19.

40. *A Scientific Autobiography of Joseph Priestley,* ed. Robert E. Schofield (Cambridge, Mass.: MIT Press, 1966), 117, 122.

Two recent articles attempt to revise, or at least to readjust, the positions of Priestley and Lavoisier and the lineage leading up to them. J. B. Gough, "Lavoisier and the Fulfillment of the Stahlian Revolution," *Osiris* n.s. 4 (1988): 15–33, esp. 23, 32, seeks to identify Lavoisier as the last and greatest in the line of French Stahlians who participated in "the Chemical Revolution of the eighteenth century . . . a revolution concerning the composition of the chemical molecule." To make this argument, Gough must deal with the obvious fact that Stahl, along with Becher, is one of the authors of the phlogiston theory. This he does by insisting that "phlogiston was but a small part of Stahlian theory." Alistair M. Duncan, "Particles and Eighteenth Century Concepts of Chemical Combination," *British Journal for the History of Science* 21 (1988): 447–53, esp. 448, 453, deemphasizes "the tradition derived from Becher and Stahl, and continuing through the modifications of the phlogiston theory," as well as "the extremes of Newtonianism [?] such as the theory of Boscovich," in order to argue that "the model of chemical change as consisting of interactions between particles, adapted by chemists to suit their own needs rather than as dictated to them by mechanical philosophers, acquired considerable explanatory power in the late eighteenth century." Although neither article is unreconstructedly internalist in its orientation, trying to separate Stahl from phlogiston in order to make him the intellectual progenitor of Lavoisier rather than Priestley, not to mention making Stahl, the source of Priestley's anti-Newtonian conception of electricity as an immanentist phenomenon, into a Newtonian extremist, raises more questions than are answered.

41. Arguably, Blake's discussion of "Poetic Genius" (*Poetry,* p. 2) in *All Religions Are One* (1788) is the earliest such discussion.

42. See Eichner, "The Rise of Modern Science," 24.

43. In *Milton* (1804), Blake names "Satan [who] is Urizen / Drawn down by Orc & the Shadowy Female into Generation" (*Poetry,* pl. 10 [11]:1–2), "Prince of the Starry Wheels" (pl. 3:43). This title, coupled with Los's recognition that Satan is "Newton's Pantocrator weaving the woof of Locke" (pl. 4:11)—that is, the *"Lord God Pantrokrator, or Universal Ruler,"* of the "General Scholium" to the *Principia* (see *Newton's Mathematical Principles,* trans. Motte,

rev. Cajori, 544), who is closely modeled on the creator-God of Genesis 1—invites the comparison of Urizen to Yaldabaoth. "The word is of Semitic (Aramaic) origin and probably means 'begetter of Sabaoth (= Abaoth)' i.e. 'the heavenly powers'; evidently an esoteric description of the God of the Jews who corresponding to the biblical tradition occupies in the gnostic systems the role of the creator" (Rudolph, *Gnosis*, 73).

As described in the gnostic codex *On the Origin of the World,* Yaldabaoth is, in several senses, the spiritless "afterbirth" or "miscarriage" of Pistis Sophia (Faith Wisdom). But lacking spirit (*pneuma*) and therefore "ignorant of the power of Pistis," Yaldabaoth knows nothing of his parent. He rules "lion-like in appearance, androgynous, and having a great authority within himself, but not knowing whence he came into being" (II, 5: *99,* 25–*100,* 20). Blake seems to have this scenario or one very much like it in mind in Urizen's description of his struggle to create the material world in a place that is the womb of Pistis whence he sprang—"A void immense, wild dark & deep, / Where nothing was: Natures wide womb" (*Poetry,* pl. 4:16–17) is how he describes the place, ignorant of the fact that his description shows him to be "ignorant of the power of Pistis."

Perhaps even more than Urizen's description, Blake's illustrations of him suggest his identity with Yaldabaoth: "the perfect ones called him 'Ariael' because he was a lion-likeness" (II, 5: *100,* 25–26). Blake, for his part, usually depicts Urizen with a leonine mane of hair and as often as not hunched or squatting in a manner suggestive of a big cat preparing to pounce. Yet another name for Yaldabaoth is "'Samuel,' that is, 'the blind god'" (II, 5: *103,* 18). Blake nearly always depicts and describes Urizen with obstructed vision—gaze averted, eyes filled with tears, pleading the dimness of the light, and so on.

44. *Trimorphic Protennoia* explains the entity thusly: "[I] am [Protennoia, the] thought that [dwells] in [the Light. I] am the movement that dwells in the [All, she in whom the] All takes its stand, [the first]-born among those who [came to be, she who exists] before the All. . . . I am intangible, dwelling in the intangible. I move in every creature" (XIII, 1: *35,* 1–13).

45. Joseph Priestley, *An History of the Corruptions of Christianity,* 2 vols. (London: Joseph Johnson, 1782), 1:6. Subsequent parenthetical volume and page references will be to *History.*

46. Pagels cites the *Tripartite Tractate* (I, 5: *99*ff.) in elaborating the contrast between the orthodox, who embrace the doctrine of particular immanence and the consequence of hierarchy, and the gnostics, who share the bond of equality effected by the working of a pervasive immanence in them.

The *Tripartite Tractate* . . . contrasts those who are gnostics, "children of the Father," with those who are uninitiates, offspring of the demiurge. The Father's children . . . join together as equals, enjoying mutual love, spontaneously helping one another. But the demiurge's offspring—the ordinary Christians—"wanted to command one another, outrivalling one another in their empty ambition"; they are inflated with "lust for power," "each one imagining that he is superior to the others." (40–41)

47. Pagels, *Gnostic Gospels,* 41.
48. Ibid., 28.

49. *Shelley's Prose, or, the Trumpet of a Prophecy,* ed. David Lee Clark, corrected ed. (Albuquerque: Univ. of New Mexico Press, 1966), 188, 279. Shelley's own gnostic sympathies are readily apparent in his prose fragment "The Assassins."

50. Pagels, *Gnostic Gospels,* 28.

51. See note 10 above.

52. Robert Alter, *The Art of Biblical Narrative* (New York: Basic Books, 1981), 145, contrasts the *P* account of the creation (Genesis 1:1–2:4a) with the *J* account (2:4b–2:25) in the following terms: "*P* is interested in the large plan of creation; *J* is more interested in the complicated and difficult facts of human life in civilization, for which he provides an initial explanation through the story of what happened in Eden. Man culminates the scheme of creation in *P*, but man is the narrative center of *J*'s story, which is quite another matter."

53. Pagels, *Gnostic Gospels,* 32–33.

Bibliography

Allogenes. Trans. John D. Turner and Orval S. Wintermute. In *The Nag Hammadi Library in English,* ed. Marvin W. Meyer, pp. 441–52. San Francisco: Harper & Row, 1977.

ALTER, ROBERT. *The Art of Biblical Narrative.* New York: Basic Books, 1981.

BACON, FRANCIS. *The Works of Francis Bacon.* Ed. James Spedding, Robert Leslie Ellis, and Douglas Denon Heath. 2d ed., 7 vols. London: Longmans, 1870.

BARNET, SYLVAN, MORTON BERMAN, and WILLIAM BURTO. *Introduction to Literature: Fiction, Poetry, Drama.* 7th ed. Boston: Little, Brown, 1981.

BERNAL, J. D. *The Social Foundations of Science.* New York: Macmillan, 1939.

BLAKE, WILLIAM. *Blake Records.* Ed. G. E. Bentley, Jr. London: Oxford University Press, 1969.

———. *Complete Poetry and Prose.* Rev. ed. Ed. David V. Erdman. Garden City: Anchor, 1982.

Corpus Hermeticum. Ed. A. D. Nock. Trans. A. J. Festugière. 1945–54. Reprint. Paris: Société d'Edition "Les Belles Lettres," 1960.

COTTRELL, ALAN P. *Goethe's View of Evil and the Search for a New Image of Man in Our Time.* Edinburgh: Floris, 1982.

CURRAN, STUART. "Blake and the Gnostic Hyle: A Double Negative." *Blake Studies* 4 (Spring 1972): 117–33.

DOBBS, BETTY JO TEETER. *The Foundations of Newton's Alchemy or "The Huntyng of the Greene Lyon."* 1975. Reprint. New York: Cambridge University Press, 1984.

DUNCAN, ALISTAIR M. "Particles and Eighteenth Century Concepts of Chemical Combination." *British Journal for the History of Science* 21 (1988): 447–53.

EICHNER, HANS. "The Rise of Modern Science and the Genesis of Romanticism." *PMLA* 97 (1982): 8–30.

EVERARD, JOHN. *The Divine Pymander of Hermes Mercurius Trismegistus, in XVII Books.* Ed. W. Wynn Westcott. London: Theosophical Publishing Society, 1894.

FERBER, MICHAEL. *The Social Vision of William Blake.* Princeton: Princeton University Press, 1985.

FUNKENSTEIN, AMOS. *Theology and the Scientific Imagination from the Middle Ages to the Seventeenth Century.* Princeton: Princeton University Press, 1986.

GOUGH, J.B. "Lavoisier and the Fulfillment of the Stahlian Revolution." *Osiris* n.s. 4 (1988): 15–33.

HESSEN, BORIS. *The Economic Roots of Newton's Principia.* 1931. Reprint. New York: Howard Fertig, 1971.

HILL, CHRISTOPHER. *The Intellectual Origins of the Puritan Revolution.* Oxford: Oxford University Press, 1965.

_____. *The World Turned Upside Down.* New York: Viking, 1972.

JAMESON, FREDRIC. *The Political Unconscious: Narrative as a Socially Symbolic Act.* 1981. Reprint. Ithaca: Cornell University Press, 1986.

MENDELSOHN, EVERETT, PETER WEINGART, and RICHARD WHITLEY, eds. *The Social Production of Scientific Knowledge.* Dordrecht: Reidel, 1977.

MERTON, ROBERT. *Science, Technology, and Society in Seventeenth-Century England.* New York: Columbia University Press, 1938.

The Nag Hammadi Library in English. Ed. Marvin W. Meyer. Trans. members of the Coptic Gnostic Library Research Project of the Institute for Antiquity and Christianity. San Francisco: Harper & Row, 1977.

NEWTON, ISAAC. *Sir Isaac Newton's Mathematical Principles of Natural Philosophy.* Trans. Andrew Motte. Rev. Florian Cajori. 1934. Reprint. Berkeley and Los Angeles: University of California Press, 1966.

On the Origin of the World. Trans. Hans-Gebhard Bethge and Orval S. Wintermute. In *The Nag Hammadi Library in English,* ed. Marvin W. Meyer, pp. 161–79. San Francisco: Harper & Row, 1977.

PAGELS, ELAINE. *The Gnostic Gospels.* New York: Random House, 1979.

PALEY, MORTON D. *Energy and the Imagination: The Development of Blake's Thought.* Oxford: Clarendon, 1970.

PLATO. *Cratylus.* In *Plato, with an English Translation,* trans. H. N. Fowler, vol. 6, rev. ed. 1939. Reprint. Cambridge, Mass.: Harvard University Press, 1953.

PRIESTLEY, JOSEPH. *Autobiography of Joseph Priestley.* Ed. Jack Lindsay. Teaneck: Fairleigh Dickinson University Press, 1971.

_____. *Disquisitions Relating to Matter and Spirit.* London: Joseph Johnson, 1777.

_____. *An History of the Corruptions of Christianity.* 2 vols. London: Joseph Johnson, 1782.

_____. *A Scientific Autobiography of Joseph Priestley (1733–1804).* Ed. Robert E. Schofield. Cambridge, Mass.: MIT Press, 1966.

REDONDI, PIETRO. *Galileo Heretic.* Trans. Raymond Rosenthal. Princeton: Princeton University Press, 1987.

RORTY, RICHARD. *Philosophy and the Mirror of Nature.* Princeton: Princeton University Press, 1979.

RUDOLPH, KURT. *Gnosis: The Nature and History of Gnosticism.* Trans. Robert McLachlan Wilson. San Francisco: Harper & Row, 1983.

SHAPIN, STEVEN. "History of Science and Its Sociological Reconstructions." *History of Science* 20 (1982): 157–211.

SHELLEY, PERCY BYSSHE. *Shelley's Prose, or, the Trumpet of a Prophecy.* Ed. David Lee Clark. Corrected ed. Albuquerque: University of New Mexico Press, 1966.

TANNENBAUM, LESLIE. "Blake's Art of Crypsis: *The Book of Urizen* and Genesis." *Blake Studies* 5 (Fall 1972): 141–64.

THOMAS, KEITH. *Religion and the Decline of Magic.* New York: Scribners, 1971.

TODOROV, TZVETAN. *Mikhail Bakhtin: The Dialogical Principle.* Trans. Wlad Gozich. Theory and History of Literature, vol. 13. Minneapolis: University of Minnesota Press, 1984.

Trimorphic Protennoia. Trans. John D. Turner. In *The Nag Hammadi Library in English,* ed. Marvin W. Meyer, pp. 461–70. San Francisco: Harper & Row, 1977.

Tripartite Tractate. Trans. Harold W. Attridge, Elaine H. Pagels, and Dieter Mueller. In *The Nag Hammadi Library in English,* ed. Marvin W. Meyer, pp. 54–97. San Francisco: Harper & Row, 1977.

VOEGELIN, ERIC. *Science, Politics, and Gnosticism.* Chicago: Henry Regnery, 1968.

WESTFALL, RICHARD S. *Never at Rest: A Biography of Isaac Newton.* New York: Cambridge University Press, 1980.

YATES, FRANCES. *Giordano Bruno and the Hermetic Tradition.* 1964. Reprint. New York: Vintage Books, 1969.

ZILSEL, EDGAR. "The Sociological Roots of Science." *American Journal of Sociology* 47 (1942): 544–62.

Romantic Drama
From Optics to Illusion

FREDERICK BURWICK

BOTH GEORGES MOYNET, in *La machinerie théâtrale. Trucs et décors* (1893), and Albert A. Hopkins, in *Stage Illusions and Scientific Diversions* (1898), look back upon the developments in staging not simply with the awareness that technological advances during the latter half of the nineteenth century had brought great new possibilities to the art of dramatic representation, but also with the sense that the theater of ages past was a primitive affair indeed. As Moynet and Hopkins expressed it, playwrights and actors of former times, in spite of their genial efforts, had been stifled in their conjuring art by the lack of proper lighting and the limitations of stage settings.[1] The theater, at the threshold of the twentieth century, had mastery over energy and machinery capable of producing powerful and spellbinding illusion.

The theater of the early nineteenth century, however, was not as primitive as Moynet and Hopkins recall. Indeed, the acute attention of playwrights and producers to the developments in physical and physiological optics and to experiments in visual perception makes the drama of the period, among all the literary genres, the most intense arena of interaction between aesthetic and scientific concerns. Not all critics of the drama welcomed that interaction. Coleridge and Lamb, for example, both advocated a reliance on the bare stage of Shakespeare's age.[2] The new technology could produce stunning stage illusion, they granted, but stage illusion, they went on to insist, is not dramatic illusion. The one works upon the eye, the other upon the imagination.

Although the optical effects of staging might well enhance the way in which a performance could stimulate the imagination, playwrights and players often felt that they were being "upstaged" by the stage itself. The audience, however, delighted in stage gimmickry, and playbills often promised the "wonders" and "marvels" of the latest technological innovations. Scientific experimentation during the romantic period had virtually claimed a theater of its own in the form of public lectures and demonstrations. Plays were often produced merely as theatrical vehicles for "recreative" science.[3] Before one sneers at the popular exploitation of science, it is worthwhile to ponder the extent to which the theater provided both motivation and patronage for experimentation in physiological optics as well as the physics of light. Important scientists such as Henry Hyde Wollaston, Thomas Young, and Sir David Brewster contributed to the new technology of the stage, and Louis Jacques Mandé Daguerre, better known as a founder of photography, launched his career as stage designer.

The romantic preoccupation with visual illusion is well documented by Sir David Brewster in his *Letters on Natural Magic, addressed to Sir Walter Scott* (1832).[4] Science, Brewster argues, always seems magical to minds unacquainted with the subtle relations between cause and effect. Every branch of science affords means for exploring illusion. The eye, he asserts, is "the most important of our organs" and "the most fertile source of mental illusions." Letters II through VI are devoted to optical illusion. Much of his investigation is devoted to the stage trickery achieved with mirrors and the magic lantern. In documenting techniques of projection with the *laterna magica,* Brewster is especially concerned with the methods of extending its possibilities in order to create illusions of motion.

The endeavor to turn pictures into moving pictures had already brought forth a number of innovations that relied on mechanical means. In preparing his *Eidophusikon* (1781), Philippe Jacques de Loutherbourg was able to provide the most stunning optical display of his day.[5] During his years as stage designer at Drury Lane, Loutherbourg had learned the tricks of enhancing scenic effects with backlighting and projected images. Visible to the audience when lighted from the front, a scene painted on a transparent screen would vanish when the front lights dimmed and the back lights revealed another scene behind. This trick was used to great effect in the Drury Lane production of *Semiramis* (1776) for the appearance of the Ghost of Ninus. In a departure from Voltaire's original play meant to allow for more appropriate supernatural conjuring, the ghost arises from his tomb to accuse Semiramis in a quiet moonlit scene rather than in a brightly lit public assembly.[6] The technique of forelighting and backlighting screen drops is turned into a veritable tour de force of scene changes in *The Wonders of Derbyshire* (1779), in which Loutherbourg, by controlling the lighting to show the scenes from dawn to dusk, manages his magical transitions through eleven different scenes.[7]

In his inventive use of light and shadow, Loutherbourg also was the first to use the moiré effect to create an illusion of motion in stage setting. The waves that ripple across the fabric of moiré silk are produced by a ribbed weave that is folded over with the face side inward and the selvedges running side by side. The dampened fabric is then pressed between heated rollers that emboss the weave pattern of one side onto the other. As a result, the weave catches the light from varying directions so that the light waves are reflected in and out of synchronization, producing a waterlike visual effect.[8] Loutherbourg was able to produce a similar effect with light and shadow by projecting two striated patterns. For the production of John O'Keefe's *Omai, or a Trip Around the World* (1785), Loutherbourg made the water seem to flow and flames to flicker by using colored lights and moiré shadows.[9] This technique was subsequently adapted for a specially designed magic lantern, the Eidotrope, which had a crank mechanism to counter-rotate two metal disks with perforated patterns to project moiré movement.[10]

Loutherbourg's most elaborate attempt to create illusions of motion was his *Eidophusikon* (1781), a pictorial entertainment designed to exhibit "Various Imitations of Natural Phenomena, represented by Moving Pictures." The pictures, as Richard Altick has described the production, brought together several popular devices: the magic lantern, transparencies, shadow figures, and mechanical figures. During the first season, the exhibit included five scenes: dawn in Greenwich Park with a view of London; noon in Tangier with a view of Gibraltar; sunset over Naples; moonlight over the Mediterranean ("the Rising of the Moon contrasted with the Effect of Fire"); "a Storm at Sea, and Shipwreck." For the following year, a new exhibit was prepared: "The Sun rising in the Fog, an Italian Seaport"; "The Cataract of Niagara"; sunset, following rain, over the cliffs of Dover with a view of the castle; a moon rising, a lighthouse on the rocky coast of Japan, a tempest with lightning and waterspout; Satan and the fallen Angels "on the Banks of the Fiery Lake, with the Raising of Pandemonium."[11] As explained in the

European Magazine, Loutherbourg's purpose was to lend dramatic space and time to an exhibition of visual art:

> He resolved to add motion to resemblance. He knew that the most exquisite painting represented only one moment of time in action, and though we might justly admire the representation of the foaming surge, the rolling ship, the gliding water, or the running steed: yet however well the action was depicted, the heightened look soon perceived the object to be at rest, and the deception lasted no longer than the first glance. He therefore planned a series of moving pictures, which should unite the painter and the mechanic; by giving natural motion to accurate resemblance.[12]

The "natural motion" is produced by two means: some of the motion is merely a mechanical moving of the setting, as when the scrim revealing the columns and arches of Pandemonium is drawn upward in front of the view of "the Lake with liquid fire" and "Mineral fury"; the flickering of the flames, however, depended upon the moiré movement (fig. 1). Mechanically operated "moving pictures" had attracted audiences in London since 1709, when William Pinkethman displayed his clockwork scenes with over a hundred animated figures.[13] For Loutherbourg, even merely mechanical movement could be enhanced by the optical ingenuity of backlighting and forelighting to make a scene gradually appear or disappear. Too, his storm scenes involved

Fig. 1. Pandemonium, from Loutherbourg's Eidophusikon *(watercolor by Edward Burney, 1781). From the British Museum, Department of Prints and Drawings.*

clouds sweeping across the sky to obscure the sun or moon. For this effect, he painted his clouds on long strips of semitransparent screen which, mounted on rollers, were gradually drawn across the scene as if impelled by the breeze.

Writing in 1832, Brewster was able to review a variety of optical illusions which had intrigued audiences in the decades following the *Eidophusikon*. The major factor limiting the use of the magic lantern was the available illumination. The lantern had been effective only in a small theater. The Argand lamp, patented in 1784, used a tubular wick and a round glass chimney for improved air flow and combustion. The addition of Carcel's clockwork pump in 1800 aided brightness by regulating the flow of oil to the wick. The next step was to provide an air pump to increase combustion. The Clegg lamps, introduced in 1809, adapted the Argand principle to gas.[14] When the limelight was introduced in 1825, the incandescence made available a powerful source of light (fig. 2). The flame of a spirit lamp, transformed into an intense torch by a jet of oxygen, was trained on a ball of quicklime. That incandescent ball of lime, no larger than three-eighths of an inch in diameter, was visible sixty-six and one-quarter miles away when Lieutenant Thomas Drummond first ignited his device on a November evening in 1825.[15] Another twelve years were to pass before the limelight had its stage debut in London.

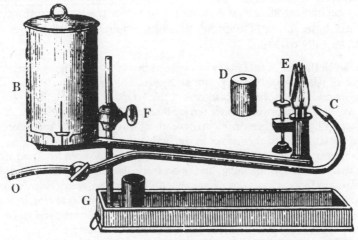

Fig. 2. Limelight apparatus (oxy-calcium lamp). Oxygen flows through hose O; *pressure regulated by valve* G; *methylated spirits contained in cannister* B; *cannister raised or lowered by clamp* F. *Spirit flame is blown by oxygen jet* C, *heating to incandescence the lime cone* D. *Lime cone is brought in line with focusing lens by adjusting spindle* E. *From* The Magic Lantern, *by a mere phantom (London: 1866).*

Loutherbourg relied on a simple oil lamp and an effective combination of mirror reflector and lens to focus a beam of light for his stage effects at Drury Lane. His stage for the *Eidophusikon* was no more than a recessed box, six feet high and eight feet deep, and his auditorium was an upstairs room in his house in Leicester Square.[16] The room had to be completely darkened for a presentation. The *Phantoscopia,* which Jack Bologna produced at the Lyceum Theatre (1796), probably made use of the new Argand lamps. For his *Phantasmagoria,* also at the Lyceum Theatre (1802), Paul de Philipstal brought to London the magic lantern developed by the Belgian physicist, Etienne Gaspard Robert. Both productions, imitating such shows in Paris, pretended to call forth ghosts and supernatural beings. Brewster describes the conjurations and explains how the uncanny effects were achieved:

> The power of the magic lantern has been greatly extended by placing it on one side of the transparent screen of taffetas which receives the images while the spectators are placed on the other side, and by making every part of the glass sliders opaque excepting the part which forms the figures. Hence all the figures appear luminous on a black ground, and produce a much greater effect with the same degree of illumination. An exhibition depending on these principles was brought out by M. Philipstal in 1802 under the name of the *Phantasmagoria,* and when it was shown in London and Edinburgh it produced the most impressive effects upon the spectators.

As Brewster's account makes evident, Robert's projector was equipped with mechanical sliders and mounted upon a track. In spite of the brighter light source, Philipstal's illusions required a small theater that could be fully darkened.

> The small theatre of exhibition was lighted by only one hanging lamp, the flame of which was drawn up into an opaque chimney or shade when the performance began. In this "darkness visible" the curtain rose and displayed a cave with skeletons and other terrific figures in relief upon its walls. The flickering light was then drawn up beneath its shroud, and the spectators in total darkness found themselves in the middle of thunder and lightning. A thin transparent screen had, unknown to the spectators, been let down after the disappearance of the light, and upon it the flashes of lightning and the subsequent appearances were represented. This screen being half-way between the spectators and the cave which was first shown, and being in itself invisible, prevented the observers from having any idea of the real distance of the figures, and gave them the entire character of aërial pictures.

The stunning transformations were wrought by series of transparencies rapidly changed in a mechanical slider. Philipstal created "moving pictures" through a variety of specially contrived sliders. He enhanced the illusion by providing eerie sound effects to accompany the projected image.

> The thunder and lightning were followed by the figures of ghosts, skeletons, and known individuals, whose eyes and mouth were made to move by the shifting of combined sliders. After the first figure had been exhibited for a short time, it began to grow less and less, as if removed to a great distance, and at last vanished in a small cloud of light. Out of this same cloud the germ of another figure began to appear, and gradually grew larger and larger, and approached the spectators till it attained its perfect development. In this manner, the head of Dr. Franklin was transformed into a skull; figures which retired in the freshness of life came back in the form of skeletons, and the retiring skeletons returned in the drapery of flesh and blood.

Movement was created by mechanical sliders and by a rapid sequence of transparencies, but also by moving projectors and changing focal distance. Because actual distances are obscured in the darkened room, the changing size of a projected figure is perceived as approaching and receding.

> The exhibitions of these transmutations was followed by spectres, skeletons, and terrific figures, which, instead of receding and vanishing as before, suddenly advanced upon the spectators, becoming larger as they approached them, and finally vanished by appearing to sink into the ground. The effect of this part of the exhibition was naturally the most impressive. The spectators were not only surprised but agitated, and many of them were of opinion that they could have touched the figures.[17]

Brewster's description closely follows the contemporary account by William Nicholson, who adds the complaint that the lightning projected by the magic lantern was too "tame." Nicholson prefers the "brisk" intensity achieved on the London stage with the flash explosion of a handful of powdered resin tossed into an open flame. The lantern images, as both Brewster and Nicholson observe, were set in motion by mechanical sliders as well as by changing the size of the focused picture. The mechanical sliders allowed for manipulating two or more glass panes within a single metal frame: "a tempest at sea is imitated, by having the sea on one slider, and the ships on other sliders, to which an undulatory motion is communicated."[18]

A secondary optical illusion, Brewster observes, may also occur with a double slider, for the motion of one lends the illusion of contrary motion to the other. In Philipstal's *Phantasmagoria*, when a head appeared with rolling eyes, the very movement of the eyes made the head seem to turn. In 1824, Wollaston read a paper to the Royal Society on that well-known optical phenomenon in which the eyes of a painting seem to follow a spectator around the room. Wollaston argued that even in looking at an actual person the viewer is "unconsciously aided by the concurrent position of the face." Using a series of engravings in which the upper half of the face, including the eyes, remained constant, and the lower half of the face, with alternative views of nose, mouth, and chin changed, Wollaston demonstrated that in viewing a portrait "the apparent position of the eyes is principally influenced by that of the adjacent parts of the face"[19] (figs. 3 and 4). "Dr. Wollaston has not noticed the converse of these illusions," Brewster points out, "in which a change of direction is given to fixed features by a change in the direc-

Fig. 3. Face with eyes toward the viewer. Henry Hyde Wollaston, "On the apparent Direction of Eyes in a Portrait." From Sir David Brewster, Letters on Natural Magic, addressed to Sir Walter Scott *(London: John Murray, 1832).*

Fig. 4. Face with eyes averted from the viewer. Only the lower portion (nose, mouth, chin) of the portrait has been altered; the engraving of the eyes is the same as in fig. 3. Henry Hyde Wollaston, "On the apparent Direction of Eyes in a Portrait." From Sir David Brewster, Letters on Natural Magic, addressed to Sir Walter Scott *(London: John Murray, 1832).*

tion of the eyes." This corollary effect, Brewster adds, "is finely seen in some magic lantern sliders, where a pair of eyes is made to move in the head of a figure which invariably follows the motion of the eyeballs."[20]

In order to make the illusion appear to advance and recede, it is necessary to change the focus. The image appears to "recede" when the lantern is brought closer to the screen, thus producing "the optical incongruity of the figures becoming more luminous when they retired from the observer." Brewster appraises Thomas Young's invention of a lantern contrived to regulate brightness and focus. Young's lantern is mounted on tracks with armatures attached to the screen which automatically adjust the focus and operate a diaphragm to damp the brightness (fig. 5).[21]

Brewster also describes how "M. Robertson at Paris introduced along with his pictures the direct shadows of living objects." Most probably, the Paris exhibit involved nothing more complex than mingling the images projected by the lantern with shadows produced by assistants moving between the projected beam of light and the screen. Brewster, however, proposes more startling effects to be achieved with his "catadioptrical phantasmagoria" (*catoptric* refers to reflection, *dioptric* to refraction) (fig. 6). In order to project the life-size image of

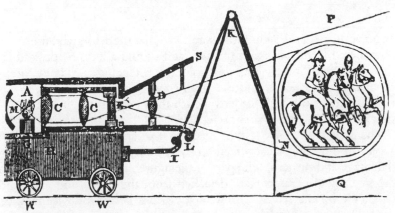

Fig. 5. Young's magic lantern. Mounted on small car H, *which runs on wheels* WW, *the light of lamp* G *is reflected by mirror* M *and condensed by lenses* CC *upon the transparent sliders at* E. *The objective lens* D *focuses the projected image on screen* PQ. *When the car is drawn back on its wheels, the rod* IK *brings down the point* K, *and, by means of the rod* KL, *pushes the lens* D *nearer to the sliders in* EF. *When the car advances toward the screen, the point* K *is raised, and the rod* KL *draws out the lens* D *from the slider, so that the image is always in focus. From Sir David Brewster,* Letters on Natural Magic, addressed to Sir Walter Scott *(London: John Murray, 1832).*

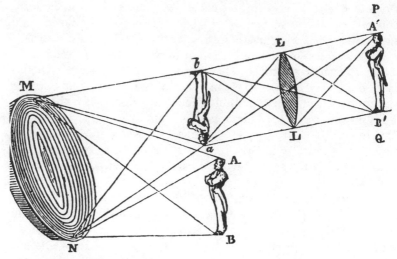

Fig. 6. Brewster's catadioptrical phantasmagoria. A living figure AB is placed
before a large concave mirror MN, by means of which a diminished and inverted
image is formed at ab. If PQ is the transparent screen upon which the image is to be
shown, a large lens LL must be so placed before the image ab to form a distinct and
erect picture A'B' upon the screen. From Sir David Brewster, Letters on Natural
Magic, addressed to Sir Walter Scott (London: John Murray, 1832).

an actor, Brewster designs his apparatus so that the actor, who must "be
illuminated in the strongest manner, and should always be dressed either in white or in very luminous colours," enters into a chamber drap-
ed in black and poses before a large concave mirror that reflects his
reduced image through the lens, which then projects the image to appear life-size on a transparent screen.[22]

The image, of course, can be made to float and hover as it is moved
about on the transparent screen. Too, by interposing a prism between
the image and the lens, "the part of the figure immediately opposite to
the prism will be as it were detached from the figure and exhibited
separately on the screen." Brewster describes how his device may be
used to stage a horrible dismembering of a living person (fig. 7).

> Let us suppose that this part is the head of the figure. It may be detached
> vertically, or lifted from the body as if it were cut off. . . . A hand may be
> made to grasp the hair of the head, and the aspect of death may be given to
> it, as if it had been newly cut off. Such a representation could be easily
> made, and the effect on the spectators would be quite overpowering. The
> lifeless head might then be made to recover its vitality, and be safely replaced
> on the figure.[23]

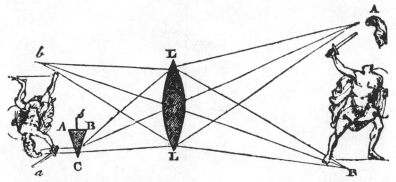

Fig. 7. Decapitating a living figure. Brewster's catadioptrical phantasmagoria with prism. A living figure is placed before a large concave mirror so that the inverted image appears at ab. A prism with a small refracting angle BCA is placed between ab and the lens LL so that the projected figure AB appears with head detached. From Sir David Brewster, Letters on Natural Magic, addressed to Sir Walter Scott *(London: John Murray, 1832).*

A simpler device, which Brewster also describes, requires only reflection. The advantage of his catadioptrical phantasmagoria is that the projected image can be easily manipulated and cast in several directions about the stage. A reflected image, by contrast, must always be presented at a specific location in relation to the viewer. The concave mirror, "the staple instrument of the magician's cabinet," is especially useful for creating phantom stage effects. Since this deception depends on backlighting, Brewster recommends that a bright lamp be used to illuminate the person or object to be reflected, while the forelighting onstage be kept relatively dim. One example of this illusion is the transformation of a portrait into a hideous demon (fig. 8). A portrait painted on a semitransparent screen is hung before an opening in the wall. A plaster cast of a demon is concealed behind the wall in an inverted position. When it is illuminated with a bright lamp, the image reflected by the concave mirror is made to appear on the screen. But a screen is not necessary. The concave mirror will seem to project an image directly toward the spectator (who must be correctly positioned) or, in rendering the image visible to a larger audience, into a cloud of smoke.[24]

Another technique Brewster recommended for stunning stage effects made use of his own invention, the kaleidoscope, for the projection of multiple images (fig. 9). When he published his *Treatise on the Kaleidoscope* (1819), the most effective source of illumination available was the recently developed oxygen lamp: "an oxygen lamp is peculiarly fitted for displaying the pictures of the Kaleidoscope to a number of spec-

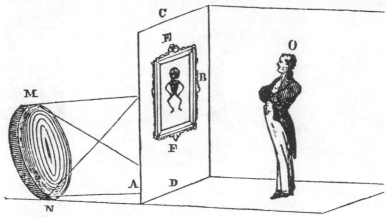

Fig. 8. Illusion with concave mirror. Wall partition CD has a square opening EF, centered about five feet above the floor. This opening might be set off with a picture frame and a semitransparent painting which would be visible when illuminated in front, but would vanish when illumination is dimmed in front and light is cast upon it from behind. A large concave mirror MN is placed on the opposite side, so that when any object is placed at A, a distinct image of it may be formed on the semi-transparent screen at EF. From Sir David Brewster, Letters on Natural Magic, addressed to Sir Walter Scott *(London: John Murray, 1832).*

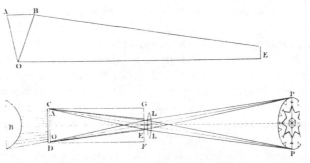

Fig. 9. Brewster's kaleidoscopic lantern. To exhibit kaleidoscopic images to a number of spectators, the tube CDGF containing three reflectors AOE is mounted on a magic lantern. The objects from which the pictures are to be created are placed in the cell CD, which may be made to have a rotary movement round the axis of the tube or to slide through a groove, like sliders of a conventional magic lantern. The objects are powerfully illuminated by lens B, which concentrates the direct light of lamp H as well as the light reflected from concave mirror MN. At the eye end E of the kaleidoscope is placed lens LL, close to the end of the reflectors, and having its center coincident with the center of the aperture at E. In order that this lens may form an image PP of the objects in cell CD, its focal length must be less than the length AE of the plates. From Sir David Brewster, Treatise on the Kaleidoscope *(Edinburgh: Archibald Constable, 1819).*

tators. One of Mr Bate's Polycentral Kaleidoscopes has been fitted up with a lamp of this kind, for exhibition, at the lectures on natural philosophy at Guy's Hospital, by that eminent chemist, William Allen, Esq. F.R.S." At the Royal Society and at the Royal Institution, Allen had delivered papers on respiration and on atmospheric gases. His kaleidoscopic exhibitions at Guy's Hospital, where he had been appointed lecturer in 1802, were primarily an occasion to demonstrate the advantages of the oxygen lamp, although he no doubt explained as well the optical principles of the illusion. Brewster himself elaborated the aesthetics of the optical effect. As in the response to music and architecture, the senses are pleased by the harmony and regularity of an object. The kaleidoscope, its very name indicating that it enables us "to see beautiful forms," serves the arts as an instrument for revealing beautifully symmetrical images. Whenever an artist seeks harmonic precision in ornamentation, whether in architecture or painting, the kaleidoscope gives him or her an exact model and an endless variety of designs. Other than his declaration that its symmetrical images will invariably please, Brewster has few specific suggestions for its use in the theater. A magical procession of figures might be made to revolve in an aerial dance. A single flame, he points out, could be transformed into "the most beautiful display of fireworks."[25]

Although Henry Hyde Wollaston's invention of the *camera lucida* (1807) was based on a relatively simple principle, another fifty years were to elapse before it was adapted to produce that truly astonishing stage illusion known as "Pepper's Ghost." Wollaston noted that by looking through a plain slip of glass held close to the eye and tilted at forty-five degrees he could see through the glass but could also see what was reflected in the glass. If the glass were held in a frame, he reasoned, so that his hands were free to draw on a sheet of paper below, he would be able to trace with precision the reflected image onto the paper. With a bit of experimentation, he substituted a silvered glass with an unsilvered slit to see through in order to obtain a more exact reflection. He went on to construct a rhombic prism (a 90° angle with a 135° angle opposite and 67½° angles at either side), which reflects a primary and a secondary image; since the secondary image can then be lined up with the clearly refracted sheet of paper, an even sharper projection is possible. Following Wollaston's experiments, Charles Wheatstone developed the first stereoscope in 1838. Brewster devised an improved twin-lens viewer; his binocular model was manufactured in Paris by Jules Duboscq, well-known maker of magic lanterns and optical equipment for the theater. The first moving-image stereoscope was devised by Czermak in 1855, and Coleman Sellers patented a stereoscopic flip-book viewer in 1864. These devices, of course, were limited to peep shows and, for the time being, seemed inapplicable to the stage.[26]

Brewster devoted continued attention to subjective illusions of motion. S. P. Thompson, in his paper on "Optical Illusions of Motion" (1880), places his own research on the visual aftereffect of motion (VAM) in the context of earlier accounts:

> a number of observations, collected at intervals over several years, have been added . . . to the stock of knowledge previously gleaned by Brewster, Wheatstone, Faraday, Plateau, and others. Brewster made a number of observations, in the early days of railways, on the various illusions which can be found by watching objects from a moving train; Wheatstone investigated a curious case of apparent fluttering motion at the border of two brightly illuminated colored surfaces—due probably to the attempt of the unachromatic eye to obtain fruitlessly a distinct focus of the border-line between the unequally regrangible colors—known as the illusion of the "Fluttering Hearts"; Faraday investigated the illusions produced by intermittant [*sic*] views of moving objects, since developed in the phenakistiscope and zoetrope, and kindred toys, and due to persistence of visual impressions. Brewster, moreover, drew attention to the existence of another class of illusions—illusions of complementary motion.[27]

The illusion of complementary motion which Brewster noted in the *Phantasmagoria,* and subsequently described as a visual aftereffect when watching the landscape from a moving train, is now usually recorded in the research on VAM as the "waterfall effect," so called because the rocks on either side of a waterfall seem to move upward after one has gazed for a while at the downward flow.[28]

What the research of Wollaston, Wheatstone, and Brewster revealed is that the eye, in its very alertness to motion, often misinterprets the sensory clues. In 1799, Alexander von Humboldt noted that stars would seem to drift while he looked at them through the telescope. Determining that the telescope had not moved and the position of the star had remained relatively fixed, he reasoned that the drift resulted from the muscular movement of the eyeball—a phenomenon now referred to as *autokinetic motion.* Another illusion of motion occurs in a darkened room when adjacent sources of light are alternately exposed and concealed: the viewer perceives a single light moving from one location to another. This illusion, called the *phi effect,* is commonplace today in electric signs that use rows of lights flashed on and off in succession to give the illusion of words or figures moving across the billboard.[29] In the early nineteenth century, such an illusion of animation could be projected on the stage by using two or three magic lanterns mounted together (bi-unial or triple lanterns) with a mechanical device for opening one aperture at a time.[30]

Among the several optical phenomena contributing to illusions of motion, those "due to persistence of visual impressions" were to have the greatest influence on the emerging technology of the theater. If one watches the wheels of a passing coach through a row of vertical slats (such as a picket fence, a palisade, or a venetian window blind), the movement of the wheel seems arrested and one seems to see the individual spokes. The spokes in the horizontal position seemed curved, while those toward the top and bottom are only slightly bent in the direction the wheel is moving. Peter Mark Roget became fascinated with this illusion. His account of the effects and his deliberation on the probable causes were presented to the Royal Society in 1824. He reasoned that the seemingly arrested motion resulted from the persistence of an image on the retina. One could, he said, measure "the duration of the impression of light on the retina by observing the apparent velocity of the visible portion of the spokes."[31] Roget estimated this duration to be one-thirtieth to one-fiftieth of a second. His account of the cinematic effect led to a number of experiments demonstrating not only how one could visually arrest objects in motion, but also how one could create moving pictures.

Shortly after Roget's announcement, Michael Faraday developed a simple demonstration of his own.[32] He cut a narrow slit in a cardboard disk and ran a pin through the center. With this circle mounted on top of a pattern, totally concealing it from view, Faraday showed that when the disk was spinning rapidly the hidden pattern was completely visible (fig. 10). Although only narrow segments of the design were exposed

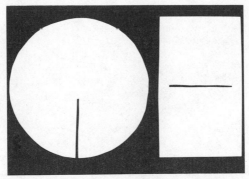

Fig. 10. Slit cards for Faraday effect and Parks effect. To observe the Faraday effect, affix the round slit card with a pin on top of a simple picture or design, concealing it from view. When the card is made to spin rapidly, the concealed picture becomes visible. For the Parks effect, see Figure 11.

in succession as the disk revolved, and then only for a fraction of a second, the fragments appeared as a whole image. The capacity of visual perception to reconstitute a whole image out of rapidly exposed parts, as recent work has shown,[33] involves more complex factors than simply the persistence of an afterimage. In a variation on Faraday's experiment, a design is moved rapidly past a stationary aperture (a vertical slit). Even under these adverse conditions (perception is limited to a single exposure through the slit of a moving image, whereas Faraday's disk passed many times over a stationary image), observers were capable of recognizing the image although it appeared foreshortened (fig. 11). Since all the various segments of the image strike the same retinal receptors, the reconstituted image cannot be adequately explained as the persistence of retinal response. The phenomenon, now referred to as *anorthoscopic perception*, apparently involves cognitive problem-solving as part of the perceptual drive to make sense of visual data. What we come to know orders and complements what we can actually see: we do not see what we think we see.

Although it was repeated throughout the rest of the century, Roget's hypothesis was nevertheless erroneous in attributing the illusion of motion to the persistence of a retinal image. Not motion but a blurred compounding of a series of images would result from mere persistence. The interesting, and still imperfectly understood, aspect of Roget's

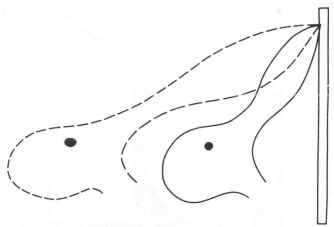

Fig. 11. Anorthoscopic illusion (Parks effect). "If a line drawing (dashed line above) is passed rapidly behind a slit in an otherwise opaque screen, viewers will often see that line faintly, briefly, and moving slightly, in the vicinity of the slit (solid line above)." From The Oxford Companion to the Mind, *ed. Richard L. Gregory, with the assistance of O. L. Zangwill (Oxford: Oxford University Press, 1987).*

demonstration is that a single coherent image is perceived. What Roget and Faraday had observed in their experiments is the *critical fusion frequency*.[34] Early motion pictures were actually just below that threshold at which the eye is still able to perceive the break in a succession of images. Even after the advent of the electric projector, the aptly named "flicks" were still slow enough to disturb the eye. Once the flicker rate reaches thirty to fifty times a second (depending on the brightness of the light), the flashing is perceived as a steady light.

In 1827, John Ayrton Paris introduced a "philosophical toy" that had immense popular appeal. He named it the "Thaumatrope": a card with a silhouette picture on each side and a loop of string affixed on two opposite edges. When the strings were wound, the card could be made to spin rapidly on its horizontal axis. The visual effect was that the silhouettes on each side of the card merged into one image. One card depicted a seated woman on one side and a trotting horse on the other; the spinning card revealed a woman riding a horse (fig. 12).[35] Within the next few years there were a number of contrivances for animating a series of drawings. Just as in Roget's experiment, these drawings were mounted on a wheel and viewed through slats. The resulting illusion was a moving picture: children tossing and catching rings, a figure climbing up and down stairs. Among the more successful of these early attempts to create a moving picture based on the hypothesis of visual

Fig. 12. Paris's thaumatrope. A card with a picture on each side is made to spin by pulling on wound strings. As the card rapidly spins, the two pictures seem to merge. Thus a card with a galloping horse on one side and a seated woman on the other would produce the illusion of the woman riding on the horse. From John Ayrton Paris, Philosophy in Sport made Science in Earnest, *with sketches by George Cruikshank, 3 vol. (London: 1827).*

persistence were Joseph Antoine Plateau's "Phenakistoscope" (Brussels, 1832), Simon Ritter von Stampfer's "Stroboscope" (Vienna, 1832), and W. G. Horner's "Zoetrope" (Bristol, 1834) (fig. 13). A magic lantern for projecting the moving pictures from Plateau-Stampfer disks was constructed by Franz von Uchatius in 1853.[36]

The popular fascination with visual display gave rise in the 1820s to the great success of the panorama and diorama. For the artists of theater scenery, this was a lucrative opportunity; too, it provided a new challenge to create special optical effects. Louis Jacques Mandé Daguerre, who had been a designer at the Théâtre Ambigu-Comique and at the Opéra, opened his first diorama in Paris in 1822 and his second one in Regent's Park, London, in 1823. Daguerre relied on a *camera obscura* to complete the realistic illusion in his grand scenes for the diorama. In

Fig. 13. Plateau's phenakistoscope. The disk depicts sixteen figures, each at consecutive stages of a pirouette. The card is cut out with the black slots removed for viewing, and mounted onto a rod (stick a pushpin through the center of the disk and into the eraser of a pencil). Face the sixteen figures toward a mirror, spin the disk, and view the reflected figures through the slots. The figures appear animated. From Joseph Antoine Plateau, "Relative à différentes expériences d'optique" (5 December 1829), in Correspondance Mathématique et Physique, *11 vols., ed. Lambert Adolphe Jacque Quetelet (Brussels, 1825–1839).*

1834, he adapted backlighting techniques to display a double-effect diorama. At the same time, he was also experimenting with photographic images; the discovery by Joseph-Nicéphor Niepce of a means to fix a camera obscura image aided Daguerre in the invention of his daguerreotype process in 1839. Photographic images on glass sliders, providing far more stunning realism than the hand-sketched glass sliders that had previously been displayed in the magic lantern, were available by 1850.[37]

Making the most of the pranks that Goethe adapted from the chapbook versions of the Faust story, such as those he gives to Mephisto in Auerbach's cellar, performances of *Faust,* in England and France as well as in Germany, freely indulged the magic of mechanical trickery. From what we know of the plans for production in 1812, the presentation of scenes from *Faust* in Berlin in 1819, and the first full performance in Weimar in 1829, Goethe called for more modest mechanical effects than the comments of his Director in the play's "Prologue in the Theater" would seem to suggest. He was especially intrigued by the use of the magic lantern in conjuring stage effects. His most elaborate architectural setting was commissioned for the "cathedral." Perhaps it was his fascination with optics and color theory[38] that prompted him to rely on the trickery of the magic lantern to introduce the supernatural into a contrastingly simple setting.

The appearance of the Earth Spirit, for example, was to be brought into Faust's study much in the manner of Rembrandt's painting of the scholar and the sign of the microcosm. Except, as Goethe sketched the scene (fig. 14), the image was to appear in giant proportions. At the time of the Berlin performance, he wrote to Count Brühl (2 June 1819):

This representation of the Earth Spirit conforms exactly with my intention. That he looks in through the window is ghostly enough. Rembrandt has used this idea very effectively in an engraved plate. When we, too, intended to take this scene and develop it for production, my conception was also simply to show transparently a colossal head and chest and I thought of adapting it from the well-known bust of Jupiter, for the words "horrible face" refer to the feelings of the observer, who would certainly be frightened by such an apparition, and could therefore be aptly addressed to the figure itself; even here there should appear nothing grimacing or disgusting. How one might, perhaps with flaming hair and beard, to some degree approach the modern idea of the supernatural, on this we had come to no agreement.[39]

Ten years later, when preparations were underway for the full production in Weimar, Goethe had decided that the supernatural scenes could be done in the manner of the popular phantasmagoria. He wrote to W. Zahn requesting him to obtain a magic lantern (12 December 1828):

> Prince Radziwill . . . had the appearance of the Spirit in the first scene presented in the phantasmagorical manner; that is, in a darkened theater an illuminated head is projected from the rear upon a screen stretched across the background, first as a small image, then gradually increasing in size, so that it seems to be coming closer and closer. This artistic illusion was appar-

Fig. 14. Apparition of the Earth Spirit, Faust, *Goethe's sketch (ca. 1810). From National Forschungs- und Gedenkstätte, Weimar, GDR.*

ently conjured with a kind of *Laterna Magica*. Could you please find out, as soon as possible, who constructs such an apparatus, how one could obtain it, and what preparations must be made for it?[40]

The conjuration in Faust's study (fig. 15), a scene written in 1800, was apparently conceived in much the same manner as the Apparition of the Earth Spirit. The demonic poodle has the "flaming hair" that Goethe associated with "the modern idea of the supernatural." Certainly, with

Fig. 15. Conjuring the poodle in Faust's study, Faust, *Goethe's sketch (ca. 1810). From National Forschungs- und Gedenkstätte, Weimar, GDR.*

the use of the *laterna magica* the "flaming" image could have been enhanced with red or orange tinted glass, and as Loutherbourg had done it, the flames could have been made to flicker with moiré shadows. Goethe's sketch shows the huge transparent head appearing in the framed alcove just beyond Faust's outstretched arm.

Another such trick was to be achieved with the mirror in the Witch's kitchen, making use of the technique of shifting from reflected image to projected image which Brewster describes in his account of stage illusions. The platinized glass developed by the Messrs. Dodé provided such a high quality of reflection that this illusion, achieved by backlighting a two-way mirror, could be staged very effectively. In Goethe's sketch (fig. 16), the flickering hearth is to the right and the magic mirror directly faces the audience from center stage. As Faust gazes at his image, his reflection is suddenly transformed into the radiant vision of the beautiful Helen of Troy.

The version of *Faustus* performed at Drury Lane in 1824, a hybrid loosely adapted from Goethe and Marlowe with a bit of Don Juan thrown in, compensated for its deficiencies in plot and dialogue with a wonderful array of stage effects. The role of Mephistopheles was shared by two actors identically costumed with large bat wings: Daniel Terry, who played the speaking role onstage; and O. Smith, who was concealed in the projection chamber offstage and appeared onstage only as

Fig. 16. Conjuring Helen in the Witch's kitchen, Faust, Goethe's sketch (ca. 1810). From National Forschungs- und Gedenkstätte, Weimar, GDR.

a phantom image. The projection apparatus was apparently much like Brewster's catadioptrical phantasmagoria. In the first conjuring scene, "a demon appears in clouds and fire" and, at Faustus's command, is transformed into human shape. Mephistopheles carries Faustus into the air and flies with him to Venice (although harness swings may have been used here, it is more likely that the simulated flight was also a projected image). In Act II, Faustus, having seduced Adine, wants to be rid of her. He calls upon Mephisto, who appears menacingly behind Adine. She lifts up her rosary; Mephisto cringes and vanishes. Faustus is next attracted to Adine's cousin Rosolia, who is carried off by Mephisto from Venice to Milan in another flight scene. In Act III, Rosolia's father, Count di Casanova, sends soldiers to arrest Faustus. Responding to Faustus's call to save him, Mephisto appears but stands idly by as the magician is carried off. Faustus tells Mephisto to kill the King, assume his shape, and order his release. The concluding scene owes all its theatrical power to the play of illusions: Mephisto decapitates the King (perhaps, as Brewster suggested, with a prism), briefly assumes the King's appearance, and then, instead of pardoning Faustus, resumes his original demon form and pronounces the magician's damnation: "the earth opens before them, and vomits forth fire."[41]

As director of Covent Garden, Charles Kemble made every effort to ensure that the production of *Oberon: or, The Elf-King's Oath* would be the most spectacular event ever seen on a London stage. In the summer of 1824, Kemble had sent an invitation to Carl Maria von Weber to appear at Covent Garden and personally conduct *Der Freischütz* and *Preciosa,* as well as a new opera to be especially composed for the occasion. Kemble suggested that a libretto might be taken either from Goethe's *Faust* or from Wieland's *Oberon.*[42] The original plan was for Weber to appear for three months of the 1825 season, but ill health forced him to postpone the engagement until March, April, and May of 1826. Following the production of *Der Freischütz* in March, the first performance of *Oberon* took place on April 12, 1826. For the "Aerial Machinery, Transformations, & Decorations" announced in the playbill, Kemble had commissioned William Bradwell, an expert in stage illusions.[43] Scenery he assigned to Thomas and William Grieve. And he arranged for James Robinson Planché to collaborate with Weber on the libretto.

Planché was an excellent choice to develop the sort of supernatural mystery and magic that Kemble knew would ensure a full house. In addition to his adaptations from Scott's *Kenilworth* (Adelphi, 8 February 1821) and Peacock's *Maid Marian* (Covent Garden, 3 December 1822), Planché had achieved considerable success with *The Vampyre; or, the Bride of the Iles* (English Opera House, 9 August 1820; Bath, 10 January 1821). *The Vampyre* opens with a stunning "Vision" and concludes with an even more stunning vanishing act. The curtain rises on a bedchamber where Lady Margaret lies asleep; by the use of backlighting, the walls of the chamber disappear and the sleeping lady is now seen within the basaltic Caverns of Staffa. In this "Vision" two spirits reveal the impending fate of the dreamer: she is about to be wed to the spirit of Cromal the Bloody, who wanders the earth by moonlight in the body of Ruthven, Earl of Marsden. He intends to drink her blood to preserve his vampire existence. In the final scene, Ronald, who has discovered Ruthven's vampire identity, struggles with the monster. The moon sets, a thunderbolt strikes Ruthven to the ground—and he vanishes before the eyes of all spectators. The trick was the first use of the English trap, or as it was also called, the vampire trap—an elevator drop built into the flooring of the stage (fig. 17).[44]

Fig. 17. English trap. From Georges Moynet, La Machinerie Théâtrale. Trucs et Décors *(Paris: La Librairie Illustrée, 1893).*

Planché made use of William Sotheby's translation of *Oberon;* the libretto was sent piecemeal to Berlin. Weber received the first act on December 30, 1824; the second and third acts arrived on January 18 and February 1, 1825. As in *The Vampire,* the opening scene involves a "Vision." Sir Huon is summoned by spirits to Oberon's bower. The surrounding foliage fades, revealing to Huon a distant view of Baghdad. Suddenly, before him appears the phantom image of Rezia, daughter of the Caliph. The harness swings of Bradwell's "Aeriel Machinery" enable Oberon's spirits to fly overhead. The "Transformation" from bower to Baghdad is managed by backlighting the screen drop; probably against this same drop is projected the image of Rezia. Act I, scene ii, reverses the visionary situation: in Namouna's cottage, Rezia has a dream vision of the stranger, Sir Huon, who will prevent her marriage to the horrid Prince Babekan.

Act II has three sumptuous scenes: the banquet hall of the Caliph, where Rezia is rescued with the aid of Oberon's magic horn; the palace gardens, where Rezia and Huon exchange vows of love; and the "Ravine amongst the Rocks of a Desolate Island," where they are shipwrecked. The first two of these scenes relied on the artistry of the brothers Grieve; the desolate island, however, called for Bradwell's optical effects as well as scene painting by Pugh. In addition to the modulation of the lighting to reveal cavern and ocean "in a Storm—a Calm—by Sunset—Twilight—Starlight—and Moonlight," Bradwell was projecting the shadowy "Spirits of the Storm" against the clouds painted on the semitransparent drop.

The most stunning effect in Act III, when Huon and Rezia are to be burned alive, may seem to repeat the magical rescue of Act II, but on this second occasion the horn's magic works more powerfully. Scherasmin, Huon's squire, arrives at the crucial moment to blow once again on Oberon's horn. A spell falls upon the Emir and his followers. "At the conclusion," writes Genest, "clouds envelop Oberon and Titania—and the scene changes to the palace of Charlemagne." If Bradwell followed Planché's *Vampyre,* which also opened with a vision and concluded with a vanishing act, he may have relied on an English trap for this last scene. Or, as in Huon's vision of Regia and Regia's dream of Huon, he may have used a projected image to cause Oberon and Titania magically to appear and disappear. His transformation of a double set through backlighting causes the Tunisian court to vanish as Charlemagne's hall of arms is brightened into view.[45]

In emphasizing the optical trickery in the production of *Oberon,* I do not mean to undervalue the musical score. The point, after all, is that stage illusion becomes part of the aesthetic ensemble. In the role of Sir

Huon, John Braham gave a moving rendition of "Ruler of this awful hour" in Act II. Enchantingly persistent from overture to finale, Weber's horn motif fully realizes, as romantic symbol, the conjuring power that Bradwell's illusions could only mimic. The overture—completed five days before the opening night, with instrumentation still being revised only the day before—was a resounding success. On the night of April 12, Weber wrote to his wife: "I obtained this evening the greatest success of my life. The emotion produced by such a triumph is more than I can describe. . . . The overture had to be executed twice. . . . At the end of the performance I was called on to the stage by the enthusiastic acclamations of the public; an honour which no composer had before obtained in England."[46] Kemble could not have realized at the time that Weber was dying of tuberculosis. He was wracked by fever and frequently coughed blood, but he managed to conduct all twelve performances (12–25 April). He died during the night of June 4, 1826.

During the 1820s the brighter illumination of the oxygen lamp made the magic lantern an increasingly useful instrument for stage effects. In the 1830s, with the intensity of the limelight, even more stunning illusions were possible. Just how an actor might make use of the projected images, however, required some experimentation. The interaction between actor and image, as we have seen in the *Faust* productions and in Planché's supernatural intrigues, could lend the optical effects a truly dramatic purpose. Edmund Kean, fascinated by the magic lantern illusions he had seen at Theodon's "Grand and Original Theatre of Arts" in Spring Gardens, was convinced that he should appropriate such effects for his production of *King Lear* (Drury Lane, 24 April 1820). Although Genest records with some surprise a month later that "King Lear and Mr. Kean continue their triumphant success," the spectacular storm scene was not an unqualified blessing.[47]

The playbill for April 27 (fourth performance) announced, "A Land Storm. After the manner of *Loutherburg's Eidophusikon*. Designed & executed by Marinari, and Assistants." The bill for May 2 (eighth performance) added the information that "The MEDIUM LIGHT has been adapted to this stage by W. A. Holland."[48] Marinari prepared the backdrop of a raging sea, and his sets for the cliff had trees that could be swayed mechanically; overhead his semitransparent screens would reveal, with appropriate lighting, the rising storm with Lear on the heath. Offstage, James Winston provided suitable sound effects for rain, wind, and thunder. From the fly gallery, Holland operated a lantern fitted with a color wheel. Joseph Leathley Cowell, a comedian at Drury Lane who had played Crack in *The Turnpike Gate* and Samson Rawbold in

The Iron Chest, viewed Kean's performance from a comic vantage that saw all too clearly how the sublime lapsed into the ridiculous: "Overhead were revolving prismatic coloured transparencies, to emit a continually changing supernatural tint, and add to the unearthly character of the scene. King Lear would one instant appear a beautiful pea-green, and the next sky-blue, and, in the event of a momentary cessation of the rotary motion of the magic lantern, his head would be purple and his legs Dutch-pink."[49] Kean's first use of the magic lantern was misdirected: unsure of how to engage the images on stage, he had the lantern focused on himself. Winston judged the storm scene "very successful,"[50] and the *European Magazine* declared that it heightened dramatic effect, "almost fixing the reality." Cowell, who saw that the magic lantern had dressed King Lear in radiant motley, also laughed at Winston's clatter: "every infernal machine that was ever able to spit fire, spout rain, or make thunder . . . were brought into full play." The *Times* agreed that "the manager, by a strange error, had caused the tempest to be exhibited with so much accuracy that the performer could scarcely be heard."[51]

As prolific writer of comedy, tragedy, melodrama, burletta, and operatic libretti, Edward Fitzball always endeavored to make the most of optical effects. In his works—from *The Flying Dutchman* (Adelphi Theatre, 1827) and *The Devil's Elixir; or, The Shadowless Man* (Covent Garden, 20 April 1829) to *Azael the Prodigal* (Drury Lane, 19 February 1851) and *Christmas Eve; or, A Duel in the Snow* (Drury Lane, 12 March 1862)[52]—the phantom images are fully integrated into the dramatic action. Daniel Terry and Frederick Yates were managing the Adelphi when Fitzball proposed *The Flying Dutchman*. When they balked because of production costs—to construct a ship for the stage would cost two hundred pounds—Fitzball pointed out that a phantom vessel would be no expense at all:

> Purchase a few yards of union [a sort of glazed calico], darken the scene by turning off the gas, then, while your invisible chorus, *rendered invisible by the darkness,* sing their corale [*sic*], draw off the flats, and Mr Child, a gentleman that I can recommend to you, will throw, with his magic lantern, on the invisible union, a better *phantom* ship than all the ship carpenters in Woolwich Dockyard could build, with Peter the Great to assist them.[53]

Phantom illusions were better and cheaper. This was a convincing argument. The production was a success, and Fitzball continued to collaborate with Henry Langdon Childe in producing optical wizardry on the stage. Among Childe's innovations in projection techniques, most important was his perfection of a shutter device for use with two or more lanterns. The lower part of the metal shutter blocked the light completely, and the upper part was cut into comblike teeth that partly obscured the light. As a shutter was cranked in front of the first lens, another shutter would open the second lens. The resulting "dissolving view" allowed one image to fade gradually into the next. Thus a barren tree could be made to blossom, bear leaves, gain its lush summer green, change to autumnal hues, shed its foliage, and gather in its bare boughs the falling snow. Childe even had an apparatus, a perforated black silk screen on rollers, that could be cranked before one lantern to make "snow" fall on the image projected by another lantern. Childe refined these techniques in a number of displays at the Adelphi Theatre and later at the Royal Polytechnic Institution (fig. 18), where he also introduced his "Chromatrope," a device with two counter-revolving glass color wheels for adding color effects.[54]

Fitzball doubtlessly owed a good measure of his success to his collaboration with Childe. Mixing motifs from Hoffmann's tale of Brother Medardus and Chamisso's Peter Schlemihl, Fitzball's *The Devil's Elixir; or, The Shadowless Man* provided, as one critic pronounced, "splendid effects of changes & scenes—but it is most silly & stupid."[55] The effect of the elixir is "that the person who drinks of it, may at his wish assume the shape of his rival—but with this distinction, that he can have no

Fig. 18. Magic lantern (with backstage effects), Royal Polytechnic Institute, 1832. From William Isaac Chadwick, The Magic Lantern Manual, with 100 practical illustrations *(London: R. Warne, 1878).*

shadow." The lighting was managed in the trial scene so that, when Count Hermogen passes a lamp, he casts a shadow on the wall, but when the Capuchin monk, his Doppelgänger, passes the same lamp, he casts no shadow. O. Smith, who by this time had played several parts assisted by the magic lantern, appeared and disappeared in his role as demon of the elixer.[56] In the final scene, Childe's "dissolving views" contributed effectively to the banishing of the demon as he attempts to pursue the repentant monk: the steps of the monk's cell crumble beneath his feet, the monastery walls begin to fade, a bolt of lightning strikes him, and he vanishes.

Twenty-two years later, when Fitzball produced *Azael the Prodigal* at Drury Lane, Childe had the advantage of limelight projection. Fitzball adapted freely from Scribe's libretto to Auber's *L'Enfant Prodigue* (Paris Opera, 6 December 1850). Childe apparently had a hand in the production of the opera at Her Majesty's Theatre as well as in the adaptations at Drury Lane (19 February 1851) and Astley's Theatre (3 November 1851). Abandoned in poverty and left to die in the desert, the prodigal son has a vision: he sees before him an image of his father, then his beloved Jepthele; from the distance an angel flies, hovers overhead, descends to stand before Azael, points the way home across the wasteland, and then disappears (fig. 19). The flight of the angel is man-

Fig. 19. Azael the Prodigal, Her Majesty's Theatre, 1851. From Illustrated London News, *XVIII (1851).*

aged by enlarging the image projected by one lantern; additional lanterns were in operation, for the vision required a sequence of many "dissolving views."[57]

"To heighten some of the effects," proclaimed the playbill for Balfe's *Joan of Arc* (Drury Lane, 30 November 1837), "a new and extraordinary Light will be introduced, called Phoshelioulamproteron." This was probably the first use of the limelight to enhance stage illusion. Because it projects a brighter image, the limelight made the magic lantern much more effective in the large theaters of London. Audiences were treated to spectral visions that deceived the eyes and perplexed the mind. Matthew Gregory Lewis's *The Castle Spectre* was revived so that the ghost of Evelina could haunt the stage in various degrees of visibility. In his retrospect on "Stage Ghosts" for *Gentleman's Magazine* (1887), W. J. Lawrence recollects a transparent Banquo in *Macbeth* and a parade of terrifying visions on Bosworth Field in *Richard III*:

> many efforts, some of them successful, were made, to render the stage ghost genuinely impressive. Thus when *Hamlet* was performed at Queen's Theatre, London, in 1846, "the appearances of the Ghost on the battlements and in the Queen's chamber were made behind some cleverly worked transparent scenery," a powerful light being so well utilized that "the shade of Hamlet's father actually acquired the semblance of being seen through."[58]

Frederick Lloyds employed a similar combination of limelight and backlit transparency in staging Queen Catherine's dream in *Henry VIII* (Princess's Theatre, 1855). When Queen Catherine slumbers, the paneled wall vanishes and her dream is revealed (fig. 20). What most astonished the spectators was the seemingly "actual presence" of countless "angels descending, gliding on a sunbeam."[59]

In 1858, Henry Dircks presented a paper to the British Association describing his invention of a mirroring device called the "Dircksian Phantasmagoria," or "Ætheroscope," for producing ethereal phantoms onstage.[60] The device was first used for a dramatization of Charles Dickens's "The Haunted Man" at the Polytechnic (24 December 1862). It involves a commonly experienced illusion: gazing out the window at twilight, we may see one of our room lamps standing in the garden; what is reflected in the window is superimposed on what is seen through the window. As noted above, Wollaston constructed his camera lucida on this principle of superimposing reflection and refraction. Dircks's device made use of a large pane of glass placed upright at a forty-five-degree angle to the front of the stage. Two concealed panels on either side, facing away from the pane, contained sets of Clegg lamps which were regulated so that when one set was brightened the other

Fig. 20. *Queen Catherine's dream,* Henry VIII, *Princess's Theatre, 1855. From* Illustrated London News, *XXVI (1855).*

was dimmed, and vice versa. An object placed at the back of the stage, directly in front of the audience, could be seen through the glass as long as the bright lamps were directed upon it; but as these lamps dimmed, an unseen object off in the left wing would be illuminated so that its reflection would appear in the glass, apparently in the very location as the first object. A living person could thus be replaced by a phantom image of a skeleton (fig. 21).

John Henry Pepper used this trickery so frequently at the Polytechnic that the illusion is still commonly referred to as "Pepper's Ghost." Among the productions at the Polytechnic were *Faust,* an "Operatic Mystery . . . with Gounod's Principal Music"; *Proteus! or, We Are Here But Not Here!;* and *The Haunted House.* Tom Taylor's *An Awful Rise in Spirits* (Olympic, 7 September 1863) provided a fine parody of the supernatural manifestations of Pepper and Dircks, who are burlesqued as Kepper and Quircks.[61] Taylor borrowed the personae of the spectre-drama—the Bleeding Nun of Lindenburg, Richardson's Ghost, and the Shade of Shakespeare—but had them comically switching places with their counterparts on the other side of the glass.

When Samuel Phelps began his long engagement at Drury Lane in 1863, he chose as his major performance of the season the title role in Byron's *Manfred.* The scenery and effects were to be arranged by

Fig. 21. John Henry Pepper's illusion: a living person transformed into a skeleton. From Albert A. Hopkins, Stage Illusions and Scientific Diversions *(New York: Munn & Co., 1898).*

William Telbin, who had acquired considerable expertise in optical techniques with his "Grand Moving Panoramas" at the Gallery of Illustration. Telbin and Thomas Grieve had been the artists for the panorama of the *Overland Mail to India* (1853) and had also built the stereorama of the *St. Gothard Route to Italy* (1860) at Cremorne Gardens. For convincing three-dimensional effects, nine hundred gallons of water per minute were piped through waterfalls and rivers, real smoke rose from chimneys, and windmills and coach wheels were mechanically turned.[62]

Phelps no doubt played a stunning Manfred, but as the *Spectator* declared, what drew the crowds "every night during the week has unquestionably been the scenery." Telbin's setting for Manfred's encounter with the Witch of the Alps (fig. 22) uses moiré shadows to create an illusion of flowing water in the waterfall painted on a semitransparent drop. Not content with a rainbow painted on the waterfall, nor even with a projected lantern transparency of a painted rainbow, Telbin used a prism and a concave mirror to project an arched rainbow onto the semitransparent drop. The sheer cliffs of the backdrop were visible behind it, and depth was enhanced by the trees, bluffs, and overarching cavern that framed the stage. The waterfall, then, was dramatically centered. It became the screen on which was projected not only the moiré

Fig. 22. *The Witch of the Alps,* Manfred, *Drury Lane, 1863. From* Illustrated London News, *XXXV (17 Oct. 1863).*

movement and the rainbow, but also the projected phantom of the Witch herself, who hovered radiantly above the mists of the waterfall. To project her giant image in motion, Telbin appropriated to the stage the Plateau-Stampfer magic lantern.[63] Even more stunning, according to the account in the *Spectator,* was Telbin's rendering of the underworld, where "Arimanes is seated on a globe of fire, in the centre of a vast amphitheatre filled with a lurid glare, and peopled by thousands of indistinctly seen spirits."[64]

When Phelps played Mephistopheles in *Faust* (Drury Lane, October 1866), he called for the same sort of stunning illusions. He obviously did not feel himself "upstaged" by Telbin's stage effects. As an actor well attuned to his audience and his age, he knew the public fascination with optical wizardry and made the most of it. He played Manfred as a character who dabbles with dangerous powers, exposes himself to awesome forces, yet is able to resist their enchantment and reassert his own will. Telbin's stage effects enhanced rather than diminished Phelps's interpretation of his role. The same claim cannot be made for all the drama of the romantic and early Victorian period. Optical effects often were the end as well as the means, and the quality of the drama was scarcely regarded. But the mechanics of illusion and the aesthetics of illusion were, in fact, not always in opposition.

In spite of his stated preference for the bare stage of Shakespeare's time, Coleridge, too, knew how to please an audience by staging a sorcerer at his dark altar suddenly dazzled by a flash of phosphorous— as in Coleridge's *Remorse* (Drury Lane, 23 January 1813). Stage illusion, after all, is not at odds with dramatic illusion. To be sure, one does work upon the eye and the other upon the imagination. But the eye, too, works upon the imagination. What is the nature of dramatic illusion? The answer requires attention to the lambent nature of visual images and the tenuous trust in perception. In exploring the physics of light and the physiology of sight, science has provided new means to challenge both perception and imagination.

That process continues to unfold. Confidence that the contemporary stage has achieved a *ne plus ultra* of technological perfection is well expressed in a review of a recent production of Wagner's *Tristan und Isolde* (Bayreuth, 1987): "It is no longer merely the boards upon which a player acts. The modern stage is high-tech equipment—without technology, aesthetic illusion would often be neglected. Soon the computer and laser-beams will provide perfect illusion."[65] The same sort of pride in the latest scientific advances will no doubt cause future critics, the Moynet or Hopkins of the next generation, to regret the sad deficiencies of the twentieth century.

Notes

1. Georges Moynet, *La machinerie théâtrale. Trucs et décors* (Paris, 1893); Albert A. Hopkins, *Stage Illusions and Scientific Diversions* (New York, 1898).

2. Samuel Taylor Coleridge, *Lectures 1808–1819, On Literature,* 2 vols., ed. Reginald A. Foakes, *The Collected Works of Samuel Taylor Coleridge,* 5 vols. (Princeton: Princeton Univ. Press; London: Routledge & Kegan Paul, 1987), 1:83, 512, 519; Wayne McKenna, *Charles Lamb and the Theatre* (New York: Harper & Row, 1978), 100–106.

3. "By 'Recreative Science', we understand the cultivation of the various branches of physical and mathematecal inquiry in a way to afford amusement as well as instruction," opening editorial in *Recreative Science* 1, 1 (1860): 1; quoted in Gerald L'E. Turner, *Nineteenth-Century Scientific Instruments* (Berkeley and Los Angeles: Univ. of California Press, 1983), 291. lications, 1983), 291.

4. Sir David Brewster, *Letters on Natural Magic, addressed to Sir Walter Scott* (London, 1832).

5. Ralph G. Allen, "The Eidophusikon," *Theatre Design and Technology* 7 (December 1966): 12–16; Richard Altick, *The Shows of London* (Cambridge, Mass.: Harvard Univ. Press, 1978), 117–27.

6. John Genest, *Some Account of the English Stage from the Restoration in 1660 to 1830,* 10 vols. (Bath, 1832), 5:549–50; W. J. Lawrence, "The Pioneers of Modern English Stage-Mounting: Philippe Jacques de Loutherbourg, R.A.,"

Magazine of Art 18 (1895): 172–77; Austin Dobson, *At Prior Park and Other Papers* (London, 1912), 94–127.

7. Ralph G. Allen, "*The Wonders of Derbyshire:* A Spectacular Eighteenth-Century Travelogue," *Theatre Survey* (1961): 54–66.

8. Carolyn M. Bloomer, *Principles of Visual Perception* (New York: Van Nostrand Reinhold, 1976), 43–44.

9. Genest, *English Stage*, 6:390; *Recollections of the Life of John O'Keefe, written by Himself,* 2 vols. (London, 1826); Ralph G. Allen, "De Loutherbourg and Captain Cook," *Theatre Research* 4 (1962): 195–211; Lillian E. Preston, "The Noble Savage: *Omai; or, A Trip Around the World,*" *Drama Critique* 8 (1965): 130–32.

10. Turner, *Scientific Instruments,* 303.

11. Altick, *The Shows of London,* 121–23.

12. *European Magazine* 1 (1782): 182; quoted in Altick, *The Shows of London,* 121.

13. Pinkethman's "landscape looks as an ordinary picture till the clock-work behind the curtain be set at work, and then the ships move and sail distinctly upon the sea till out of sight; a coach comes out of the town, the motion of the horses and wheels are very distinct, and a gentleman in the coach that salutes the company; a hunter also and his dogs, &c. keep their course until out of sight" (11 February 1708/9), *The Diary of Ralph Thoresby, F.R.S.,* ed. Joseph Hunter (London, 1830), 1:47–48; quoted in Altick, *The Shows of London,* 59.

14. T. C. Hepworth, *The Book of the Lantern, being A Practical Guide to the working of the Optical (or Magic) Lantern* (London, 1889; 4th ed., 1891), 3–15.

15. Terence Rees, *Theatre Lighting in the Age of Gas* (London: Society for Theatre Research, 1978), 42–43.

16. Altick, *The Shows of London,* 121.

17. Brewster, *Natural Magic,* 80–81.

18. William Nicholson, "Narrative and Explanation of Phantoms and other Figures in the Exhibition of Phantasmagoria. With Remarks on the Philosophical Use of common Occurances," *Journal of Natural Philosophy* 1, 2 (February 1802): 147–50.

19. Henry Hyde Wollaston, "On the apparent Direction of Eyes in a Portrait" (read 27 May 1824), *Philosophical Transactions of the Royal Society of London. 1824* (London, 1825), 247–56.

20. Brewster, *Natural Magic,* 118–24.

21. Ibid., 82–85.

22. Ibid., 85–87.

23. Ibid., 87–88.

24. Ibid., 61–66.

25. Brewster, *Treatise on the Kaleidoscope* (Edinburgh, 1819), 103–7.

26. Wollaston, "On a Camera Lucida," *Philosophical Magazine* 27 (1807): 343; Wollaston, "On a Periscopic Camera Obscura and Microscope" (read 11 June 1812), *Philosophical Transactions of the Royal Society of London. 1812,* 370; Charles Wheatstone, "Contributions to the Physiology of Vision. Part the First. On some remarkable, and hitherto unobserved, Phenomena of Binocular

Vision," *Philosophical Transactions of the Royal Society. 1838,* 371–94; Wheatstone, "On some remarkable, and hitherto unobserved, Phenomena of Binocular Vision (Part the Second)," *Philosophical Transactions of the Royal Society. 1852,* 1–17; Sir David Brewster, *The Stereoscope: Its History, Theory and the Construction, with Its Application to the Fine and Useful Arts and to Education* (London, 1856); see also Lenny Lipton, *Foundations of the Stereoscopic Cinema* (New York: Van Nostrand Reinhold, 1982), 16–31.

27. Silvanus Phillips Thompson, "Optical Illusions of Motion," *Brain* 3 (1880): 289–98. See also Michael Faraday, "On a Peculiar Class of Optical Deceptions" (read 10 December 1830), *Journal of the Royal Institution* (February 1831); Joseph Antoine Plateau, "Relative à différentes expériences d'optique" (5 December 1829), in *Correspondance mathématique et physique,* 11 vols., ed. Lambert Adolphe Jacque Quetelet (Brussels, 1825–39), 5.

28. Brewster, "On observing objects from a train window," *Proceedings of the British Association. 1848,* 47; R. Addams, "An Account of a peculiar optical phenomenon seen after looking at a moving body," *Philosophical Magazine* 5 (3rd ser., 1834): 373–74.

29. William N. Dember and Joel S. Warm, *Psychology of Perception,* 2d ed. (New York: Holt, Rinehart and Winston, 1979), 326–28.

30. *The Magic Lantern; its history and effects* (London, 1854).

31. Peter Mark Roget, "Explanation of an Optical Deception in the Appearance of the Spokes of a Wheel seen through vertical Apertures" (Royal Society of London, read 9 December 1824); Roget, "The Laws of Sensation and Perception" (Royal College of Physicians, Gulstonian Lectures, 1831).

32. Faraday, "On a Peculiar Class of Optical Deceptions."

33. T. E. Parks, "Post-retinal Visual Storage," *American Journal of Psychology* 78 (1965): 145–47; Irvin Rock and F. Halper, "Form Perception without Retinal Image," *American Journal of Psychology* 82 (1969): 425–40; I. Rock, "Anorthoscopic Perception," *Scientific American* 244 (1981): 145–53.

34. J. Hochberg and V. Brooks, "The Perception of Motion Pictures" (1978) in *Handbook of Perception,* ed. E. C. Carterette and M. P. Friedman, vol. 10 (New York: Academic Press, 1974–   ).

35. John Ayrton Paris, *Philosophy in Sport made Science in Earnest,* with sketches by George Cruikshank, 3 vols. (London: 1827), 3:14–19.

36. Martin Quigley, *Magic Shadows: The Story of the Origin of Motion Pictures* (Washington, D.C.: Georgetown Univ. Press, 1948), 85–97.

37. Louis Jacques Mandé Daguerre, *Historique et description des procédés du daguerréotype et du diorama* (Paris, 1839); trans. J. S. Memes, under the title *History and Practice of Photogenic Drawing on the true Principles of the Daguerréotype, with the new Method of Dioramic Painting* (London: Smith, Elder & Co.; Edinburgh, 1839); Altick, *The Shows of London,* 128–210.

38. Johann Wolfgang von Goethe, *Werke,* 143 vols. (Weimar: Hermann Böhlau, 1887–1912), II Abt., Bd. 1; *Goethes Farbenlehre,* ed. Rupprecht Matthaei (Ravensburg: Otto Maier, 1971); Goethe, *Theory of Colours,* trans. and annotated by Sir Charles Lock Eastlake (London, 1840). See also Frederick Burwick, *The Damnation of Newton: Goethe's Color Theory and Romantic Perception* (Berlin and New York: de Gruyter, 1986).

39. Goethe, *Werke,* IV Abt., Bd. 31, pp. 163–64 (my translation). The undated sketches for *Faust* were collected with Goethe's *Theaterzeichnungen,* presumably executed during his tenure as director of the Weimarer Hoftheater, 1791–1817. Now in the collection of the Nationale Forschungs- und Gendenkstätte, Weimar (NFG/GNM Corp. IVb 222, 223, 224, 227), they may have been sketched when the scenes were composed or, more probably, in anticipation of performance in 1812, 1819, or 1829. In his *Tag- und Jahresheften,* Goethe records that Pius Alexander Wolff had persuaded him to have *Faust* performed in 1812, and he had even begun to prepare stage settings ("Dekorationen und sonstiges Erfordernis"), *Werke,* III Abt., Bd. 4.

40. Goethe, *Werke,* IV Abt., Bd. 45, p. 80.

41. Genest, *English Stage,* 9:294–95.

42. Michael Leinert, *Carl Maria von Weber* (Hamburg: Rowolt, 1978), 115–17.

43. Lord Drogheda, Ken Dawson, and Andrew Wheatcroft, *The Covent Garden Album* (London: Routledge & Kegan Paul, 1981), 55; Altick, *The Shows of London,* 154–55.

44. Genest, *English Stage,* 9:123–24; James Robinson Planché, *Recollections and Reflections and Extravaganzas,* 2 vols. (London, 1872), 1:118.

45. Carl Maria von Weber, *Oberon: or, The Elf-King's Oath* (London, 1826); Genest, *English Stage,* 9:349.

46. *Reisebriefe von Carl Maria von Weber an seine Gattin Caroline,* ed. Carl von Weber (Leipzig, 1886), 111; Leinert, *Carl Maria von Weber,* 127–30.

47. Genest, *English Stage,* 9:35–36; Altick, *The Shows of London,* 214.

48. Rees, *Theatre Lighting,* 84–85.

49. Joseph Leathley Cowell, *Thirty Years Passed among the Players in England and America* (New York, 1845), 47.

50. *Drury Lane Journal. Selections from James Winston's Diaries, 1819–1827,* ed. Alfred L. Nelson and Gilbert B. Cross (London: Society for Theatre Research, 1974), 8.

51. *European Magazine* 77 (1820): 428; *Times* (25 April 1820), p. 2: quoted in Rees, *Theatre Lighting,* 84–85.

52. W. Davenport Adams, *A Dictionary of the Drama,* 3 vols. (Philadelphia: Lippincott, 1904), 1:520.

53. Edward Fitzball, *Thirty-five Years of a Dramatic Author's Life,* 2 vols. (London, 1859), 2:13–14.

54. *The Magic Lantern; its history and effects,* 21–25; *The Magic Lantern, Dissolving Views, and Oxy-hydrogen Microscope, described* (London, 1865), 11; William Isaac Chadwick, *Magic Lantern Manual* (London, 1878), 104–5; Hepworth, *The Book of the Lantern,* 7–15; Hepworth, "The Evolution of the Magic-Lantern," *Chamber's Journal* 1 (6th ser., 1897–98): 213–15; G. A. Household, *To Catch a Sunbeam: Victorian Reality through the Magic Lantern* (London: M. Joseph, 1979).

55. John Waldie, Journal, 85 vols., Special Collections, University of California, Los Angeles, 56:344 (1 June 1829).

56. His shared role with Terry as Mephistopheles in *Faustus* (Drury Lane, 1824) was apparently O. Smith's first such "phantom" part in a magic-lantern

production. He played Charlemagne in the Drury Lane version of *Oberon, or the Charmed Horn* (27 April 1826), produced as a rival to Weber's opera at Covent Garden. Another part requiring him to play in and out of magic-lantern images was his role as the monster in *Presumption, or the Fate of Frankenstein* (Covent Garden, 9 July 1824). Just the week before his appearance as the demon in Fitzball's *The Devil's Elixer,* O. Smith again performed as Frankenstein's monster (Covent Garden, 26 April 1829). Genest, *English Stage,* 9:259–60, 482–83.

57. *Illustrated London News* 18 (1851): 586; *The Standard* (20 February 1851), p. 3; Rees, *Theatre Lighting,* 88–91.

58. Adams, *A Dictionary of the Drama,* 1:575, quoting from W. J. Lawrence, "Stage Ghosts," *Gentleman's Magazine* (1887).

59. Frederick Lloyds, *Practical Guide to Scene Painting* (London, n.d. [1875?]), 86–87; *Illustrated London News* 26 (1855): 531; Godfrey Turner, "Show and Its Value," *The Theatre* 3 (1884): 231–32; Rees, *Theatre Lighting,* 52–53, 140.

60. Henry Dircks, *The Ghost, as produced in the Spectre-Drama, popularly illustrating the marvellous optical illusions obtained by the Apparatus called the Dircksian Phantasmagoria* (London, 1863); Altick, *The Shows of London,* 504–5. See also Terry Castle, "Phantasmagoria: Spectral Technology and the Metaphorics of Modern Reverie," *Critical Inquiry* 15 (Autumn 1988): 26–61.

61. Adams, *A Dictionary of the Drama,* 1:94–95.

62. Altick, *The Shows of London,* 207, 460, 480, 481n, 485.

63. Rees, *Theatre Lighting,* 78, notes that a rainbow was produced in a similar manner by Duboscq for the performance of Rossini's *Mosé* (Paris Opera, 1860). Duboscq had developed lanterns for projecting Plateau-Stampfer disks as well as for creating other special effects; see Jules Duboscq, *Catalogue des appareils employés pour la production des phénomènes physiques au théâtre* (Paris, 1877), and Quigley, *Magic Shadows,* 104–5, 109–10, 171.

64. *Spectator* 36 (17 October 1863): 2631; *Illustrated London News* (17 October 1863): 389; Martin Meisel, *Realizations: Narrative, Pictorial, and Theatrical Arts of the Nineteenth Century* (Princeton: Princeton Univ. Press, 1983), 178–79.

65. Hans-Peter Kurr, "Hinter den Kulissen," *Scala* (January–February 1988): 46–49.

Bibliography

ADAMS, W. DAVENPORT. *A Dictionary of the Drama.* 3 vols. Philadelphia: Lippincott, 1904.

ADDAMS, R. "An Account of a peculiar optical phenomenon seen after looking at a moving body." *Philosophical Magazine* 5 (3rd ser., 1834): 373–74.

ALLEN, RALPH G. "De Loutherbourg and Captain Cook." *Theatre Research* 4 (1962): 195–211.

———. "The Eidophusikon." *Theatre Design and Technology* 7 (December 1966): 12–16.

———. "*The Wonders of Darbyshire:* A Spectacular Eighteenth-Century Travelogue." *Theatre Survey* 2 (1961): 54–66.

ALTICK, RICHARD. *The Shows of London*. Cambridge, Mass.: Harvard University Press, 1978.

BLOOMER, CAROLYN M. *Principles of Visual Perception*. New York: Van Nostrand Reinhold, 1976.

BREWSTER, SIR DAVID. *Letters on Natural Magic, addressed to Sir Walter Scott*. London, 1832.

_____. "On observing objects from a train window." *Proceedings of the British Association. 1848*, 47.

_____. *The Stereoscope: Its History, Theory and the Construction, with Its Application to the Fine and Useful Arts and to Education*. London, 1856.

_____. *Treatise on Optics*. London, 1831.

_____. *Treatise on the Kaleidoscope*. Edinburgh, 1819.

BURWICK, FREDERICK. *The Damnation of Newton: Goethe's Color Theory and Romantic Perception*. Berlin and New York: de Gruyter, 1986.

CASTLE, TERRY. "Phantasmagoria: Spectral Technology and the Metaphorics of Modern Reverie." *Critical Inquiry* 15 (Autumn 1988): 26–61.

Catalogue of the Special Loan Collection of Scientific Apparatus at the South Kensington Museum. London, 1876, 3d ed., 1877.

CHADWICK, WILLIAM ISAAC. *The Magic Lantern Manual, with 100 practical illustrations*. London, 1878.

COLERIDGE, SAMUEL TAYLOR. *Lectures 1808–1819, On Literature*. 2 vols. Ed. Reginald A. Foakes, *The Collected Works of Samuel Taylor Coleridge*, 5 vols. Princeton: Princeton University Press; London: Routledge & Kegan Paul, 1987.

COWELL, JOSEPH LEATHLEY. *Thirty Years Passed among the Players in England and America*. New York, 1845.

DAGUERRE, LOUIS JACQUES MANDÉ. *Historique et description des procédés du daguerréotype et du diorama*. Paris, 1839.

_____. *History and Practice of Photogenic Drawing on the true Principles of the Daguerréotype, with the new Method of Dioramic Painting*. Trans. J. S. Memes. London: Smith, Elder & Co.; Edinburgh, 1839.

DEMBER, WILLIAM N., and JOEL S. WARM. *Psychology of Perception*. 2d ed. New York: Holt, Rinehart and Winston, 1979.

DIRCKS, HENRY. *The Ghost, as produced in the Spectre-Drama, popularly illustrating the marvellous optical illusions obtained by the Apparatus called the Dircksian Phantasmagoria*. London, 1863.

DOBSON, AUSTIN. *At Prior Park and Other Papers*. London, 1912.

DROGHEDA, LORD, KEN DAWSON, and ANDREW WHEATCROFT. *The Covent Garden Album*. London: Routledge & Kegan Paul, 1981.

DUBOSCQ, JULES. *Catalogue des appareils employés pour la production des phénomènes physiques au théatre*. Paris, 1877.

FARADAY, MICHAEL. "On a Peculiar Class of Optical Deceptions" (read 10 December 1830). *Journal of the Royal Institution* (February 1831).

FITZBALL, EDWARD. *Thirty-five Years of a Dramatic Author's Life*. 2 vols. London, 1859.

GENEST, JOHN. *Some Account of the English Stage from the Restoration in 1660 to 1830*. 10 vols. Bath, 1832.

GOETHE, JOHANN WOLFGANG VON. *Goethes Farbenlehre.* Ed. Rupprecht Matthaei. Ravensburg: Otto Maier, 1971.

———. *Theory of Colours.* Trans. and annotated by Sir Charles Lock Eastlake. London, 1840.

———. *Werke.* 143 vols. (Weimar: Hermann Böhlau, 1887–1912).

Handbook to the Special Loan Collection of Scientific Apparatus, South Kensington Museum. London, 1876.

HEPWORTH, T. C. *The Book of the Lantern, being A Practical Guide to the working of the Optical (or Magic) Lantern.* London, 1889; 4th ed., 1891. 4th ed., 1891.

———. "The Evolution of the Magic-Lantern." *Chamber's Journal* 1 (6th ser., 1897–98).

HOCHBERG, J., and V. BROOKS. "The Perception of Motion Pictures" (1978). In *Handbook of Perception,* ed. E. C. Carterette and M. P. Friedman, vol. 10. New York: Academic Press, 1974– .

HOPKINS, ALBERT A. *Stage Illusions and Scientific Diversions.* New York, 1898.

HOUSEHOLD, G. A. *To Catch a Sunbeam: Victorian Reality through the Magic Lantern.* London: M. Joseph, 1979.

Lantern. London: M. Joseph, 1979.

HUTTON, CHARLES. *Recreations in Mathematics and Natural Philosophy.* Trans. from the French of Montucula. 4 vols. London, 1803.

KURR, HANS-PETER. "Hinter den Kulissen." *Scala* (January–February 1988): 46–49.

LAWRENCE, W. J. "The Pioneers of Modern English Stage-Mounting: Philippe Jacques de Loutherbourg, R.A." *Magazine of Art* 18 (1895): 172–77.

———. "Stage Ghosts." *Gentleman's Magazine* (1887).

LEINERT, MICHAEL. *Carl Maria von Weber.* Hamburg: Rowolt, 1978.

LEREBOURS, N. P. *A Treatise on Photography.* Trans. J. Egerton. London, 1843.

LIPTON, LENNY. *Foundations of the Stereoscopic Cinema.* New York: Van Nostrand Reinhold, 1982.

LLOYDS, FREDERICK. *Practical Guide to Scene Painting.* London, n.d. (1875?).

MCKENNA, WAYNE. *Charles Lamb and the Theatre.* New York: Harper & Row, 1978.

Magic and Pretended Miracles. London, 1848.

The Magic Lantern, Dissolving Views, and Oxy-hydrogen Microscope, described. London, 1865.

The Magic Lantern; its history and effects. London, 1854.

MARION, F. *Wonders of Optics.* New York, 1869.

MAYHEW, EDWARD. *Stage Effect: or, The Principles which Command Dramatic Success in the Theatre.* London, 1840.

MEISEL, MARTIN. *Realizations: Narrative, Pictorial, and Theatrical Arts of the Nineteenth Century.* Princeton: Princeton University Press, 1983.

MOYNET, GEORGES. *La machinerie théâtrale. Trucs et décors.* Paris, 1893.

NICHOLSON, WILLIAM. "Narrative and Explanation of Phantoms and other Figures in the Exhibition of Phantasmagoria. With Remarks on the Philosophical Use of common Occurances." *Journal of Natural Philosophy* 1, 2 (February 1802): 147–50.

O'KEEFE, JOHN. *Recollections of the Life of John O'Keefe, written by Himself.* 2 vols. London, 1826.

PARIS, JOHN AYRTON. *Philosophy in Sport made Science in Earnest.* With sketches by George Cruikshank. 3 vols. London: 1827.

PARKS, T. E. "Post-retinal Visual Storage." *American Journal of Psychology* 78 (1965): 145–47.

PIESE, G. W. S. *Chymical, Natural, and Physical Magic.* 3d ed. London, 1865.

PLANCHÉ, JAMES ROBINSON. *Recollections and Reflections and Extravaganzas.* 2 vols. London, 1872.

PLATEAU, JOSEPH ANTOINE. "Relative à différentes expériences d'optique" (5 December 1829). In *Correspondance mathématique et physique,* 11 vols., ed. Lambert Adolphe Jacques Quetelet, vol. 5. Brussels, 1825–39.

PRESTON, LILLIAN E. "The Noble Savage: *Omai; or, A Trip Around the World.*" *Drama Critique* 8 (1965); 130–32.

QUIGLEY, MARTIN. *Magic Shadows: The Story of the Origin of Motion Pictures.* Washington, D.C.: Georgetown University Press, 1948.

REES, TERENCE. *Theatre Lighting in the Age of Gas.* London: Society for Theatre Research, 1978.

ROCK, IRVIN. "Anorthoscopic Perception." *Scientific American* 244 (1981): 145–53.

ROCK, IRVIN, and F. HALPER. "Form Perception without Retinal Image." *American Journal of Psychology* 82 (1969): 425–40.

ROGET, PETER MARK. "Explanation of an Optical Deception in the Appearance of the Spokes of a Wheel seen through vertical Apertures." 9 December 1824.

———. "The Laws of Sensation and Perception." Royal College of Physicians, Gulstonian Lectures, 1831.

Thaumaturgia; or, Elucidations of the Marvelous. By an Oxonian. London, 1835.

THOMPSON, SILVANUS PHILLIPS. *Faraday: His Life and Work.* 1898.

———. "Optical Illusions of Motion." *Brain* 3 (1880): 289–98.

THORESBY, RALPH. *The Diary of Ralph Thoresby, F.R.S.* Ed. Joseph Hunter. London, 1830.

TURNER, GERALD L'E. *Nineteenth-Century Scientific Instruments.* Berkeley and Los Angeles: University of California Press, 1983.

TURNER, GODFREY. "Show and its Value." *The Theatre* 3 (1884): 231–32.

WALDIE, JOHN. Journal. 85 vols. Special Collections, University of California, Los Angeles.

WEBER, CARL MARIA VON. *Oberon: or, The Elf-King's Oath.* London, 1826.

———. *Reisebriefe von Carl Maria von Weber an seine Gattin Caroline.* Ed. Carl von Weber. Leipzig, 1886.

WHEATSTONE, CHARLES. "Contributions to the Physiology of Vision. Part the First. On some remarkable, and hitherto unobserved, Phenomena of Binocular Vision." *Philosophical Transactions of the Royal Society. 1838,* 371–94.

———. "On the apparent Direction of Eyes in a Portrait" (read 27 May 1824).

Philosophical Transactions of the Royal Society of London. 1824, 247–56. London, 1825.

WINSTON, JAMES. *Drury Lane Journal. Selections from James Winston's Diaries, 1819–1827*. Ed. Alfred L. Nelson and Gilbert B. Cross. London: Society for Theatre Research, 1974.

WOLLASTON, HENRY HYDE. "On a Camera Lucida." *Philosophical Magazine* 27 (1807): 343.

————. "On a Periscopic Camera Obscura and Microscope" (read 11 June 1812). *Philosophical Transactions of the Royal Society of London. 1812*, 370.

————. "On the apparent Direction of Eyes in a Portrait" (read 27 May 1824). *Philosophical Transactions of the Royal Society of London. 1824*, 247–56. London, 1825.

Reviews

Review of the performance of *Azael the Prodigal*, Drury Lane. *The Standard* (20 February 1851).

Review of the performance of *Azael the Prodigal*, Drury Lane. *Illustrated London News* 18 (1851): 586.

Review of Loutherbourg's *Eidophusikon*. *European Magazine* 1 (1782): 182.

Review of performance of *Henry VII*, Princess Theatre. *Illustrated London News* 26 (1855): 531.

Review of performance of *King Lear*, Drury Lane. *European Magazine* 77 (1820): 428.

Review of performance of *King Lear*, Drury Lane. *Times* (25 April 1820), 2.

Review of performance of *Manfred*, Drury Lane Theatre. *Illustrated London News* (17 October 1863), p. 389.

Review of performance of *Manfred*, Drury Lane Theatre. *Spectator* 36 (17 October 1863): 2631.

Self-Reflexive Metaphors in Maxwell's Demon and Shannon's Choice
Finding the Passages

N. KATHERINE HAYLES

IN A SENSE, all language is metaphoric. When a carpenter says that a room is seven yards long, he is comparing the length of the room to the length of an Anglo-Saxon girdle. When a scientist says that a molecule has a diameter of 2.5 angstroms, the standard has changed but the principle is the same; the object is still understood in terms of its relation to something else.[1] A completely unique object, if such a thing were imaginable, could not be described. Lacking metaphoric connections, it would remain inexpressible.[2] The question is thus not whether metaphors are used in science as well as literature, but rather how metaphors are constituted in the two disciplines, how they change through time, and how they are affected by the interpretive traditions in which they are embedded.

In discussing how metaphors work, Paul Ricoeur points out that it is misleading to analyze a metaphor at the level of individual words, for the essence of a metaphor is the relation it establishes between words.[3] A metaphor posits a connection rather than a congruence. It points to a similarity, but the similarity is striking because in other respects the concepts are very different. A metaphor is vital only for as long as the relation is problematic—that is to say, as long as similarity and difference are both perceived to be present. When differences in the relation have been so successfully suppressed through use and habit that they are no longer capable of putting a torque or, as Ricoeur says, a "twist" on our understanding of the concepts, the metaphor is dead. "There are no live metaphors in a dictionary," Ricoeur asserts.[4] In this he is not quite correct, for metaphors that appear dead may be brought back to active tension again through their interplay with the surrounding context, as the split writing of deconstruction has taught us. Dead metaphors too easily suggest corpses that can be safely buried and forgotten. Rather than thinking of metaphors as dead or alive (adjectives that are themselves dead as metaphors), I prefer to consider them dormant or active. The distinction is important to the story I have to tell, for it is a narrative of metaphors expanding and collapsing, fading into dormancy and being tightened into tension by changing cultural contexts in interplay with disciplinary traditions.

The story begins with a thought experiment proposed by James Clerk Maxwell in 1879 which came to be known as "Maxwell's Demon." Maxwell's Demon is one of the most famous conundrums in the history of science and has provoked over a hundred years of commentary, interpretation, revision, and speculation. It sparked a crucial development in information theory, marking the inscription into scientific discourse of a new attitude toward chaos and disorder. This development I call "Shannon's Choice," after the decision Claude Shannon made to equate information with entropy, rather than oppose them as had been accepted practice until then. This decision was possible, I argue, because the underlying heuristic had changed, allowing the problem that Maxwell's Demon had posed to be conceptualized in a new way. The example illustrates how scientific theory can be guided by conceptual sets embodied in heuristic narratives, even though these are not part of the theory as such. If this is true, then metaphor may play a larger and more active role in scientific theorizing than has hitherto been recognized.

Heuristic fictions such as Maxwell's Demon are like metaphors in that they posit a relation between the fiction and the theory which gestures toward similarity at the same time that it encounters the resistance of difference. The loose bagginess of the fit between the heuristic fiction and the theory is important, for it can open passages to new interpretations. Equally important is the language used to construct the heuristic. Following Max Black, Ricoeur observes that "to describe a domain of reality in terms of an imaginary theoretical model is a way of seeing things differently by changing our language about the subject of our investigation."[5] The detour through language which the heuristic represents creates polysemous connections not present in the theory itself.[6] Overlaying a heuristic onto a theory is never merely an inert transposition of concepts, for it generates a surplus of signification that can lead to interpretations not intended by the person who proposed the theory or, for that matter, the heuristic.

Within the redescription process the heuristic entails, moments of special complexity appear when this process contains a metaphor that self-reflexively mirrors the heuristic itself. A traditional visualization of a metaphor images it as a geometric compass, with one leg grounded and one leg moving free. The grounded leg alludes to the similarities between concepts brought into relation by the metaphor; the freely moving leg evokes the differences between them which can cause our understanding to land at unexpected points. A metaphor that self-reflexively mirrors itself in another metaphor threatens to lose the grounding that reassures us the comparison is not entirely free-floating. Postmodern writers have exploited this lack of ground to reveal the intrinsic reflexivity of all language. Borges's emblem of a staircase that ends in space, leading not to a door but to vertigo, speaks to the dangerous potential of metaphors to expose the ungrounded nature of discourse.

From a scientist's viewpoint, the vertiginous staircase explains very well why metaphors have not been admitted as valid components of the scientific process. Already suspicious of the looseness that a freely moving compass leg would imply, they are even warier of a mode of speaking, thinking, and writing which can lose its ground entirely. What this response misses is the fact that language is always already metaphoric. If we do not feel vertigo, it is because long usage has inured us to balancing over the abyss. At moments of dangerous reflexivity, when polysemy of metaphor threatens to overwhelm scientific denotation with too much ambiguity, the tradition confronts the new possibilities that metaphor has brought into play. My story is thus also about the interplay between the inertia of disciplinary traditions and the free-floating possibilities of self-reflexive metaphors. What the tradition would close off, the metaphor opens up; what the metaphor would destabilize, the tradition tries to recuperate.

In an early essay, Roland Barthes distinguishes between science and literature through their different attitudes toward language.[7] Science, Barthes says, regards language instrumentally. For science, language (which is nothing) serves only to transmit concepts (which are everything). In literature, language is not a vehicle transmitting the object, but the object itself. Barthes is interested in what happens to this dichotomy between literature and science when structuralism is injected into it. Structuralism prides itself on being a science but has its roots in linguistics. Derived "from linguistics, structuralism encounters in literature an object which is itself derived from language."[8] The question Barthes raises is whether structuralism will (like a science) pose itself above its object or whether it will recognize that it is itself composed of the language it would take for its object. Anticipating the advent of deconstruction and other poststructuralist theories, Barthes predicts that structuralism "will never be anything but one more 'science' . . . if it cannot make its central enterprise the very subversion of scientific language . . . [it must work to] abolish the distinction, born of logic, which makes the work into a language-object and science into a meta-language, and thereby to risk the illusory privilege attached by science to the ownership of a slave language."[9]

Since Barthes wrote these lines, the project he outlined for structuralism has, of course, spread far beyond its boundaries.[10] So pervasive is the recognition today that language is never transparent that it seems almost quaint to associate the insight exclusively with structuralism. If structuralism has been superseded, however, the project Barthes set forth has not. The task of understanding how scientific languages are implicated in the concepts they convey remains one of the important problems of literature and science. To this project the study of self-reflexive metaphors can offer distinctive contributions, for at these moments science necessarily confronts the enfolding of language-as-object into its assumed stance as a meta-language. That is to say, at these moments science confronts its literariness.

The self-reflexive metaphor is analogous to the encoding scheme that Kurt Gödel worked out in proving his Incompleteness Theorem, whereby statements about numbers were made simultaneously to function as statements about statements about numbers.[11] Gödel's theorem proves that it is always possible to devise a coding scheme (for formal systems complicated enough to allow arithmetic to be done in them) that will collapse the distance between statements and meta-statements. The result of this conflation of a meta-language with an object language is an inherent undecidability that defeats all attempts at formal closure. If we take Gödel's theorem as itself a metaphor for self-reflexive metaphors, it suggests that at these moments an inherent undecidability emerges that cannot be resolved within the system itself. This is why reflexive metaphors often function as crossroads or junctures, for the undecidability opens up passages that result in new directions.

At this point I am obliged to address a difficulty in which I immediately become involved if I suggest that the remarks above constitute a theory that the rest of my essay will apply in practice. Insofar as my comments about self-reflexive metaphors imply a theory, it is a theory about the impossibility of separating theory from practice, formal results from heuristics, language-as-concept from language-as-vehicle. To illustrate how my own practice already determines my theory even as I articulate it, consider the lines in which I attempt to explain how metaphor works: they are shot through with metaphors, from corpses to compasses. Since I can explain metaphor only through metaphors, practice interpenetrates theory from the beginning—a situation I will henceforth recognize by putting "theory" in quotation marks. If my "theory" is correct, it implies that the attempt to arrive at a theory about literature and science is hopeless from the outset, for theory is always already determined by disciplinary practices that are necessarily different for literature and for science.[12]

In science, "theory" generally means a set of interrelated propositions which has predictive power and therefore has the potential to be falsified. By contrast, in literature, "theory" means a set of speculative statements which serves as a guide to reading and interpreting texts. Literary critics do not attach much importance to the predictive power of literary theories, for most would agree that one's theoretical orientation determines what will be seen, at least in part. A literary "theory" falls into disuse not because it has been falsified, but because its assumptions have become so visible to those who practice it that it can no longer effectively create the illusion that it is revealing something about the text which is intrinsically present, independent of its assumptions.

What does it mean, then, to posit a theory about literature and science? To answer this question, one would have to presuppose a set of disciplinary practices which constitutes literature and science as a field of its own. Supposing that such distinctive practices exist (a proposition I regard as problematic), the resulting "theory" will be different from theories about literature and theories about science. It will not, however, be a meta-theory capable of subsuming theories in other disciplines it surveys. The only hope for a truly interdisciplinary theory, it seems to me, is a "theory" about the impossibility of creating a theory that will not be implicated in disciplinary practice. Such a "theory" is interdisciplinary not because it transcends disciplines, but because it recognizes the rootedness of every theory in the discursive practices characteristic of its discipline.

In this essay, I intend to explore the implications of a "theory" about scientific metaphor by engaging in a recursive analysis that traces the play of surplus meaning in Maxwell's Demon until the interpretive tradition arrives at a self-reflexive moment, that is, a point where the heuristic becomes a metaphor for itself. At that moment, a new interpretive fiction is born which differs fundamentally from the heuristic that fathered it. This fiction is Shannon's Choice, in which Shannon associates information with disorder rather than order. In its turn, Shannon's Choice also engendered a self-reflexive metaphor that opened new passages, this time into the paradigm known as chaos theory.

In retrospect, it appears that these self-reflexive moments acted like switches on a railroad track, sending the train of thought in a different direction. Or perhaps they occurred because the views to which they led had been highly energized by cultural events, and the self-reflexive moments acted as conduits or fissures that allowed culturally energized ideas to erupt into the scientific traditions. However the self-reflexive moments came about, they created instabilities within the heuristics which were amplified into vortices of turbulent signification. Out of these vortices, like Venus from the sea, arose new attitudes toward chaos which called into question the traditional relation of order to disorder, information to meaning, human understanding to that which it understands.

To appreciate the complexities of Maxwell's Demon, it is first necessary to understand *entropy*—a formidable task, because the word has undergone so many changes in meaning that the term actually refers to a group of different concepts. It makes no sense to ask what entropy "is," as though it were possible to find in this protean signifier a transcendent signification. Instead, we must ask what it meant to whom, for what reasons, in what context, and with what consequences.[13]

The word *entropy* entered the language when Rudolf Clausius coined it from a Greek word meaning "transformation." To Clausius, entropy was linked to the inevitable degradation of heat that occurs in any heat exchange.[14] Entropy is a measure of the heat lost for useful purposes. Suppose you boil water in a kettle, pour the water into a mug, and put your hands around the cup. Some of the stove's heat is lost to the air and kettle; some to the mug and your hands. If we consider the heat exchanges in the room as a whole, we find that the total amount of heat remains nearly constant (neglecting that lost to the environment outside the room). But after the transactions are complete, much of the heat is in such diffuse form that it can no longer be harnessed for useful purposes. Clausius expressed the fact that no energy is lost through the first law of thermodynamics, which states that the total amount of energy in a closed system remains constant. The first law says nothing, however, about the *form* in which this energy exists. This issue is addressed by the second law, which decrees that in a closed system entropy always tends to increase. The second law implies that no real heat transfer can be 100 percent efficient.[15]

It did not take scientists long to realize that, if some energy is always lost for useful purposes in every heat exchange, there will eventually come a time when no heat reservoir exists anywhere in the universe. At this point the universe experiences "heat death," a final state of equilibrium in which the temperature stabilizes at about −270 degrees centigrade and there is no longer any heat differential to do work or sustain life. These implications of the second law were made explicit in 1852 by William Thomson (Lord Kelvin), the great British thermodynamicist. Kelvin summarized them in three "general conclusions."[16] First, "there is at present in the material world a universal tendency to the dissipation of mechanical energy"; second, "any restoration of mechanical energy, without more than an equivalent of dissipation, is impossible . . . and is probably never effected by means of organized matter, either endowed with vegetable life or subjected to the will of an animated creature"; and third, "within a finite period of time . . . the earth must again be unfit for the habitation of man as at present constituted."[17]

Implicit in Kelvin's rhetoric are connotations that link these scientific predictions with the moral concerns of Victorian society.[18] The convergence of social formation with scientific concept is registered through language, illustrating how language-as-instrument is always already enfolded into language-as-concept. The "universal tendency toward dissipation" places entropic heat loss in the same semantic category as deplorable personal habits. To reverse this tendency requires a "restoration." But any attempt at reform only creates more dissipation. To achieve a *net* restoration is beyond the power of "organized matter"; the adjective implicitly acknowledges that matter may be unorganized, itself subject to entropic decay. As the passage builds to its climax, it moves up the chain of being. "Vegetable life" cannot conquer entropy; neither can "animate creatures," even though they possess wills capable of "subjecting" matter. As a result of these failures, "the earth *must again* be unfit for the habitation of man." Human existence is thus bracketed between a prehistoric past and a thermodynamic future. As the earth reverts back to the primordial chaos from which divine will had fashioned it, man must inevitably perish if he remains "as at present constituted." For man to escape this dismal prediction, some unimagined transformation would have to take place.

These connotations are embedded within a text and a discipline concerned with the transfer and conservation of heat—concerns that had direct application to the expansion of the British Empire, which is why thermodynamics is sometimes called the science of imperialism. To Kelvin and his fellow thermodynamicists, entropy represented the tendency of the universe to run down, despite the best efforts of British rectitude to prevent it. In Kelvin's prose, the rhetoric of imperialism confronts the inevitability of failure. In this context entropy represents an apparently inescapable limit on the human will to control.

The very slight margin of escape Kelvin allowed himself in his prediction was well advised, for the second law quickly became one of the most controversial results of thermodynamics. An important development came in 1859, when James Clerk Maxwell published a paper deriving the properties of a gas from the most probable speeds of its particles.[19] The implications of Maxwell's methodology were not at first apparent, for it was thought that his statistical treatment was merely a convenient way of treating systems about which one has incomplete information. Later it was recognized as a philosophical landmark, because it supported the view that thermodynamic laws are statistical generalizations rather than laws in an absolute sense. According to this interpretation of the second law, there is nothing to prevent the air molecules in a room from clustering in one corner. Such an event has an infinitesimally low probability; calculations show that it is quite unlikely to happen once during the time the universe has been in existence. Small as it is, this tiny margin of improbability keeps the second law from having the force of absolute truth. Strict determinism thus yielded to probabilistic prediction in Maxwell's interpretation of entropy.

Another important step came when Ludwig Boltzmann extended Maxwell's statistical method to arrive at a more general understanding of entropy as a measure of the randomness or disorder in a closed system. Boltzmann calculated the entropy S as $S = k (\log W)$, where k is a universal constant and W is the number of ways the system can be arranged to yield a specified state. Suppose we flip a coin four times, and for each set of four tosses record the results. Only one arrangement gives four heads—$HHHH$. But there are six ways to get two heads and two tails:

$$HHTT \quad HTHT \quad HTTH$$
$$TTHH \quad THTH \quad THHT$$

The quantity W in Boltzmann's formula is therefore larger for the two heads/two tails state than for four heads, because there are more ways to arrive at the mixed state. This result corresponds with our common-sense intuition that it is safer to bet that a poker hand has cards of different suits than cards all in the same suit. The more mixed up or randomized the final state, the more probable it is because the more configurations there are that lead to it. Thus in Boltzmann's formula the entropy increases with the probability of a given distribution, with the most dispersed being the most probable.

Although Boltzmann and Clausius interpreted entropy differently, it is possible to reconcile the two interpretations. Heat is essentially a measure of internal energy. For gases, this correlates with how fast molecules are moving. The hotter the gas, the more entropic it is in Clausius's terms because the more heat it loses as it undergoes heat exchanges. It is also more entropic in Boltzmann's sense because the faster molecules move, the more mixed up they become. The two formulations are thus equivalent—but they are not identical. The statistical interpretation contains important implications that the heat formulation lacks. To think of entropy as a statistical measure of disorder allows its extension to systems that have nothing to do with heat engines. In fact, so rich in significance is the statistical view of entropy that its full implications are still being explored. Its immediate consequence was to weaken further the absoluteness of a predicted heat death by giving entropy an interpretation that was overtly probabilistic rather than deterministic.

With this background, we are now ready to consider the thought experiment that Maxwell proposed to test the second law. In a short note near the end of *Theory of Heat*, Maxwell envisioned a microscopic being who could separate fast molecules from slow ones in a closed system and so decrease the system's entropy without doing work. So concise is Maxwell's description that it may be quoted directly.

> If we conceive a being whose faculties are so sharpened that he can follow every molecule in its course, such a being, whose attributes are still as essentially finite as our own, would be able to do what is impossible for us. . . . Now let us imagine [that a vessel full of air] is divided into two portions, *A* and *B*, by a division in which there is a small hole, and that a being, who can see the individual molecules, opens and closes the hole, so as to allow only the swifter molecules to pass from *A* to *B*, and only the slower ones to pass from *B* to *A*. He will thus, without expenditure of work, raise the temperature of *B* and lower that of *A*, in contradiction to the second law of thermodynamics.[20]

It is difficult to know how seriously Maxwell took this heuristic fiction. Its brevity and location suggest that the passage was almost an afterthought. Nevertheless, Maxwell's Demon generated a debate that continues to engage the attention of mathematicians, physicists, and engineers. We may wonder why, since the second law was never seriously

the same frequency as they absorb it. Since vision depends on sensing a difference between absorbed and radiated light frequencies, the demon would have no way to "see" the molecules. Imagine trying to see a black object in an absolutely dark room; that is the Demon's position inside the box.

Then Brillouin demonstrated that, if a source of illumination is introduced (for example, a headlamp), the absorption of this radiation by the system increases the system's entropy more than the Demon's sorting decreases it. Thus information gathered by the Demon is "paid for" by an increase in entropy. This result resolves the conundrum by showing that for the system as a whole the second law is not violated. More important than saving the second law (a quixotic adventure, since it was not in jeopardy) was Brillouin's intuition that entropy and information were connected. This insight led directly to Brillouin's conclusion that information is defined by the corresponding amount of negative entropy.[24]

Just as Brillouin sought out Szilard's paper and retrospectively established it as his predecessor, so his work has been read retrospectively by himself and others. In these readings, the aspect of Brillouin's solution that is underscored is the creation of a context in which information could be divorced from human intelligence. Ehrenberg's article reviewing the controversies over Maxwell's Demon points out that "[in Brillouin's analysis] the agent does not rely on his intelligence, since he needs physical means to obtain the information—but given the physical means we do not need the agent any longer because we can replace him by a machine!"[25] Brillouin expanded upon this aspect of his interpretation by later emphasizing that information theory completely eliminates the "human element."[26] The threshold was passed; the Demon no longer functioned as a liminal figure mediating between human limitations and inhuman entropy. The dream behind the Demon was realized in another sense, however, for the potent new force of information had entered the arena to combat entropy.

As the implications of Brillouin's analysis were explored, the tensions embedded in the subtext of Maxwell's Demon were transformed rather than resolved. One viewpoint, which set human intelligence and will against entropy, became irrelevant; another, which pitted information and machines against entropy, had emerged. From now on, control was increasingly seen not in terms of human will fighting universal dissipation, but as information exchanges processed through machines. As the world vaulted into the information age, the limiting factor became the inability of human intelligence to absorb the information that machines could produce.[27]

This current of thought surfaced explicitly in the most recent addition to the heuristic, based on work by Rolf Landauer and Charles H. Bennett.[28] Following Brillouin, scientists in the 1950s thought that data-processing operations were thermodynamically irreversible, that is, that they required heat dissipation as the price paid for performing the information-processing operation. Because the amount of heat involved was extremely small, the question was of little practical consequence. But it was important theoretically, for it posited a connection between entropy and information that reinforced Brillouin's interpretation of Maxwell's Demon. When Landauer performed calculations to test this hypothesis, he found that only some data-processing operations were thermodynamically costly. Specifically, he discovered that the irreversible (or costly) processes were those requiring the destruction of information.[29]

Armed with this demonstration, Bennett returned to Szilard's paper to clarify that the Demon's operation really consisted of two steps: a measurement step and a memory step (because the Demon has to remember where he put the slow and fast molecules). Brillouin had suggested that the entropic increase was a result of the measurement step. Bennett refuted this idea by devising a reversible measuring device that allowed measurements to be made without increasing the entropy.[30] In effect, he showed how the Demon could find out where the molecules were without needing to shine a headlamp. He then proposed that the true source of the increasing entropy was in the memory step. Since the demon will eventually run out of memory space if he does not clear outdated information out of his memory, at some point he must destroy information, which according to Landauer's demonstration has to be paid for by an increase in entropy. If one supposes a demon (or a computer) with a very large memory, he could of course simply remember all the measurements. The trouble with this scenario, Bennett explains, is that "the cycle would not then be a true cycle: every time around, the engine's memory, initially blank, would acquire another random bit [of information]. The correct thermodynamic interpretation of this situation would be to say that the engine increases the entropy of its memory in order to decrease the entropy of its environment."[31]

Acknowledging that "we do not usually think of information as a liability," Bennett proposes an analogy to make his conclusion plausible. "Intuitively, the demon's record of past actions seems to be a valuable (or at worst a useless) commodity. But for the demon 'yesterday's newspaper' (the result of a previous measurement) takes up valuable space, and the cost of clearing that space neutralizes the benefit the demon derived from the newspaper when it was fresh." Arriving belatedly in the tradition surrounding Maxwell's Demon, Bennett can appreciate more easily than his predecessors that there is a strong correlation between his explanation and his historical moment. He ends his article with the conjecture that perhaps "the increasing awareness of environmental pollution and the information explosion brought on by computers have made the idea that information can have a negative value seem more natural now than it would have seemed earlier in this century."[32] The surplus meaning characteristic of heuristic fictions thus receives explicit acknowledgment from within the scientific community. Moreover, the play of excess meaning has brought forth interpretations of the heuristic which are concerned with how information is created and destroyed. The stage is set for a self-reflexive moment to occur.

To see how this moment arrives, consider the multileveled, self-reflexive nature of Bennett's interpretation. When he argues that the crux of the problem lies in the destruction of information, his interpretation is engaging in an erasure of previous information analogous to what is happening within the heuristic, according to his interpretation. Of course, earlier interpretations also had to compete against received ideas to gain acceptance. But in Bennett's case, the operation performed by his interpretation is mirrored by the operation that he sees the Demon performing. Moreover, he recognizes that his interpretation reinscribes within the heuristic cultural forces operating at the moment of interpretation. Thus the heuristic is seen as a kind of permeable membrane connecting the culture to the disciplinary tradition. Just as the culture is becoming aware that old newspapers do not spontaneously disappear but pile up, so the demon is interpreted as needing to clear "yesterday's newspaper" out of his head. As metaphor is enfolded into metaphor, the scientific tradition is forced to confront the fact that thought, language, and social context evolve together. Social context affects language, language affects thought, thought affects social context. The circle is closed. Objectivity has given way to hermeneutics.

I want now to turn to another juncture in the cascading bifurcations that mark interpretations of Maxwell's Demon. The juncture occurs when Leon Brillouin and Claude Shannon diverge in their opinions about what the relationship between information and entropy should be. In Brillouin's analysis of Maxwell's Demon, the Demon's information allowed him to sort molecules, thus decreasing the system's entropy; but this information had to be paid for by an even greater increase in entropy elsewhere in the system. For Brillouin, then, information and entropy are opposites and should have opposite signs. He emphasized the inverse connection between information and entropy by coining "negentropy" (from *negative entropy*) as a synonym for information.

To Shannon, an engineer at Bell Laboratories who published two papers that were to form the basis of modern information theory,[33] information and entropy were not opposites. They were identical. When Shannon devised a probability function that he identified with information, he chose to call the quantity calculated by the function the "entropy" of a message. Why he made this choice is unclear. Rumor has it that von Neumann told Shannon to use the word because "no one knows what entropy is, so in a debate you will always have the advantage."[34] One could argue that von Neumann's comment was only one element and that the choice of entropy was overdetermined, with multiple factors leading to its conflation with information. On a conceptual level, an important consideration was the similarity between Shannon's equation for information and Boltzmann's equation for entropy. Because the two equations had similar forms, it was tempting to regard the entities they defined as the same. On the level of language, entropy was compelling because it was a term of recognized importance and could be expected to grant immediate legitimacy to the concept of information. On a cultural level, Shannon's choice anticipated the contemporary insight that proliferating information is associated with the production of entropy. Recall, for example, Landauer's conclusion that it is not obtaining but *erasing* information that dissipates energy. The proposition implies that too much information, piling up at too fast a rate, can lead to increasing disorder rather than order. For postmodern society, the compelling fable is not Maxwell's Demon but *My Brother's Keeper,* the story about two reclusive brothers who were finally buried under the *New York Times* they compulsively saved. What we fear most immediately is not that the universe will run down, but that the information will pile up until it overwhelms our ability to understand it.

Whatever the reasons for Shannon's choice, it is regarded by many commentators within the scientific tradition as a scandal, for it led to the (metaphoric) knotting together of concepts that are partly similar and partly dissimilar. Typical is Denbigh and Denbigh's reaction in their careful study of how the quantity defined by Shannon's equation differs from thermodynamic entropy. Recounting the story about von Neumann's advice, they write that thus "confusion entered in and von Neumann had done science a disservice!"[35] Jeffrey S. Wicken is even more explicit, calling Shannon's choice "loose language" that served "the dark god of obfuscation." "As a result of its independent lines of development in thermodynamics and information theory, there are in science today two 'entropies,'" Wicken writes. "This is one too many. It is not science's habit to affix the same name to different concepts. Shared names suggest shared meanings, and the connotative field of the old tends inevitably to intrude on the denotative terrain of the new."[36]

Clearly Wicken's concern is to restore scientific univocality by closing off the ability of the information-entropy connection to act as a metaphor rather than a congruence. Yet at the same time, he admits that shared language creates an inevitable "intrusion" into the "denotative terrain" of one term by the "connotative field" of another. The problem is more scandalous than he recognizes, for whenever a heuristic is proposed, it necessarily uses "shared names" that cause scientific denotation to be interpenetrated with cultural connotations. For what else is language but "shared names"? As Wittgenstein has observed, there are no private languages. Moreover, the distinction between denotative and connotative language is itself part of the distinction between language-as-vehicle and language-as-concept which metaphors, and particularly self-reflexive metaphors, bring into question. To turn Wicken's argument on its head, we might say he recognizes that metaphors in general, and the information-entropy connection in particular, directly threaten science's ability to separate ideas from the language it uses to express them.

In his anxiety to suppress the metaphoric potential of Shannon's choice, Wicken misses the richly complex and suggestive connections that were instrumental in enabling a new view of chaos to emerge.[37] By the simple fiat of using information and entropy as if they were interchangeable terms, Shannon's choice gave rise to decades of interpretive commentary that sought to explain why information should be identified with disorder rather than order. For the alliance between entropy and information to be effective, information first had to be divorced from meaning (a premise made explicit in Shannon's 1948 papers) and had to be associated instead with novelty. Suppose, for example, that a random number generator produces a tape that we can read. No matter how long we watch the tape, numbers keep appearing in unpredictable sequences. From one point of view, this situation represents chaos; from another, maximum information.

Once randomness was understood as maximum information, it was possible to envision chaos (as Robert Shaw does) as the source of all that is new in the world.[38] Wicken is correct in noting that denotative and connotative fields overlap; in the case of information, the connotation that "intruded" upon the denotative field of chaos was complexity. In the interdisciplinary research front known as the science of chaos,

chaos does not mean simply disorder. Rather, it names a kind of behavior that is distinct both from classical order and statistical disorder. Chaotic or complex systems are disordered in the sense that they are unpredictable, but they are ordered in the sense that they possess complex recursive symmetries that almost, but not quite, replicate themselves over time. The metaphoric joining of entropy and information was instrumental in bringing about these developments, for it allowed complexity to be seen in information rather than deficient in order.[39]

To see how Shannon's choice embodies a self-reflexive moment, it will be necessary to understand more precisely how informational entropy is like and unlike thermodynamic entropy. Shannon defined information as a function of the probability distribution of the message elements.[40] Information in Shannon's sense does not exist in the same way as the dimensions of this book exist. A book can be measured as twelve inches long, even if there are no other books in the world. But the *probability* that a book has that dimension is meaningful only if there are other books to which it can be compared. If all books are twelve inches long, the probability that a given book has that dimension is one, indicating complete certainty about the result. If half of the books are twelve inches, the probability is one-half; if none are, it is zero. Similarly, information cannot be calculated for a message in isolation. It has meaning only with respect to an ensemble of possible messages.

Shannon's equation for information calculated it in such a way as to have it depend *both* on how probable an element is *and* on how improbable it is. Having information depend on the probability of message elements makes sense from an engineer's point of view. Efficient coding reserves the shortest code for the most likely elements (for example, the letter *e* in English), leaving longer codes for the unlikely ones (for instance, *x* or *z*). Improbable elements will occupy the most room in the transmission channel because they carry the longest codes. Thus for a channel of given capacity, fewer improbable elements can be sent in a unit of time than probable ones. This explains why an engineer would think it desirable to have a direct correlation between probability and information.

Why have information correlate with improbability? Partly compensating for the longer codes of improbable elements is the greater information they carry. To see why improbable elements carry more information, suppose that I ask you to guess the missing letter in *ax_*. It is of course *e,* the most probable letter in an English text. Because it is so common, *e* can often be omitted and the word will still be intelligible. In *axe,* the letter e carries so little information that *ax* is an alternate spelling. Suppose, by contrast, that I ask you to guess the word *a_e*. You might make several guesses without hitting the choice I had in mind—*ace, ale, ape, are, ate*. When you find out that the expected letter is *x*, you will gain more information than you did when you learned that the final letter is *e*. Shannon's equation recognizes this correspondence by having the information content of a message increase as elements become more improbable.

This dual aspect of information is immediately apparent when information is plotted as a function of probability. The resulting curve is a parabolic arc, as shown in figure 1. (This diagram describes the simplest case, when the probabilities of message elements are independent of one another.) The diagram illustrates that, as the probability increases, the information increases until it reaches a maximum, when the probability is one-half. Then it begins to decrease as the message becomes highly probable. When the probability is one—that is, when there is no uncertainty about what the message will be—the information drops to zero, just as it does when the message is completely improbable. Maximum information is conveyed when there is a mixture of order and surprise, when the message is partly anticipated and partly surprising.

We are now in a position to understand exactly how Shannon's equation for informational entropy differs from thermodynamic entropy. Although Shannon's equation for information has the same form as Boltzmann's equation for entropy, what the probabilities *mean* in the two equations is different. In Boltzmann's equation, the probabilities derive from a lack of specific information about the system's microstates. Thermodynamic quantities such as temperature and entropy are macrostate properties; that is, they are statistical averages that represent the collective actions of millions of molecules. According to the

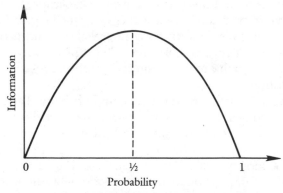

Fig. 1. Information as a function of probability

uncertainty principle, we have no way to know how a single particle behaves. Our ignorance of the microstates is reflected in the probabilistic form of Boltzmann's equation. By contrast, in Shannon's equation the probabilities derive from *choice* rather than ignorance; they reflect how probable it is that we would choose one message element rather than another, given a known ensemble (for example, the alphabet).

Wicken has a good example that can be adapted to illustrate this difference.[41] Suppose that I ask you to place a die on a table for a thousand consecutive times, each time choosing which face you want to place upward. Shannon's equation calculates the information of the resulting sequence as a function of the number of times a face actually turns up, compared to how often it could be predicted to turn up based on how many die faces there are. The uncertainty implied by the probability function reflects my ignorance about which choices you will make, not about which die faces have appeared. To imagine an analogous case for thermodynamic entropy, suppose that a thousand dice are cast all at once, and a measuring instrument records the total amount of light reflected from the die faces. We do not know how each individual die landed. However, after calibrating the light instrument, we could figure out the average face count, based on the amount of light reflected. In this case the probability function reflects ignorance of the microstates, not ignorance of our choices in assembling a series of such states.

In the heuristic that evolved around Shannon's choice, the difference between informational entropy and thermodynamic entropy is not made clear. On the contrary, since the point of the heuristic is to justify Shannon's choice, differences between informational and thermodynamic entropy are suppressed in favor of similarities. But as in metaphors, the differences are not negligible. They put a torque on the heuristic that twists how entropy is understood. This torque registers itself as a perturbation in the language of the commentators, as they struggle to suture the gap created by difference without ever quite acknowledging that there *is* a gap.

Warren Weaver was Shannon's first, and perhaps most important, commentator.[42] His explanation for why information correlates with disorder rather than order set a precedent that other commentators would follow for at least twenty years. Reasoning that if a message is perfectly ordered the receiver will be able to guess what it will say, Weaver suggests that a "noisy" message will be more surprising and hence will convey more information. This leads him into a quandary, for by this reasoning gibberish should convey the maximum possible information. To close off this possibility, Weaver introduces a distinction between desirable and useless information. True, gibberish is maximum information. But since it is not desired, it does not really count as information. Hence, the maximum amount of information is conveyed by a message that is partly surprising and partly anticipated.

This explanation produces the result required by the theory, which as we have seen defines information through a curve whose maximum occurs precisely at the midpoint between certainty and uncertainty. To arrive at this conclusion, the heuristic must inject the receiver's knowledge as a factor. But the probabilities defined by Shannon's equation do not depend on the receiver's knowledge of the message. They are determined solely by the frequency with which a given element appears, relative to its predicted frequency of appearance in the ensemble. To suture this gap, attention was turned to a quantity in one of Shannon's equations which did depend on the receiver's knowledge—an ambiguous quantity that Shannon called, appropriately, the "equivocation."

One of Shannon's important contributions was to create a schematic of the communication situation which made clear that there is no such thing as an unmediated message. By dividing the communication situation into a sender, an encoder, a channel, a decoder, and a receiver, Shannon demonstrated that any message is always subject to the intrusion of "noise." Noise can be anything that interferes with the receiver's receiving the same message that the sender sent—misprints in a book, lines in a television image, static on a radio, coding errors in a telegram, mispronunciations in speech. Noise is measured in the same units as information; indeed, it *is* information, but information not intended by the sender. The amount of information contributed by noise is called the "equivocation."

As an employee of American Telephone & Telegraph, Shannon was interested in transmitting messages as accurately as possible, and he naturally considered the equivocation as an unwanted intrusion that should be subtracted from the received message to get the original message back again. But Weaver, in his commentary on Shannon's papers, proposed that in some instances the equivocation might be seen as a desirable addition to the message rather than as an interference. This ambiguity in the sign of the equivocation turned out to be extremely fruitful, for it led to a new view of the communication process in which noise was seen as playing a constructive rather than a destructive role.

Henri Atlan's article "On a Formal Definition of Organization" illustrates this view.[43] Atlan points out that equivocation in a message can sometimes lead the system to reorganize itself at a higher level of complexity—for example, when a genetic mutation results in a positive adaptation trait. He therefore proposes that we distinguish between two different kinds of equivocations—a "destructive" one that interferes negatively with a message and an "autonomy-producing" one that stimulates a system to undergo reorganization. How an "autonomy-producing" equivocation is seen depends on where the observer is stationed. If he or she is inside the channel, the equivocation is an interference, for from this frame of reference one is interested only in the message. However, if outside the channel, he or she can see the effect on the system as a whole. The observer's knowledge thus reenters the picture, but it is constituted differently than in the Shannon-Weaver heuristic. For Atlan it is not knowledge of the message that counts, but knowledge of the system as a whole.

The point I want to make in tracing the genealogy from Shannon's theory to Weaver's commentary to Atlan's proposal is that it was precisely the multivocality of the information-entropy connection which allowed new views to emerge. At the center of this multivocality is a self-reflexive moment. When the equivocation came to be seen as a potentially positive quantity within the Shannon heuristic, the heuristic became a metaphor of itself, for in making equivocation an equivocal quantity, the heuristic acknowledged that there was surplus meaning not only within the communication channel, but within itself also. The constructive role that surplus meaning can play was then metaphorically incorporated into the "order out of chaos" paradigm in the recognition that noise can sometimes cause a system to reorganize at a higher level of complexity. Thus, as with Maxwell's Demon, my story ends with a heuristic that had become self-reflexive on multiple levels.

It remains to clarify what role disciplinary practices had in shaping the heuristics of my story, as well as in-forming my story of the heuristics. I can illustrate by returning to an unresolved crux in my story—the disagreement between Shannon and Brillouin on whether information should have the same or opposite sign as entropy. When I surveyed several dozen textbooks on information theory to see how they treated the information/entropy crux, I found a clear division along disciplinary lines. Almost without exception, textbooks written by electrical engineers followed the Shannon-Weaver heuristic, explaining that the more uncertain a message was, the more information it could convey.[44] Like Weaver, these writers withdrew from the obvious conclusion that gibberish is maximum information by saying that a mixture of surprise and certainty was needed. Also like Weaver, they did not recognize the implicit contradiction with Shannon's theory. On the whole, they did not devote much space to the question of how thermodynamic entropy was related to informational entropy.

Textbooks written by chemists, physicists, and thermodynamicists, by contrast, usually adopted the Brillouin explanation, developing the concept of information through its connection with thermodynamic entropy.[45] Maxwell's Demon figured prominently in these explanations and led to the expected conclusion that entropy and information should have opposite signs. For these authors, the problem of how thermodynamic entropy related to informational entropy was compelling; most of them devoted several pages to the question. The ability of both heuristics to replicate themselves through several generations of textbooks is striking evidence of the effectiveness of disciplinary traditions in erecting boundaries that marginalize or trivialize what happens outside them.

In fact, the problem of how Brillouin's negentropy relates to Shannon's entropy is not especially complex or difficult. In 1968, John Arthur Wilson demonstrated that Brillouin's proofs still hold true if the signs are reversed and the "negentropy" concept dropped.[46] But the debate continues because the heuristics are informed by other associations. Brillouin's heuristic grew out of his analysis of Maxwell's Demon, and this analysis makes sense *only* if information and entropy are opposites. By contrast, Shannon's heuristic concentrates on the circuits necessary to transmit messages, and these circuits emphasize the intrinsic uncertainty of message transmissions. Embodied in the heuristics are values extraneous to the formal theories but essential to the mindsets out of which they grew.

The crucial differences revealed by the heuristics are two opposite ways of valuing disorder. These differences are implicit in Wilson's reasons for dropping "negentropy." He argues that by defining information as the opposite of entropy, Brillouin is "attributing to information a quality which it does not have—the quality of being organized."[47] It is the connotation that disorder is the enemy of order and thus of information that is debated in the heuristics, not the denotative results of the theories themselves. When information could be conceived of as *allied* with disorder, a passage was opened into the new paradigm of chaos theory which is still in the process of unfolding.

Within the heuristics, the crux of the disagreement lies in where the commentator positions himself or herself with respect to the transmission process. Both heuristics agree that entropy correlates with uncertainty. But the Shannon heuristic foregrounds the uncertainty present before the message is sent, whereas the Brillouin heuristic focuses on the uncertainty that remains after the message had been received. The difference between the two viewpoints can now be succinctly stated. *Shannon considers the uncertainty in the message at the source, whereas*

Brillouin considers it at the destination. To ask which is correct is like asking whether a glass is half-empty or half-full. The answer is important not because it is correct, but because it reveals an orientation toward the glass and, by implication, an attitude toward life. Similarly, the Brillouin and Shannon heuristics reveal different attitudes toward chaos by their orientations toward the message.

Like the optimist and pessimist regarding a glass of water, Shannon and Brillouin locate themselves at the halfway point of the information-probability arc and look in opposite directions (fig. 2). Shannon, looking forward, sees a downward sloping curve and argues that the more certain the message is, the less information there is. Brillouin, looking backward, also sees a downward curve and argues that the more surprising a message is, the less information there is. Both recognize that maximum information comes when there is a mixture of certainty and surprise. But where Brillouin emphasizes certainty, Shannon stresses surprise.

These different orientations are no doubt related to the different contexts in which the two men lived and worked. Brillouin began his career in thermodynamics, a discipline that had traditionally envisioned disorder as humanity's enemy. From Kelvin on, entropy had been seen by thermodynamicists as an inhuman chaos that would win in the end, try as we might to resist it. Shannon, by contrast, worked for AT&T, a company that made its living satisfying people's curiosity. The more uncertain people were—about the stock market, national news, or events in other cities—the more they sent telegrams, made phone calls, required information. No wonder Shannon thought of uncertainty as

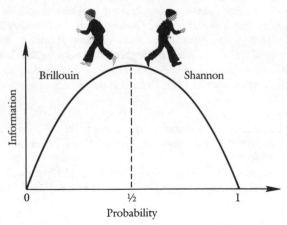

Fig. 2. Locating Shannon and Brillouin on the information curve

information's ally, whereas Brillouin saw the two as antagonistic. The controversy illustrates how scientific traditions are seen in a false light if they are regarded solely as self-contained, rationally coherent discourses. Concepts and theories are important. But so are the heuristics that explain them, the language that constitutes them, the disciplinary practices that inform them, and the cultural contexts that interpenetrate them.

Within the heuristic I have created to tell my story—that is, the self-reflexive moment—the values of my own discipline are clearly inscribed. For someone steeped in literary analysis, it is a given that multiple signification is a plus rather than a minus, or to use metaphors more appropriate to literature, a story rather than a scandal. The metaphoric play that I have been excavating throughout this essay leads me to a different interpretation of Borges's image of a stairway ending in space. Although it does not lead to the expected door, it can sometimes turn into a passage that opens onto previously unrecognized and unconstituted territory. As chaos theory has taught us, disorder is not necessarily bad, and the void is not always empty.

Notes

1. This point is made by George Lakoff and Mark Johnson in *Metaphors We Live By* (Chicago: Univ. of Chicago Press, 1981). They emphasize that the "essence of metaphor *is understanding and experiencing one kind of thing in terms of another*" (p. 5). I am also indebted to F. C. McGrath's manuscript, "How Metaphor Works: What Boyle's Law and Shakespeare's 73rd Sonnet Have in Common" (unpublished). Also important in informing my remarks on metaphor is Max Black's definitive study, *Models and Metaphors: Studies in Language and Philosophy* (Ithaca: Cornell Univ. Press, 1962).

2. Gillian Beer's fine discussion of metaphor in Darwin and his contemporaries also makes this observation; see *Darwin's Plots: Evolutionary Narrative in Darwin, George Eliot and Nineteenth-Century Fiction* (London: Routledge & Kegan Paul, 1983). I am indebted throughout this essay to Beer's insights.

3. Paul Ricoeur, *Interpretation Theory: Discourse and the Surplus of Meaning* (Fort Worth: Texas Christian Univ. Press, 1976), 46–52.

4. Ibid., 50, 52.

5. Ibid., 67.

6. Mary Hesse draws attention to the importance of what she calls "redescription" in *Models and Analogies in Science* (Notre Dame: Univ. of Notre Dame Press, 1966).

7. Roland Barthes, "From Science to Literature" (1976); rpt. in *The Rustle of Language*, trans. Richard Howard (New York: Hill & Wang, 1986).

8. Ibid., 6.

9. Ibid., 7.

10. The question of whether a meta-language could be created that would

not be contaminated with the assumptions of an object language was central to the raveling of the positivist program, as well as to the attempted formalization of mathematics. In *The Structure of Scientific Inference* (Berkeley and Los Angeles: Univ. of California Press, 1974), Hesse addresses the question of whether there is an independent observation language in science (pp. 9–45). Frederick Suppe's collection remains a landmark in the debate: *The Structure of Scientific Theories*, 2d ed. (Urbana: Univ. of Illinois Press, 1977).

11. Kurt Gödel, *On Formally Undecidable Propositions in* Principia Mathematica *and Related Systems*, trans. Bernard Meltzer, ed. R. B. Braithewaite (New York: Basic Books, 1962).

12. Stanley Fish made a similar point in his paper on interdisciplinarity read at the 1988 Modern Language Association convention, "Being Interdisciplinary Is So Very Hard To Do." According to Fish, the very idea of interdisciplinary work engenders an unresolvable paradox. How his own work in literature and law is possible he did not address, rather like the aeronautical engineer who proved that a bumblebee could not fly.

13. The changing meanings of *entropy* in thermodynamics, statistical mechanics, and information theory are reviewed in K. G. Denbigh and J. S. Denbigh, *Entropy in Relation to Incomplete Knowledge* (Cambridge: Cambridge Univ. Press, 1985).

14. R. J. E. Clausius, "On the Motive Power of Heat, and on the Laws Which Can Be Deduced from It for the Theory of Heat," *Annalen der Physik* 84 (1850): 368–500; D. S. L. Cardwell, *From Watt to Clausius: The Rise of Thermodynamics in the Early Industrial Age* (Ithaca: Cornell Univ. Press, 1971).

15. It is possible to imagine an idealized system in which changes occur with infinite slowness. Because the system is always at equilibrium, the entropy remains constant. However, this condition cannot be attained in the real world. In all real heat transfers, entropy increases.

16. Sir William Thomson (Lord Kelvin), *Mathematical and Physical Papers*, vol. 1 (Cambridge: Cambridge Univ. Press, 1881).

17. Ibid., 514.

18. A persuasive argument for the cultural subtext of Kelvin's theory of heat is presented by Crosbie Smith, "Natural Philosophy and Thermodynamics: William Thomson and the 'Dynamical Theory of Heat,'" *British Journal of the Philosophy of Science* 1 (1976): 293–319.

19. James Clerk Maxwell, *Scientific Papers of James Clerk Maxwell*, 2 vols., ed. W. D. Niven (Cambridge: Cambridge University Press, 1890; rpt. New York: Dover, 1952).

20. James Clerk Maxwell, *Theory of Heat* (London and New York: Longmans, Green, 1871), 328.

21. Later commentators argued that resistance on the door could be made negligibly small; see, for example, Charles Bennett, "Demons, Engines and the Second Law," *Scientific American* 258 (1987): 108–16. My purpose in highlighting the assumption is not to bring this assertion into question, but to point out that it was never rigorously tested in the same way that Brillouin, Landauer, and Bennett questioned other aspects of the heuristic.

22. Leo Szilard, "On the Reduction of Entropy as a Thermodynamic System Caused by Intelligent Beings," *Zeitschrift für Physik* 53 (1929): 840–56; Leon Brillouin, "Maxwell's Demon Cannot Operate: Information and Entropy. I," *Journal of Applied Physics* 22 (1951): 334–57. See, for example, W. Ehrenberg, "Maxwell's Demon," *Scientific American* 217 (1967): 103–10. Ehrenberg's account of the thirty-year gap between the publication of Szilard's paper and its reappearance in Brillouin is typical. "Physicists were preoccupied with so many basic developments that Szilard's postulate was not seriously reviewed until 1951," Ehrenberg writes (p. 109). The assertion is a transparent attempt to create narrative continuity in the face of an obvious gap and shows how the idea of a "tradition" is reinforced through a retrospective reading of history. J. R. Pierce, *Symbols, Signals and Noise: The Nature and Process of Communication* (New York: Harper & Row, 1961), argues that Szilard's paper had little or nothing to do with the development of information theory, other than its impact on Brillouin (pp. 21–44).

23. Ehrenberg, "Maxwell's Demon," 109.

24. Brillouin, "Maxwell's Demon Cannot Operate."

25. Ehrenberg, "Maxwell's Demon," 109.

26. Leon Brillouin, *Science and Information Theory* (New York: Academic Press, 1956), x.

27. For a full discussion of the connections between information technologies and the idea of control, see James R. Beninger, *The Control Revolution: Technological and Economic Origins of the Information Society* (Cambridge, Mass.: Harvard Univ. Press, 1986).

28. Charles H. Bennett and Rold Landauer, "The Fundamental Physical Limits of Computation," *Scientific American* 253 (1985): 48–71; Bennett, "Demons, Engines."

29. Bennett and Landauer, "Physical Limits of Computation."

30. Bennett, "Demons, Engines."

31. Ibid., 116.

32. Ibid.

33. Claude E. Shannon, "A Mathematical Theory of Information," *Bell System Technical Journal* 27 (1948): 379–423, 626–56.

34. This version comes from Jeremy Campbell, *Grammatical Man: Information, Entropy, Language and Life* (New York: Simon & Schuster, 1982), 32. Slightly different phrasing is cited in Denbigh and Denbigh, *Entropy,* 104, who give their source as Myron Tribus, *Boelter Anniversary Volume* (New York: McGraw-Hill, 1963).

35. Denbigh and Denbigh, *Entropy,* 104.

36. Jeffrey S. Wicken, "Entropy and Information: Suggestions for a Common Language," *Philosophy of Science* 54 (1987): 176–93.

37. Wicken cites some of the order-out-of-chaos work in "Entropy and Information," but he sees these developments occurring in spite of the ambiguity in informational entropy, rather than being facilitated by it. Drawing from this work, Wicken proposes that what Shannon's function actually measures is the

"complexity" of a message (p. 184). Wicken suggests that using this term instead of entropy would remove confusion about whether information is or is not ordered.

38. Robert Shaw, "Strange Attractors, Chaotic Behavior, and Information Flow," *Zeitschrift für Naturforschung* 36A (1981): 79–112. Among contemporary chaologists, Shaw is perhaps the best known for positing and developing a strong connection between chaos and information. A more accessible treatment is presented by the so-called Santa Cruz collective in James P. Crutchfield, J. Doyne Farmer, Norman H. Packard, and Robert S. Shaw, "Chaos," *Scientific American* 255 (1986): 46–57. Also informative is James Gleick's narrative history, *Chaos: Making a New Science* (New York: Viking, 1987). The link between information and chaos is explored more thoroughly in my book, *Chaos Bound: Orderly Disorder in Contemporary Literature and Science* (Ithaca: Cornell University Press, forthcoming).

39. Also relevant here is Ilya Prigogine's reconceptualization of entropy as the engine that drives a system toward self-organization. An accessible account of this work can be found in Ilya Prigogine and Isabelle Stengers, *Order Out of Chaos: Man's New Dialogue with Nature* (New York: Bantam, 1984). Particularly relevant is "Irreversibility—The Entropy Barrier" (pp. 257–90).

40. Shannon's equation calculated the information H as $H =$

$$- \sum_{i=1}^{n} P_i(\log_2 P_i),$$

where n is the number of different kinds of symbols that could be used in the message (for example, twenty-six alphabet letters) and P_i is the probability of the ith kind.

41. Wicken, "Entropy and Information," 185.

42. Warren Weaver's commentary, which first appeared in *Scientific American,* was bound together with Shannon's two papers in Claude Shannon and Warren Weaver, *The Mathematical Theory of Communication* (Urbana: Univ. of Illinois Press, 1949).

43. Henri Atlan, "On a Formal Definition of Organization," *Journal of Theoretical Biology* 45 (1974): 295–304.

44. Typical of commentators who follow the Shannon-Weaver heuristic is Gordon Raisbeck, *Information Theory: An Introduction for Scientists and Engineers* (Cambridge, Mass.: MIT Press, 1964), esp. 1–11. Raisbeck is steeped in the engineering tradition; he was Norbert Wiener's son-in-law.

45. For an example of the Brillouin tradition, see D. A. Bell, *Information Theory and Its Engineering Applications* (London: Pitman and Sons, 1953), esp. v and 120–25. Bell's discussion is noteworthy because he considers untangling the relation between entropy and information one of the important problems his book addresses. Sometimes hybrid explanations would result, as, for example, in a heuristic used by Jagjit Singh, which mixes a microstate/macrostate analogy with the Shannonian uncertainty-in-the-message argument in *Great*

Ideas in Information Theory, Language and Cybernetics (New York: Dover, 1966).

46. John Arthur Wilson, "Entropy, Not Negentropy," *Nature* 219 (1968): 535–36.

47. Ibid., 535.

Bibliography

ATLAN, HENRI. "On a Formal Definition of Organization." *Journal of Theoretical Biology* 45 (1974): 295–304.

BARTHES, ROLAND. "From Science to Literature." 1976. Reprinted in *The Rustle of Language*, Trans. Richard Howard. New York: Hill & Wang, 1986.

BEER, GILLIAN. *Darwin's Plots: Evolutionary Narrative in Darwin, George Eliot and Nineteenth-Century Fiction*. London: Routledge & Kegan Paul, 1983.

BELL, D. A. *Information Theory and Its Engineering Applications*. London: Pitman and Sons, 1953.

BENINGER, JAMES R. *The Control Revolution: Technological and Economic Origins of the Information Society*. Cambridge, Mass.: Harvard University Press, 1986.

BENNETT, CHARLES H. "Demons, Engines and the Second Law." *Scientific American* 258 (1987): 108–16.

BENNETT, CHARLES H., and ROLD LANDAUER. "The Fundamental Physical Limits of Computation." *Scientific American* 253 (1985): 48–71.

BLACK, MAX. *Models and Metaphors: Studies in Language and Philosophy*. Ithaca: Cornell University Press, 1962.

BRILLOUIN, LEON. "Maxwell's Demon Cannot Operate: Information and Entropy. I." *Journal of Applied Physics* 22 (1951): 334–57.

———. *Science and Information Theory*. New York: Academic Press, 1956. 2d ed., 1962.

CAMPBELL, JEREMY. *Grammatical Man: Information, Entropy, Language and Life*. New York: Simon & Schuster, 1982.

CARDWELL, D. S. L. *From Watt to Clausius: The Rise of Thermodynamics in the Early Industrial Age*. Ithaca: Cornell University Press, 1971.

CLAUSIUS, R. J. E. "On the Motive Power of Heat, and on the Laws Which Can Be Deduced from It for the Theory of Heat." *Annalen der Physik* 84 (1850): 368–500.

CRUTCHFIELD, JAMES P., J. DOYNE FARMER, NORMAN H. PACKARD, and ROBERT S. SHAW. "Chaos." *Scientific American* 255 (1986): 46–57.

DENBIGH, K. G., and J. S. DENBIGH. *Entropy in Relation to Incomplete Knowledge*. Cambridge: Cambridge University Press, 1985.

EHRENBERG, W. "Maxwell's Demon." *Scientific American* 217 (1967): 103–10.

FISH, STANLEY. "Being Interdisciplinary Is So Very Hard To Do." Paper presented at 1988 Modern Language Association convention.

GLEICK, JAMES. *Chaos: Making a New Science*. New York: Viking, 1987.

GÖDEL, KURT. *On Formally Undecidable Propositions in* Principia Mathematica *and Related Systems*. Trans. Bernard Meltzer, ed. R. B. Braithewaite. New York: Basic Books, 1962.

HAYLES, N. KATHERINE. *Chaos Bound: Orderly Disorder in Contemporary Literature and Science.* Ithaca: Cornell University Press, 1990.

HESSE, MARY. *Models and Analogies in Science.* Notre Dame: University of Notre Dame Press, 1966.

——. *The Structure of Scientific Inference.* Berkeley and Los Angeles: University of California Press, 1974.

LAKOFF, GEORGE, and MARK JOHNSON. *Metaphors We Live By.* Chicago: University of Chicago Press, 1981.

McGRATH, F. C. "How Metaphor Works: What Boyle's Law and Shakespeare's 73rd Sonnet Have in Common." Unpublished.

MAXWELL, JAMES CLERK. *Scientific Papers of James Clerk Maxwell.* 1890. 2 vols. Ed. W. D. Niven. Cambridge: Cambridge University Press, 1890. Reprint. New York: Dover, 1952.

——. *Theory of Heat.* London and New York: Longmans, Green, 1871.

PIERCE, J. R. *Symbols, Signals and Noise: The Nature and Process of Communication.* New York: Harper & Row, 1961.

PRIGOGINE, ILYA, and ISABELLE STENGERS. *Order Out of Chaos: Man's New Dialogue with Nature.* New York: Bantam, 1984.

RAISBECK, GORDON. *Information Theory: An Introduction for Scientists and Engineers.* Cambridge, Mass.: MIT Press, 1964.

RICOEUR, PAUL. *Interpretation Theory: Discourse and the Surplus of Meaning.* Fort Worth: Texas Christian University Press, 1976.

SHANNON, CLAUDE E. "A Mathematical Theory of Information." *Bell System Technical Journal* 27 (1948): 379–423, 626–56.

SHANNON, CLAUDE, and WARREN WEAVER. *The Mathematical Theory of Communication.* Urbana: University of Illinois Press, 1949.

SHAW, ROBERT. "Strange Attractors, Chaotic Behavior, and Information Flow." *Zeitschrift für Naturforschung* 36A (1981): 79–112.

SINGH, JAGJIT. *Great Ideas in Information Theory, Language and Cybernetics.* New York: Dover, 1966.

SMITH, CROSBIE. "Natural Philosophy and Thermodynamics: William Thomson and the 'Dynamical Theory of Heat.'" *British Journal of the Philosophy of Science* 1 (1976): 293–319.

SUPPE, FREDERICK. *The Structure of Scientific Theories.* 2d ed. Urbana: University of Illinois Press, 1977.

SZILARD, LEO. "On the Reduction of Entropy as a Thermodynamic System Caused by Intelligent Beings." *Zeitschrift für Physik* 53 (1929): 840–56.

THOMSON, SIR WILLIAM (Lord Kelvin). *Mathematical and Physical Papers,* vol. 1. Cambridge: Cambridge University Press, 1881.

——. *Mathematical and Physical Papers,* vol. 5. Cambridge: Cambridge University Press, 1911.

WICKEN, JEFFREY S. "Entropy and Information: Suggestions for a Common Language." *Philosophy of Science* 54 (1987): 176–93.

WILSON, JOHN ARTHUR. "Entropy, Not Negentropy." *Nature* 219 (1968): 535–36.

Contributors

CHARLES M. ANDERSON, assistant professor of English at the University of Arkansas at Little Rock, teaches writing and rhetoric. He is co-director of the Little Rock Writing Project and teaches literature and medicine at the University of Arkansas Campus for the Medical Sciences. He has presented numerous papers at national conventions, published essays and reviews in books and journals, and completed a monograph on the early essays of surgeon-writer Richard Selzer entitled *Richard Selzer and the Rhetoric of Surgery* (Southern Illinois University Press, 1989).

JAMES J. BONO is an assistant professor in the Departments of History and Medicine at the State University of New York at Buffalo. His research concentrates on the cultural contexts of science and medicine in the Renaissance and the seventeenth century, and on the role of language and literary theory in the history of science. Professor Bono has published a number of articles and is currently working on two books: *The "Word of God" and the "Languages of Man": Interpreting Nature and Texts in Early Modern Science and Medicine* (Wisconsin), and *Medicine and the Life-Sciences in Early Modern Culture, 1450–1700* (Twayne's History of Science and Society series).

FREDERICK BURWICK is professor of English and comparative literature at the University of California, Los Angeles. His contributions to literature and science have explored optics and perception theory. Recent books include: *The Damnation of Newton: Goethe's Color Theory and Romantic Perception* (Walter de Gruyter, 1986); *The Haunted Eye: Perception and the Grotesque in Romantic Literature* (Carl Winter Universitätsverlag, 1987); *Approaches to Organic Form* (Reidel, 1987); *Coleridge's Biographia Literaria: Text and Meaning* (Ohio State University Press, 1989); and, with Paul Douglass, a facsimile edition of *Hebrew Melodies* by Lord Byron and Isaac Nathan (University of Alabama Press, 1988).

EDWARD DAVENPORT is associate professor of English in the SEEK Program at the John Jay College of Criminal Justice in New York City. He specializes in the theory of literature and criticism. Since 1980 he has been a founding and continuing member of the New York Circle for Theory of Literature and Criticism. He has published widely on the philosophy of science as it relates to methods of literary inquiry. His chapter, "The Scientific Spirit," appears in *Literary Theory's Future(s)* (University of Illinois Press, 1989).

MARK L. GREENBERG is associate professor of humanities and director of graduate studies in the Department of Humanities and Communications at Drexel University. From 1984 to 1989 he served on the Executive Committee of the Modern Language Association's Division of Literature and Science. In 1989 he became president of the Society for Literature and Science. His research concentrates on eighteenth- and nineteenth-century British literature and on social relations among literature, science, and technology. Studies of poetic responses to science and technology have appeared in *Eighteenth-Century Culture, Journal of the History of Ideas, Annals of Scholarship,* and *Colby Library Quarterly.* He is contributing editor of two forthcoming books: *Blake's Poetical Sketches and Criticism* (Wayne State University Press) and, with Lance Schachterle, *Literature and Technology* (Lehigh University Press). He has been named guest editor for a special issue of *Modern Language Studies* devoted to "New Models for the Study of Literature and Science" to appear in autumn 1990.

N. KATHERINE HAYLES, associate professor of English at the University of Iowa, holds degrees in chemistry and English and conducts research in contemporary literature and science. She is the author of *The Cosmic Web: Scientific Field Models and Literary Strategies in the Twentieth Century* (Cornell University Press, 1984) and *Chaos Bound: Orderly Disorder in Contemporary Literature and Science* (Cornell University Press, 1990).

STUART PETERFREUND is associate professor of English at Northeastern University. He has published three volumes of poetry and numerous articles on English romanticism, eighteenth-century British literature, and literature and science. Recent examples of the last sort include "The Way of Immanence, Coleridge, and the Problem of Evil" in *ELH* 55 (1988); "Organicism and the Birth of Energy" in *Approaches to Organic Form* (Reidel, 1987); and "Science's Fictions: The Problem of Language and Creativity" in *Creativity and the Imagination* (University of Delaware Press, 1987). Peterfreund also edits *PSLS*, the newsletter of the Society for Literature and Science, as well as *Nineteenth-Century Contexts*. His book on Shelley and language is forthcoming.

ERIC WHITE, assistant professor of English and comparative literature at the University of Colorado at Boulder, teaches critical theory and twentieth-century literature. He is the author of *Kaironomia: On the Will-to-Invent* (Cornell University Press, 1987). He began his research project, in which he explores the implications of contemporary scientific discourse for theories of cultural postmodernity, during his 1986–87 fellowship at the Cornell Society for the Humanities. A second pilot study appears in *Chaos and Order: Complex Dynamics in Literature and Science*, edited by N. Katherine Hayles (Princeton University Press, 1990).

Index